# Llewellyn's

# *Herbal Almanac*
## 2010

© 2009 Llewellyn Worldwide
Llewellyn is a registered trademark
of Llewellyn Worldwide.
Editing/Design: Sharon Leah
Interior Art: © Fiona King,
excluding illustrations on pages 2–4,
which are © Mary Azarian
Cover Photos: © Digital Vision, © Brand X,
© Digital Stock, © Photodisc
Cover Design: Kevin R. Brown

You can order annuals and books
from *New Worlds*, Llewellyn's
catalog. To request a free copy
call toll-free: 1-877-NEW WRLD, or visit our
Web site at http://subscriptions.llewellyn.com.

ISBN 978-0-7387-0691-7
Llewellyn Worldwide
2143 Wooddale Drive
Woodbury, MN 55125-2989

# Table of Contents

## Growing and Gathering Herbs

## Culinary Herbs

# Herbs for Health

# Herbs for Beauty

# Herb Crafts

## Herb History, Myth, and Lore

## Moon Signs, Phases, and Tables

# Introduction to Llewellyn's Herbal Almanac

The herbal landscape is an ever-evolving one. The slow warming of our planet has temperate climates creeping toward the poles, while consumer trends prompt more immediate changes. But through it all, home-grown herbs still make a lasting impact. *Llewellyn's 2010 Herbal Almanac* takes a look at the year-round effects of herbs, re-examining the research on uses of herbs as medicine, as culinary spices, as cosmetics, and more. This year we once again tap into practical, historical, and just plain enjoyable aspects of herbal knowledge—using herbs to help people stop smoking; to attract bees to our gardens; to make infusions and smudges; and, of course, trying out new recipes. And we bring to these pages some of the most innovative and original thinkers and writers on herbs.

Growing, preparing, and using herbs allows us to focus on the old ways—when men and women around the world knew and understood the power of herbs. Taking a step back to a simpler time is important today as the pace of everyday life quickens and demands more and more of our energy—leaving precious little room for beauty, good food, health, love, and friendship. This state of affairs is perhaps not terribly surprising considering so many of us are out of touch with the beauty, spirituality, and health-giving properties of the natural world. Many of us spend too much of our lives rushing about in a technological bubble. We forget to focus on the parts of life that can bring us back into balance and harmony.

Though it's getting more difficult, you can still find ways to escape the rat race once in a while. People are still striving to make us all more aware of the uplifting, beautiful ways that herbs can affect our lives. In the 2010 edition of the *Herbal Almanac*, the various authors pay tribute to the ideals of beauty and balance in relation to the health-giving and beautifying properties of herbs. Whether it comes in the form of natural herbal baths, crafting your own skin lotion, or a new favorite recipe, herbs can clearly make a positive impact in your life.

Herbs are the perfect complement to the power of the mind, an ancient tool whose time has come back around to help us restore balance in our lives. More and more people are using them, growing and gathering them, and studying them for their enlivening and healing properties. We, the editors and authors of this volume, encourage the treatment of the whole organism—of the person and of the planet—with herbal goodness.

# Growing
# and
# Gathering
# Herbs

# Grow Herbs that Give Back to the Bees

≫ by Suzanne Ress ≪

I f you want to start a new herb garden or enhance an existing one,
take time to consider which herbs
are attractive and useful to bees before
you select all of your plants. Yes, bees!
It's easy to forget what an essential
part they play in agriculture, but they
do more than provide us with honey.
By planting herbs that they like, we're
actually giving back to the bees.

Rock carvings found in southern
Spain indicate that humans were sys-
tematically hunting for honey as early
as 6000 BC. By about 2000 BC, people in Egypt were building clay bee
hives and keeping domesticated bees
for an annual honey harvest, much as
beekeepers do today.

Honey was the only sweetener available for sweetening and preserving fruits, nuts, and meats for thousands of years. Sugar was in use by 510 BC in Polynesia and India, but it remained a very rare and precious commodity that was used sparingly by nobility. Honey was the base for the alcoholic beverage mead (with its variations: metheglin, hydromel, and melomel). Town and city dwellers could not risk drinking plain water, but people of all ages drank meads and ales from first thing in the morning until last thing at night.

Once bees were living in man-made hives, humans became aware that the flavor of honey varied greatly according to what flowering plants were blooming within about a two-mile radius around the hives. So people began to purposefully locate their beehives near flowering plants that produced the best honeys, and many of these plants were common herbs.

Honeybees (*Apis mellifera L.*) were brought to America from Europe in 1622. Through swarming, abandonment, and other means of escape, they became naturalized and can easily live in the wild in hives they construct themselves—usually in trees. Honeybees kept by beekeepers are social insects. These bees will readily live in a man-made hive, knock themselves out collecting nectar and transforming it into honey, and they don't even complain much if we take most of it away from them for our own uses.

## Field-worker Bees Collect the Honey

Using her senses of sight and smell, a field-working honeybee alights inside or close to the selected flower. She inserts her tiny tube-like proboscis into the part of the flower where its nectar is, and sucks it up into her mouth, from where it then goes to her honey sack. A bee gathers nectar from 50 to 1,000 blossoms to fill one tiny sack.

All field-worker honeybees are infertile females. While she visits each flower, she is also packing pollen into the miniscule pollen baskets located on her hind legs. This pollen will be used as food for new bees back at the hive. Since a field-working honeybee only visits a single type of flower on each flight out of the hive, with every new flower landing she makes, she carries and leaves some pollen from the previous flowers, and thereby performs the invaluable job of pollination.

Without pollination there would be no fruit, vegetables, nuts, or berries. Without bees, pollination is less likely to happen. While butterflies and other insects, as well as the wind, can also do it, bees, with their fuzzy bodies and single flower type at each outing, do it best.

So, while a field-working honeybee is busy gathering nectar to be transformed into honey, she is also doing an essential part in providing the world with food.

## Keep Herbs in Bloom all Season

To offer the best to bees, as well as to get the greatest use and pleasure out of an herbal bee garden, a variety of herbal plants should be used. Select plants according to their blooming times. That way, something will always be in flower for as long as the growing season lasts in your temperate zone.

Bees have favorite colors. Generally, they are attracted to purple, blue, yellow, and white flowers. I've also found that they seem to prefer many smaller blossoms crowded together on one plant rather than a few large blossoms.

The common dandelion (*Taraxacum officinale*) is considered a weed by many. But as one of the earliest herbal flowers to bloom in the spring, it is a lifesaver for hungry bees. Bees adore dandelion nectar, and dandelions should not ever be eradicated from lawns. Besides being essential to bees, the dandelion's tender spring leaves are delicious as salad greens. Dandelions have also been used to treat urinary tract disorders and arthritis.

## Spring Herbs

Other excellent bee-attracting herbs that bloom from spring into early summer are horehound, with its rings of delicate white flowers, and borage, with its magical celestial-blue blossoms. The leaves on both of these early blooming herbs have an unusual texture, so even when the plant is not in flower it looks dazzling in the garden. Old-fashioned horehound can be used to make syrup or hard candies that work as effective sore-throat and cough soothers. The bitter liqueur is also useful to quell digestive upset. Borage leaves have a fresh taste reminiscent of cucumber that is a nice complement to salads. Check to make sure any herbs you plant are appropriate for your temperate zone.

## Summer Herbs

The Mediterranean trio—rosemary, sage, and lavender—blossom in early summer. These herbs love full sun and can tolerate very dry conditions and poor soil. They produce lovely blue to purple and violet flowers between May and July and, if they are grown in a zone that has a long growing season, these wonderfully fragrant plants will bloom a second time in September. Bees love them and they are extremely useful as culinary herbs, natural antiseptics, and in sachets and potpourri mixes. Bees also like sweet-scented chamomile, an early bloomer that will self-seed if the flowers have been pollinated for another bloom later in the summer. The dried flower heads make a wonderful soothing tea, especially when served with honey. And don't forget to let some chives go to flower for the bees.

Midsummer-blooming herbs include thyme, hyssop, fennel, oregano, and marjoram. Bees make a most delicious and highly prized honey from the tiny pink or purple flowers on thyme. The old-fashioned perennial hyssop, with its beautiful blue, pink, and white blossoming spires, can be counted on for a second bloom in September. Fragrant wild fennel (also delicious sprinkled in salads or on fish), Melissa lemongrass (comes from the Greek word that means bee), garlic chives, soft lemony-scented white verbena, bergamot (also called bee balm), and silvery-leafed lambs' ears are also good choices for this time of year.

### *Autumn Herbs*

In late summer and early autumn, all kinds of bee-attracting mints come into flower. Low-growing summer and winter savory, with their myriad tiny white blossoms, are a bee magnet. So are the long lavender-colored lacy spires of Russian sage (*Perovskia abrotanoides*).

Succulent-leaved purslane, with its small yellow flowerets, and its cousin, the striking multicolored single moss rose are appreciated by hungry bees, and their leaves and stems can be added to salads.

Probably the last herb to put forth its flowers is the gorgeous red-blossomed pineapple sage (*Salvia elegans*), so named because its leaves, when rubbed, give off a refreshing pineapple scent.

Once the last bloom of the pineapple sage plant has given its nectar to a bee and withered and fallen to the ground, the warm days of Indian summer may just be starting. The bees, feeling the sun's warmth, will still be frantically looking for something to eat before starting their long winter rest. Dandelions, which opened the season for the bees, will, along with goldenrod, also close it. But if nothing else is available, bees can battle it out with the wasps and suck nectar from wind-fallen apples and pears.

## Herbs that Bees Dislike

Though there are many flowering herbs that bees like, there are a few that will actually repel bees from your garden. Avoid planting strong-scented curry plant (*Helichrysum italicum*) near herb plants that bees are attracted to, or they will avoid the entire area. Feverfew produces many tiny daisy-like blossoms at midsummer and again in early fall, and bees hate them! The artemisias, including tarragon, wormwood, southernwood, and mugwort are not known for their blossoms, and the scents of their leaves seem to repel bees.

## Bees Love the Sun

When it comes to sun, more is better for both your herb plants and the bees. Consider the ambient temperature when deciding where to locate an herb garden for bees. If the temperature goes below 72°F, bees go into a semi-lethargic state and are barely able to move. The ideal location for growing herbs and attracting bee pollinators will be protected from the wind and facing south, with maximum daily sun exposure. Another thing to keep in mind is that bees need water to drink but cannot swim, so you might place a shallow, tray-like container filled with pebbles and clean water somewhere amongst the herbs.

To improve the environment for bees, avoid using chemical pesticides or herbicides anywhere on your property. If your lawn is sprayed with a wide-range insecticide, you can be certain no bees, butterflies, or ladybugs will come to your herb garden. And very few of your plants will produce viable seed to be self-sown for the following season. Weed-killing herbicides will kill important nectar-producing flowers such as dandelions and clover in a lawn.

Instead, think green. Reduce or even eliminate the space devoted to neatly mown grass and plant more herbs, wildflowers, or native flowering grasses. You won't have to worry that aphids will take over. The aphids will attract more ladybugs, and ladybugs bring good luck!

Human beings have reached the point where we seem to have dominion over all other species and sometimes, it seems, over Mother Earth herself. Every time a field of wildflowers or grain, an empty lot, or an abandoned fruit orchard is transformed into neatly planned housing developments, apartment complexes, office space, parking lots, or other commercially developed property, some wildlife loses its home and foraging area. Bees that depend on wildflowers and flowering wild herbs and grasses for their survival may relocate, or simply die off, when their natural foraging territory is destroyed. We owe it to the bees to give back to them at least a little bit of what we've taken.

If you are contemplating whether or not to plant a new herb garden or add to an existing one, be sure to include plenty of flowering herbs for the bees. Or consider taking a course with your local beekeepers' association if you are really concerned and have enough free time. You could become a beekeeper yourself.

## Bees, Bees, and More Bees

Aside from honeybees, there are many other species of bees in any locale. One of these is the large furry-looking black-and-yellow-striped bumblebee. The bumblebee, like most other bees (aside from honeybees), is a solitary bee. Solitary bees do not live in caste societies as honeybees do. Some other wild solitary bees are yellow-faced bees, sweat bees, sand bees, and mason bees. All of these solitary bees, especially the bumble-bee, are excellent pollinators.

We can't domesticate solitary bees (or collect honey from them) since they do not live in large groups, but we can appreciate the important part they play in the ecosystem and do what we can to help make both solitary and social bees' lives a little better.

If you fear or dislike bees because you're afraid of being stung, remember that most bees, most of the time, would rather avoid having to use their stingers. Bees will not attack a human unless they feel they are in danger. If you swat at an approaching bee, or at one that has mistakenly landed on your arm, she may sting because she feels threatened. It's worth remembering that a bee can sting a person only one time, because once she does, she dies.

# Plantscaping: Bring the Outdoors In

≈ by Alice DeVille ≈

In the dead of winter, when outdoor gardens have faded, vibrant indoor gardens can still be enjoyed. Sun-loving houseplants benefit from basking in a window, and you'll benefit from having them there. Besides screening you from strong floods of light and conferring extra privacy, plants create leafy, live window trims of branches and foliage—and sometimes bright flowers.

You can savor the presence of plants in small quarters and enjoy a year-round growing season, whether space is limited or expansive, when you plant for success by choosing the right species. This article focuses on creating room to grow flowers, herbs, plants, vegetables, trees, and shrubs by maximizing use of available space both inside and outdoors.

If you have a south-facing kitchen window, nothing is prettier than adding an easy-to-install greenhouse window to put a small and colorful garden just over the kitchen sink. You can display herbs and flowers, mixing a variety of easy-to-grow herbs such as basil, rosemary, and chives with colorful flowers such as flowering cactus, African violets, or begonias. If you would rather display different textures and colors, you can place flowing ivy, table fern, and hydrangea on the next shelf; bicolor caladium, cyclamen, and a prayer plant on another shelf; and yellow kalanchoe, lady's slipper, and maidenhair fern on the lower shelf.

Decorating with plants brings significant value to indoor spaces. Into any room that's missing greenery, introduce a fabulous potted fern, a twining ivy, a graceful fig, or a stately palm. Lots of bare walls or missing furniture? Why not introduce several of these varieties? What's the least that can happen? The whole room suddenly comes alive, feels fresher and more inviting. The chairs and rugs seem warmer than before the addition of plants, inviting you to relax. Windows and tables seem to soften their angles, and walls look "finished."

Living houseplants clear the air and clean the air quality. If you prefer water gardens, you can engage in *hydroponics*, a technique for growing plants without using soil. (Most hydroponic gardens are in indoor settings.) All plants—even hydroponically grown plants—need a regular supply of fresh air, and indoor gardeners use carbon plant filters to circulate air around plants grown in alternative media like rock wool, water, and *coir* (coconut fiber).

## Help Your Indoor Plants Thrive

Potted plants have different needs from their ground-dwelling relatives. In designing your indoor paradise, remember that potted plants may require specific watering and fertilization schedules, container sizes, light preferences, and soil content. Find out which plants thrive in indirect lighting and which prefer to bask in a generous amount of sunlight.

Many people buy houseplants solely for their wonder-working effects rather than considering their botanical properties. To keep any plant healthy, it really helps to know more about the biological nature of the species. Living plants need loving care. After you make your selection and have safely installed your plants in their new habitat, purchase a good plant care book that covers total maintenance requirements. Nurseries, master gardeners, horticulturalists, and other plantgrowing aficionados have favorite manuals. Ask for a recommendation. Many of these books offer comparisons among the species and give both Latin and English names for identifying the plants as well as a description of their physical characteristics and expected growing dimensions.

### Good Air

The more stable the environment you provide for your leafy "friends," the healthier they will be. Extreme air temperatures and sudden drafts can throw a plant into shock. Since potted plants have limited soil resources, it is crucial to get into the habit of fertilizing your indoor charges. Use liquid fertilizer, a special soil mix, or fertilizing sticks to keep them healthy.

### Good Grooming

Plants thrive on good grooming. When you leave dead flowers on a live plant the plant tends to wither away and develop seedpods, which shorten its ornamental life. The best way to keep plants blooming is to "deadhead," or remove spent flowers. Some plants grow in wild spirals or may have an unusual growth spurt on one side. These plants may be routinely clipped according to plant care recommendations to keep an attractive shape.

## Right Amount of Watering

No two plants use water at exactly the same rate. For maximum results, make sure your plant has a properly draining container and potting soil. Feel the soil to a depth of one inch below the surface and, if it's dry to the touch, add tepid water to the soil surface—never shock the plant with hot or icy water. Overwatering plants can kill them just as much as forgetting to give them at least a weekly sprinkling. If you have a variety of plants that require diverse care techniques, keep a notebook recording the treatment and watering schedule for each item and helpful notes so that you don't confuse requirements. For example, palms and palm-like plants aren't too fussy about soil requirements and grow well in indoor potting soil. During spring and summer, most palms actively grow and need regular watering to keep soil consistently moist (not soggy.) During winter months, allow the top inch or so of soil to dry out between waterings so that palm roots do not rot. While adaptable to varying light conditions, palms prefer filtered light that screens out direct rays of sunshine. Palms thrive on higher humidity and benefit from misting or showering lightly.

## Pest Control

Pests and diseases are the bane of houseplants. Insects can be so small you hardly notice their presence while diseases show more noticeable symptoms such as dark spots, discoloration, mildew and shrinkage. Crown rot occurs when the plant has poor drainage or has been overwatered; this disease turns plants brown or makes them wilt suddenly. Pests like aphids, green, reddish or black creatures with soft, round, or pear-shaped bodies tend to cluster on buds, or new plant growth, where they suck plant juices. An attack leads to stunted growth or curled leaves or flowers. Aphids secrete a substance that forms a growth of sooty mold. Some of the preferred treatments include use of insecticidal soaps, scraping, wiping off residue with a soft cloth, or repotting in containers that have better drainage.

### *Room to Grow*

The bottom line is that your baby blossoms and herbs outgrow their initial pots. When they do, it is time to transplant them into larger containers to keep their roots from growing out through the pot's drainage holes and coiling up around the container's edges. Repotting shifts an uncomfortably crowded plant from a pot-bound environment to a new and roomier space. When using decorative and often expensive cachepots (the word means "conceal") for your plants, put a layer of pebbles or stones in the bottom to facilitate drainage and then put the actual planter inside. Never plant directly in a fancy pot—your plant will die within weeks if you don't allow for air and water circulation. A cachepot should measure at least an inch more in diameter than the plant's container.

Specimens that you arrange in clusters on garden window shelves, and in massive groupings in a common bed, need careful maintenance. If they grow into one another, the aesthetics change and the likelihood of insect and disease damage increases even if only one of the plants is the actual carrier.

## Feng Shui and Indoor Plants

Houseplants provide life and vitality to your indoor environment; they are an integral component of the feng shui energy balance in your home. Plants connect you to the natural world and increase the flow of *chi* (positive energy) throughout your home. All objects, including plants, have energy that is either yin (feminine) or yang (masculine). Too much of either tilts the balance of a room and can actually make you feel uncomfortable. Take full advantage of feng shui philosophy by following these guidelines:

- Create a positive impression in the entry of your home by placing a plant or floral arrangement near your front door.

- Use plants for their oxygen-creating properties to help neutralize toxic materials found in plastics, fibers, and paints.

- Choose plants that have round or soft edges instead of spiky, pointed, or aggressive-looking species, especially if you are placing them near groups of chairs or in a dining area.

- Stagger plants strategically along a straight corridor to relax and soften the space.

- Place bushy plants near windows or doors to slow down the flow of chi.

- Avoid negative energy by getting rid of sick or dead plants. No plants are better than ones that are sick.

- Keep in mind the angles and corners prominent in Western architecture that are dumping grounds for negative energy and "poison arrows" known as *shars*. Note how many people put wastebaskets in corners—they block the flow of positive energy and clog prosperity. Let the energy flow freely by placing plants or indoor trees in the corners of rooms.

- Plants with pointy leaves, such as palms, snake plants, and cacti radiate more yang energy. Species with narrow, droopy leaves, such as spider plants, generate yin energy. A bushy, leafy ficus plant slows down fast-moving chi. But adding a draping or trailing plant (such as grape or Swedish ivy, strawberry begonia, or wandering Jew) nearby will create more water chi energy. They look best in hanging baskets or placed on a pedestal to create a statement and add flow.

Fresh flowers radiate living chi energy and bring the chi energy associated with their color into a room. Existing energy transforms to a higher plane the moment you bring flowers into the space. Yellow flowers create sociability; blue flowers help you communicate better and encourage travel and connections; red flowers like roses foster romance while red tulips generate wealth; green ferns represent vitality and freshness.

## Improving Outdoor Spaces

A little greenery goes a long way toward improving the image your home projects. Whether you have a large plot of ground with diverse landscaping possibilities or a front stoop with hanging basket options, you make a statement with artistic plantings that welcome visitors to your home.

The simplest way to create color and a high-impact first impression is to grow flowers. Don't let appearances fool you; hard work is not necessary for a beautiful flower garden. All you really need are the right plants, a few minutes each day to maintain them, and lots of time to enjoy them. With a few savvy tips, you can add considerable value to your cozy cottage, one floor rancher, or stately colonial. A trendy townhouse, a sophisticated condo, or your leased apartment comes alive with green accents or, with time and money, a complete makeover. The American Nursery & Landscape Association reports that landscaping can add up to 15 percent to a home's value. That's incentive to give visitors an eye-opening first impression with the natural environment you create in and around your home.

## *Invigorate Your Green Spaces*

First, figure out where you could use the most improvement from Mother Nature by answering these questions.

1. What do you want to achieve?

2. Are you preparing your home for sale or is your aim to beautify your home for personal satisfaction?

3. Do you want to work on making a particular outdoor feature, such as your deck, more attractive? If so, do you have room to landscape around the deck with a variety of herbs, plants, flowers, and shrubs?

4. Does your exterior need a complete makeover or do you need specific cosmetic upgrades? Take note of any areas with dead plants or trees.

5. Do you live in quarters that do not have outdoor planting space but may have a patio, balcony, small deck, or courtyard?

6. Do you like home-grown vegetables and can you accommodate them?

7. What's going on inside your home? Have you allocated space for house plants or an herb garden? Which rooms could use a boost?

8. Will you need the assistance of a professional landscaper, horticulturalist, or expert gardener?

Next, make a plan, starting with the basics. You can always expand your vision at a later date. To help you understand the scope of your project, make a sketch. A visual aid will help you select a variety of greenery that pops. To keep exterior maintenance low, choose mostly shrubs that stay green or colorful all year long rather than plants or trees that shed leaves or wither. Maybe your preference is to make use of deck space with a variety of hanging plants, deck planters, or deck boxes strategically placed along the rails.

If you are one of the millions of residents who rents an apartment, owns a condo, or simply doesn't have a plot of ground, there are plenty of opportunities for showing off your green thumb in windows, balconies, zero-lot-line courtyards, or any corner of your home that could use aesthetic appeal. Perhaps your dwelling has windows that can accommodate exterior planter boxes to show off brilliant spring flowers or a variety of seasonal plants. It's a good idea to assess your available land, the features of your home, and the available indoor space. Be sure to take into consideration the amount of sun that hits those areas—it will determine what you can plant and where. Houseplants thrive in the outdoor climate approximately six months of the year in most regions and longer in warmer climates. When you pot them, place them in a decorative planter for indoor use and remove it for their outdoor exposure. Remember that many perennial garden, herbs, and deck plants may be transplanted for use in your home when the weather turns cooler.

## Working within a Budget

Plantscaping requires money. It is important to determine right up front how much money you have in your annual budget for this project. If you follow the lead of experts, who consider an exterior landscape plan a multi-year project, you can spread the cost of your dream over a number of years instead of bearing a heavy cash outlay in a single year. For example, with a landscape plan you can plant your trees and some flowers in year one; shrubs around front windows and bulbs in year two; design and plant garden beds in year three; add larger border shrubs for privacy in year four and, by the fifth year, you'll be ready to finish landscaping the deck area. You should have nicely maturing plants all around your lot that readily compliment your deck, patio, or gazebo. Add a water feature or an arbor in year six and you'll be in competition for the trendy Home and Garden shows. During any of these years, you can bring the outdoors into your home through strategic decorating with plants.

Research the cost of all supplies and plants before you buy. Make a list of everything you will need to determine the price associated with obtaining and installing each item. If you balance these costs against your budget, you will be able to see when you can actually fund each phase. Most gardeners are in a big hurry, eager to see the fruits of their labor. The "rush" is a big mistake and can be very costly in the long run, because you tend to purchase fast-growing but not particularly hardy species and will have to replace them in a few years. Be realistic about what you can actually tackle in a given year. Do the job right and you won't regret your investment of time and money.

The payoff can be bountiful if you are building an edible landscape. Outdoor soil often needs amendments, such as fertilizer and clay cutter, and it may take a few years to produce plants and vegetables that are truly lush. A 100- to 200-square-foot bed is a reasonable starter size for producing a variety of herbs and vegetables. Choose plant varieties that are highly productive to get your best yield. Berries, pumpkins, melons, and cucumbers need space to spread out; if your plot is small, you won't be able to diversify the crops as much as you can with tall-growing or more compact species. Indoor soil needs a boost as well, so remember to add fertilizer to your houseplants according to plant care recommendations.

Seek referrals from friends and neighbors as you design and plan your landscape. Don't hesitate to pay for a consultation with a professional. It is the least costly investment for a big project. Nurseries often set a minimum fee, typically $2,500 for specific area plantings, stock purchases, and installation. This amount won't buy much. Be wary of firms that push certain species unless you have done your homework and know these trees or plants work well in your climate. Don't be talked into planting anything that does not visually appeal to you. When nurseries are low on stock they sometimes discount less desirable trees and shrubs. These items are a bargain only if you really like them; just as often these plants or trees have a limited shelf life, are less disease-resistant, and have less attractive shapes or sparse leaves if they are deciduous trees. The shortfalls or deficiencies affect the shape and symmetry of your plan and you won't have the desired visual effects.

If an indoor/balcony planting project is your top priority, call a houseplant professional to give you guidance and help you make selections for blooming plants, indoor trees, patio shrubs, and herb gardens. Be sure to ask about care of your choices—you can lose considerable money investing in difficult to care for plants that are delicate and susceptible to plant disease.

Explore the rich, diverse world of plants. Whether you place them indoors or out, the best way to enhance your home's balance is to decorate with plants. They perk up rooms and inspire the occupants. Their gentle, natural beauty invites you to wander in, sit down, and relax for a while. Plants work wonders. These ethereal blooms impart a mood of contentment and draw your thoughts away from the busy world outside. With a little imagination, you too can enjoy the magnificent artistry from nature.

# Basil: We Love It or Hate It

*⁂ by Elizabeth Barrette ⁂*

*Pounding fragrant things—
particularly garlic, basil, parsley—is a
tremendous antidote to depression.*
~Patience Gray

**B**asil delivers a wide array of benefits despite its cantankerous reputation. It stars in Mediterranean cuisine and many other recipes. Its diverse colors and shapes make it ideal for ornamental plantings. Its magical properties earn it a place on the altar. Grow your own basil and you can enjoy it fresh, when it presents its best qualities, because this herb loses much of its charm when dried.

# Varieties

Basil (*Ocimum basilicum*), a member of the mint family, is prized by cooks for its culinary uses; it also has medicinal properties. Some basil varieties are annuals, while others are perennials and, depending on the climate, perennials may be grown as annuals or annuals may survive as short-lived perennials. All varieties are tender to varying degrees and require warm temperatures.

Gardeners enjoy the diversity of sweet-spicy basil; it comes in dark green, light green, purple, and variegated. Its small flowers are white or lavender; it ranges from 12 to 18 inches in height, and some varieties are columnar while others are globular in shape. Leaves tend toward pointed ovals, but can be broad or quite narrow, usually with shallow serrations around the edges. They are smooth and glossy, and they exude strong fragrance when bruised.

**African blue basil** (*O. basilicum L.* 'African Blue') grows from 18 to 24 inches high. This vigorous grower is a favorite in ornamental landscapes. Its soft, blue-green leaves and pale lavender flowers provide a resting place for the eyes. It has a definite camphoraceous scent. In warm climates, it behaves as a perennial; in cool climates, it may reseed itself.

**Anise basil** (*O. basilicum L.* 'Licorice') reaches 15 to 18 inches high. This culinary variety has medium-sized leaves and a faint anise flavor. Use in savory salads.

**Aussie sweet basil** (*Ocimum spp.*) is a vigorous variety that grows to 24 inches or more. Its light-green leaves and sweet flavor make it a favorite for culinary purposes. This cultivar does not flower or set seed, which is a great convenience for busy gardeners!

**Baja basil** (*O. basilicum L.* 'Baja') hails from Baja, Mexico. It bears medium-sized green leaves and white flowers. The flavor is intensely sweet, with a cinnamon spice note, making it useful in fruit salads, chutney, dips, and other fruit recipes.

**Bush basil** (*O. basilicum L.*) tolerates most growing conditions and thrives in containers. It only grows about 6 inches high, and it has small leaves and a pungent flavor.

**Camphor basil** (*O. basilicum L.*) has a sharp scent. It is often grown for medicinal use, and it makes an excellent tea for colds or nausea. It also bushes beautifully when clipped, and can be trimmed into a miniature hedge or topiary. It's too pungent for most cooks, though.

**Cinnamon basil** (*O. basilicum L.* 'Cinnamon') has violet stems, leaf veins, and flower bracts that contrast with rich green leaves topped by delicate lavender flowers. It makes a dramatic ornamental; its strong cinnamon scent and flavor also suit it for culinary purposes. Use in Asian or Middle Eastern recipes, especially fruit salads or dressings.

**Compact genovese basil** (*O. basilicum L.* 'Compact Genovese') is a small version of the standard Italian basil. It grows only 12 to 15 inches high and thrives in a pot. However, it still bears full-size leaves, making it good for a kitchen plant.

**Fino verde basil** (*O. basilicum piccolo*) is a small plant with tiny narrow leaves. Its flavor is sweeter and less sharp than other varieties.

**Genovese basil** (*O. basilicum L.* 'Genovese Gigante') is the traditional Italian plant used in pasta sauces, pesto, and garlic dishes. It grows 18 to 20 inches tall, and it has bright green leaves and white flowers. It has a strong flavor and readily sprouts new leaves after picking.

**Greek column basil** (*Ocimum* x *citriodorum* 'Lesbos') grows tall and narrow, adding vertical interest to ornamental herb gardens. It can only be propagated by cuttings.

**Green ruffles basil** (*O. basilicum L.* 'Green Ruffles') has fluffy ripples on its bright lime-green leaves. It makes a gorgeous ornamental plant.

**Holy red and green basil** (*Ocimum sanctum*) from Thailand bears glorious green leaves splashed with red. It grows 18 to 24 inches tall, and its musky flavor includes a clove note; it makes excellent tea. This variety is used for culinary, spiritual, and ornamental purposes. Consider growing it between a purple and a green variety.

**Lemon basil** (*O. basilicum* var. *citriodorum*) grows into a small, compact plant. Its potent lemon scent makes this cultivar go well with fish, poultry, fruits, or light vegetables. It makes a good addition to a fragrance garden, too.

**Lettuce leaf basil** (*O. basilicum* var. *crispum*) is a vigorous, flavorful variety with white flowers. Its huge, crinkly leaves spice up salads; it pairs well with fish.

**Lime basil** (*O. americanum*) reaches 18 to 24 inches high. This culinary variety has a delicate lime flavor—very sweet rather than spicy—making it suitable for fruits and desserts. Its light green leaves and white flowers that are visually interesting when it's planted next to a lemon variety.

**Mrs. Burns lemon basil** (*O. basilicum* var. *citriodora* 'Mrs. Burns') is an antique cultivar from southeastern New Mexico. It blooms quite late, making it a more slow-bolt variety than other lemon-scented basils. It also has an exceptionally strong lemon flavor with a bright aroma and is favored for fish or chicken. This cultivar grows 18 to 24 inches tall, with white flowers and bright green leaves.

**New Guinea basil** (*O. basilicum L.* 'New Guinea') grows 18 to 24 inches high. Its narrow leaves can reach two inches in length, and it's dark green on top with dark-purple in places. The undersides and veins of leaves are also purple. Flavors include a combination of licorice, mint, and spice. This edible ornamental is a showpiece in kitchen, fragrance, or decorative gardens.

**Nufar basil** (*O. basilicum L.* 'Nufar F1') is a relative of genovese basil with resistance to fusarium wilt. Try this if your garden has disease problems.

**Perennial basil** (*O. basilicum* var. *gratissimum*) is a giant among its miniature relatives. Officially considered a bush, it can reach heights of 6 feet, with individual leaves 6 inches long! Grow this plant in a greenhouse or in a tropical climate where it can flourish long term.

**Purple basil** (*O. basilicum purpureum*) has aubergine (dark purple) leaves and pale pink flowers. It makes a spectacular ornamental plant, especially contrasted with other colors of basil. Although rarely used for culinary purposes, it is still edible and a few of the purple leaves make a vivid addition to salads or herbal vinegar.

**Purple ruffles basil** (*O. basilicum L.* 'Purple Ruffles') looks similar to plain purple basil, but with dramatic rippled edges on its maroon leaves. Grow this 18- to 24-inch-high ornamental basil for its foliage. It provides a striking contrast when set off against green or white plants, and it looks especially striking when alternated with green ruffles.

**Red rubin basil** (*O. basilicum L.* 'Red Rubin') grows 18 to 24 inches high. This culinary and ornamental variety has a sweet Italian flavor and its leaves have a distinctive coppery-purple color.

**Sacred basil** (*O. basilicum L.* 'Sacred'), known as "Tulsi" in India and "Kaprao" in Thailand, bears coarse grey-green leaves, topped with spires of lilac-colored flowers. It has a musky, faintly minty scent. This cultivar appears in Hindu tradition as a holy herb, making it the most suitable for spiritual uses. It's also a favorite for medicinal uses but is too sharp for the kitchen. In the garden, it reseeds itself reliably.

**Spicy globe basil** (*O. basilicum L.* 'Spicy Globe') forms a compact 12- to 15-inch-ball without pruning. It makes an interesting ornamental plant but its tiny leaves have zesty flavor. It grows well in pots, too.

**Sweet basil** (*O. basilicum L.*) ranks among the most famous. Its broad smooth leaves and strong clove scent make it a culinary and fragrance favorite.

**Thai basil** (*O. basilicum* var. *thyrsiflorum* 'Siam Queen') adds a faint licorice flavor and scent. It goes well with rice and vegetables, appearing in numerous Asian recipes. Also consider planting this in a fragrance garden. Its Thai name is "Horopa."

**Zulu basil** (*O. basilicum* var. *urticifolum*) blends a mild hint of lemon with the spicy-sweet basil base notes.

### Best Culinary Varieties

Anise, Aussie sweet, 'Baja', bush, 'Cinnamon', fino verde, Genovese, holy red and green, lemon, lettuce leaf, lime, 'Mrs. Burns', 'New Guinea', 'Red Rubin', 'Sacred', 'Spicy Globe', sweet, and 'Siam Queen'.

### Best Ornamental Varieties

'African Blue', camphor, Greek column, 'Green Ruffles', holy red and green, 'New Guinea', 'Nufar F1', purple, 'Purple Ruffles', 'Red Rubin', 'Sacred', and 'Spicy Globe'.

### Best Medicinal and Magical Varieties

Camphor, holy red and green, 'Sacred'.

### Best Fragrance Garden Varieties

Anise, 'Cinnamon', genovese, lemon, lime, 'Mrs. Burns', 'New Guinea', 'Spicy Globe', sweet, 'Siam Queen', and Zulu.

# Propagation

It was believed in Greek and Roman times that to have a good basil crop, it was necessary to yell loudly and swear when planting the seeds. Today, there is a French idiom for ranting which, translated literally, means "to sow the basil."

As a tender tropical plant, basil requires warm conditions. It is hardy in Zone 10 or higher. Sow the seeds outdoors only after the last frost has passed and the soil has warmed; temperatures must not drop below 10°C. Space seeds about one inch apart, covering them with one-fourth-inch of compost. Basil germinates in about one week. After two pairs of true leaves have developed, thin to leave the strongest sprouts 6 to 8 inches apart.

Indoors, sow the seeds at least a month before the last frost. Use growth medium with good drainage, and provide a strong grow light or full sunlight. Keep the medium moist at all times. Transplant seedlings outdoors after soil has warmed. Space the plants 8 to 10 inches apart. Provide shade over transplants for several days, then remove the covering to allow full sun.

Basil can also be grown from cuttings; this is the only option for the non-seeding cultivars such as 'Greek Columnar', and the best way to get a pure strain of any cultivar. Before the plant flowers, cut off a 4-inch piece from the end of the stem. Remove the bottom pair of leaves. Place the cut end of the stem in a glass of water and leave it in a sunny window. Change water daily. After roots have emerged, plant the basil in a small pot. When it's growing strongly, transplant outdoors or into a larger pot.

This herb is easy to cross-pollinate. Try making your own crosses to get many different types of basil.

The most peculiar thing about growing basil is an old belief that it thrives on negative energy. Try planting your basil in two patches. Revile one and praise the other and see which grows better!

## Cultivation

For best results, use soil or potting medium that is light and well-drained. Basil needs plenty of water but also good drainage. Water when the soil begins to lighten or flake; do not allow the leaves to start wilting. Basil tolerates a wide range of soil chemistry from 5.1 (very acidic) to 8.5 (very alkaline). Ideal pH is 5.5 (acidic) to 6.5 (slightly acidic). It responds well to many fertilizers, especially fish emulsion or kelp. Use a balanced fertilizer because too much nitrogen may produce larger leaves, but at the cost of flavor. Compost aids feeding, aeration, and water absorption.

Basil grows best outdoors, either in pots or in the ground. There it prefers a sheltered site with full or almost full sun. In midsummer or other very hot conditions, a little midday shade helps prevent sunburn. Growing basil between tomatoes or other vegetables benefits both the herb and the vegetables; this enhances flavors and discourages insects. This herb also attracts butterflies and bees to aid pollination.

Indoors, basil may be cultivated under grow lamps or in a south-facing window. Standard fluorescent lights are acceptable; high-output fluorescent, compact fluorescent, or metal halide lamps yield superior results. Use potting soil or hydroponic systems with vermiculite or rockwool and nutrient solution. A greenhouse or cold frame helps with overwintering mature plants or starting new ones. Keep basil away from any drafts or other sources of cold. However, an oscillating fan turned on seedlings for two to three hours a day encourages sturdy, bushy growth so they don't get weedy.

To encourage maximum growth, pinch off flower buds when they appear, because any stem that flowers will stop growing. You can also cut back some stems while leaving others to flower. Later, seedpods full of small black seeds will appear; harvest these and save them to sow next year. Picking off the leaves also encourages regrowth, as the area just below the break will sprout new stems.

In rich soil, basil may regrow after harvesting. You can dig it up in autumn and transplant it into a pot, where it will grow indoors through the cold season.

Beware of pests such as aphids, thrips, and white flies. They love the taste of basil too! Spray plants with insecticidal soap, then rinse with plain water after infestation ceases. Fusarium wilt can also occur, and affected plants should be destroyed. Prevent this soil-borne fungal disease by using sterile potting medium.

## Harvest and Preservation

Harvest basil by frequent pruning. This makes the plant bushy and vigorous. Start pruning when the plant has between three and six pairs of leaves, or when it reaches 12 inches in height. Cut off the top two-thirds of each stem, leaving at least two pairs of leaves on the bottom third. If you shear off all the stems at once, do so every three or four weeks. However, you can also cut only part of the stems each time, allowing for weekly or even more frequent harvests. Choose a schedule that suits your needs: small frequent harvests for fruit or meat dishes that need just a little basil, or heavy harvests for pesto or other sauces that require masses of basil.

You may want to mist your basil plants the evening before harvest to remove any dust from the leaves. The best time for harvesting is midmorning, after any dew has evaporated but before the heat of the day. This catches the essential oils at maximum strength.

For best flavor, use basil fresh. Whole sprigs can be wrapped in damp paper towels, then sealed inside a plastic bag and stored in the refrigerator for a few days.

One interesting method of preserving basil is to pack it in salt. For this you need a glass jar with an airtight lid. Start with a layer of sea salt, then add a layer of individual fresh basil leaves, and continue alternating layers until the jar is full. The basil leaves will keep for months this way, and the salt—complete with faint spicy flavor—can be used to flavor soups or vegetables.

To store basil in the freezer: lay individual leaves on a cookie sheet, freeze, and then transfer them to a plastic bag or container for storage. (Frozen basil may turn black.) The appetizing green color survives better if the basil is chopped and mixed with just enough olive oil to form a thick paste. Freeze the mixture in an ice cube tray for convenient portions. Add frozen cubes of olive oil and basil to sauces or soups.

Drying is the least felicitous method of preserving basil, but often the most convenient. Basil may be hung in bundles and air-dried like any other herb, although this tends to blacken the leaves. Drying individual leaves pressed between sheets of paper helps prevent oxidation and discoloration. In any case, keep dried basil leaves whole to preserve as much flavor as possible. Store them in a tightly sealed jar of dark glass for up to a year.

## Culinary Uses

Basil complements tomatoes, onions, olives, garlic, fish, fruit, and many other foods. It's a great choice for soups and sauces. In salads, its leaves add color, texture, and zest. Some herbs can overpower basil's flavor and fragrance. However, it combines well with oregano, sage, summer savory, sweet marjoram, thyme, and rosemary. Add basil near the end of cooking, because prolonged heat burns away its essential oils.

Remove stems and thick veins from the tender portions of the leaves. The tough parts have bitter flavors and encourage the leaves to blacken when chopped. Tearing rather than cutting the leaves may also reduce this tendency. Before adding them to a recipe, bruise the leaves by placing them between two sheets of paper and pressing with a rolling pin.

Two famous pastes consist primarily of chopped basil. Pesto is a mix of basil with oil, pine nuts, and grated hard cheese. Pistou is a mix of basil with oil and garlic. When serving these over pasta, add a dash of lemon juice to the water while boiling the pasta to prevent discoloration when the ingredients combine.

Basil stimulates the appetite, relieves nausea, and aids digestion. It also reduces gas and flatulence.

Basil is the ultimate edible herb. It characterizes ethnic cuisines and ancient religions. It makes bold contrasts in ornamental gardens. It likes most soil types, so you can grow it almost anywhere. And if you get frustrated and swear at it—well, it likes that, too.

# Reference

Schlosser, K. K. *The Herb Society of America's Essential Guide to Growing and Cooking with Herbs*. Baton Rouge, LA: Louisiana State University Press, 2007.

# Winter Solstice-sown Herbs

### ⇜ by Danny Pharr ⇝

We wake to darkness. The sun will rise in a couple of hours, around eight in the morning, and set only eight hours later. The Winter Solstice has arrived. This shortest day of the year, and the week or so on either side, brings less sunlight on a clear day than on any other day of the year. Snow may cover the countryside, and looking at the garden, one can imagine lush herbs, vegetables, and flowers growing there in six months.

This is the first day of the solar year and every day for the next six months will grow longer. Winter Solstice marks the depths of winter. In many places around the Northern Hemisphere, winter has considerable strength and cold still to be unleashed; however, and most importantly, this winter day is the first day of the planting season.

## Cold Stratification

Cold stratification is the process of breaking the dormancy of a seed so it can germinate. In nature, cold stratification begins when any plant—be it herb, flower, vegetable, or tree—drops its seeds on the ground in the autumn. The seeds are propagated by wind, creatures, and the gravity of the fall, and in the natural course of their journey, they find a place to rest for the winter. The seeds that find cover—a hiding place from the birds—and the right amount of drainage, sunlight, and insulation from the coming cold will be dormant. The winter cold and snow will encourage the dormancy to take its course and crack the seed's outer protection. Once the weather warms in the spring, the dormant stage will end and the seeds will germinate. This is nature's way. Plants are hardiest, healthiest, and most productive when they're sown by way of nature's cold stratification.

Modern gardeners tend to resist natural cold stratification as they consider the process too risky and beyond their control. Risky because natural germination rates are reduced during natural cold stratification and survival rates are decreased as the variances in temperature, moisture, bugs, birds, and critters fluctuate beyond anyone's control. Gardeners in general tend to display a controlled and patient demeanor when practicing their craft, at once waiting for the natural germination and growth to occur, while trading plant strength and longevity for artificially induced increases in germination and growth rate.

The most involved method to cold stratify your seeds is the most reliable and it's not all that difficult. You will need some supplies, but if you think of this as a recycling project, you will save a good deal of cash. This method still involves outdoor stratification that will produce hardened plants ready for planting when the time is right. Do consider how involved you want to become in winter sowing, as it can be addictive. You may end up being the busiest winter gardener on the block.

### *Container Stratification*

Prepare for winter sowing by drinking your soda pop from two-liter clear plastic bottles and your milk from one-gallon plastic jugs. Of course, the point of this is to save the bottles and jugs for planting.

- Cut the bottles and jugs in half horizontally. Discard the spout tops. Be sure to wear hand protection when cutting, drilling, and punching.

- Drill or punch some drainage holes in the bottom halves of the containers. Make the holes small enough that the soil doesn't fall through them. The holes should not leave internal ridges, which would prevent drainage.

- Fill the bottoms with four to six inches of suitable damp potting material, including some coarse sand to facilitate drainage throughout the winter.

- Sow your seeds as you would normally. Smaller seeds should be planted to a depth of one-quarter to one-half inch, and larger seeds can go as deep as one inch. Of course, if the seeds packets include instructions different from the norm, follow those instructions.

The soil should remain moist. Never provide so much water that it pools in the containers, but never let the soil get too dry, either. Now that you have sown your seeds, reassemble the containers by taping, with duct tape, the tops to the bottoms. This will create a number of tiny greenhouses, vented through their dispensing holes. Be sure to write the herb names on the tape for identification, or put a marked tag inside each bottle. If reattaching container tops to the bottoms proves to be too difficult, cover the bottoms with plastic wrap and secure the wrap with rubber bands. This method works well to keep the soil moist, but plant growth will be restricted unless the container bottoms have fairly high walls.

Once the seedlings sprout, remove the plastic wrap and, if the weather is still harsh, place the containers in warm, sun-lit areas in the garden. Select areas that are exposed to the weather, and in full sun. Set the containers so that they do not fall over, and check them from time to time. Water or fertilizer can be added through the top holes. Hopefully, the humidity and moisture will keep the soil suitably damp, but not so much that fungus will grow. When spring arrives and the weather is conducive to transplanting, move the hardened herbs from the containers to the garden soil.

Mother Nature would sow her seeds in the fall, but you could choose to use the above method of sowing your herbs in mini-greenhouses to extend the growing season. January and February are typically low, or no, activity months for garden-ers. Assuming you live in an area that still has snow or hard freezes to come, cold container stratification could be started late and still be successful.

## Plastic Bag Stratification

The whole process can also be completely simulated in the home using your refrigerator, and this method works any time of the year. The only negatives are that the plants will be less hardy and you will have less available space in your fridge.

Obtain some large freezer zip-lock bags. Fill the bags with vermiculite and sow your seeds therein. Seal the bags and place them in the refrigerator, not the freezer. The bags should be kept in the refrigerator for three months and turned occasionally. Remove the bags, re-sow the seeds in prepared trays or containers and place them near a sunny window. The seeds should germinate more quickly. If the seeds sprout while the bags are in the refrigerator, remove them and transplant immediately.

## Cold Frame Stratification

The riskiest method of cold stratification, but also the least involved, is to build a cold frame in a spot that is fully exposed to the elements and in full sun. Prepare planting trays with seed compost. Sow the seeds and cover with a thin layer of coarse sand. Put the trays in the cold frame in the autumn. Keep a watchful eye on your seeds to make sure they do not become too dry or moist, either of which will inhibit germination. Early spring will bring seedlings that should be moved to larger pots and then transplanted into the garden in late spring.

## Scatter Stratification

Now, for the advanced method of natural cold stratification. This method is not for the faint of heart, so don't be surprised if you find yourself having some resistance to this method. I have done it, and I know you can, too. Wait for the Winter Solstice. Snow or shine, grab a double handful of seeds, maybe marigold or poppy to start, and walk out into the garden, or anywhere on the property, to the spot that feels right to you. Cast the seeds upon the ground. Cast the seeds with sweeping arm motions, like you are sending forth life. Bring the children along—they will love planting in this way. When your hands are empty, rest and observe your work. Go inside, have a cup of tea and relax. Choose to be happy.

# Five Top Herbs to Get You Started

Selecting the right seeds for cold stratification is important to successful solstice sowing. There are three methods for determining which seeds can be sown in the winter months. The easiest and most accurate method for determining which seeds require cold to germinate is to consult a germination table that is a list herbs along with their stratification and germination temperatures. They can be found in herb catalogs and online. Identifying an herb's origin is one method for determining which herbs require stratification. An herb name that includes a reference to cold, such as a snowy mountain, or a cold climate—Canada or Russia, for example—is likely to require cold stratification.

The Old World method of determining which herbs need stratification is simple observation. Pay attention to the plants in your garden, around your house, around your neighborhood, and in the local woods and parks. Those that germinate and sprout early are likely candidates for cold stratification, as are the genetic relatives of these plants. Many herbs thrive from cold stratification, but we will focus on just a few. These are of interest as they all have healing properties attributed to them, all require cold stratification, and most have the either a purple or lilac color in their leaves or flowers.

## *Cinquefoil*

Cinquefoil (*Potentilla*), also known as five-leaf grass, is a fast propagating creeper with large yellow flowers that secrete honey and close at night. The leaves are divided into five fingers, each on its own stalk from the main runner. This herb has been used for love spells, to heal inflammations and fevers, coughs and arthritis, and it was said to attract fish to the nets. The tender leaves and stems are edible if gathered prior to the flowers blooming, and the high tannin content gives it an astringent taste. Freshly rendered juice mixed with a bit of clover honey will ease sore throats, including hoarseness and coughing. A tonic will break fevers and a decoction will act as an antiseptic. The herb will stop bleeding and has been used to treat addiction to nicotine.

## Mugwort

Mugwort (*Artemisia vulgaris*), also known as felon herb, is native to the British Isles, thus a candidate for cold stratification. Mugwort is believed to have been named for its use in flavoring mugs of beer before hops was used. The plant grows to a height of three feet or more, and has dark green leaves hanging from purple stems. The small oval heads of red or yellow flowers are clustered. This herb has been in use for thousands of years and in a variety of ways. Many of the uses of mugwort are in the realm of childbirth, mostly to induce the birth of stubborn babies, and involve pressing mugwort against the body for a period of time. Ancient soldiers are said to have walked with mugwort in their sandals to care for their feet and reduce injury during long marches.

Today, mugwort has many medicinal uses. A tea made of mugwort and ginger will ease menstrual pain, and a tonic made from mugwort can be taken to increase appetite, as mugwort is more mild in its action in the digestive tract than other similar acting herbs. Mugwort tonic will increase nutrient absorption and help to solve other digestive issues. Mugwort tonic will also help regulate menstrual bleeding.

## Red-topped Sage

Red-topped sage (*Salvia viridis*), a variety of common sage, grows from the banks of the northern Mediterranean Sea to the mountains of Spain. For centuries, the herb has been cultivated in Britain and Germany. Red-topped sage grows to be about a foot high and is named for its red and purple leaves that terminate at the base of the purple flowers. The remainder of the leaves are gray-green. Sage has been a remedy for centuries and red-topped sage has similar medicinal properties to common sage as they are similar in their botany. Sage is often administered as a tea, which can be flavored with honey and lemon to improve the taste, and taken in varying quantities and potencies. When treating acute periods of illness, such as colds or flu, three cups a day for a maximum of four days is appropriate.

However, when using sage tea as a health drink, one cup a day for ten to twelve days is the proper course. Daily sage drinks will reduce breast milk production, hot flashes, perspiration, and salivation; increase hormone and estrogen production; enhance memory; improve digestion and liver function; relieve muscle spasms; and will act as an antibiotic and astringent.

### *Vervain*

Vervain (*Verbena officinalis*), also called Herb of Cross, has opposite toothed leaves hanging below a spear of small lilac flowers without a scent, and it is found in England. Vervain has been used since Roman times as a medicinal and spiritual treatment. Vervain was used in ancient times as an aphrodisiac, and is said to have been used to stop the blood flow from the wounds of Jesus on the cross. This also made vervain useful for consecrating spiritual places and property.

The Puritans brought vervain to North America and, since then, it has been used to treat nearly every common ailment from fevers, colds, flu, and gout, to nervous disorders and skin disorders. Ancient Romans chewed vervain to relieve mouth ulcers and sensitive, bleeding gums. A tonic made from vervain is used today to relieve stress and nervous exhaustion, mitigate headaches and migraines, calm nerves, relieve anxiety, and elevate the mood. As with other bitter herbs, vervain enhances digestion and improves gastrointestinal functioning. The wisdom of the ancient people has again been proven as vervain does improve the health of skin sores and wounds, and when used as a mouthwash, it promotes healthy gums. The antiseptic nature of vervain works well on insect bites and wounds, too.

### *Yarrow*

Yarrow (*Achillea millefolium*) has had many names, including knight's milfoil. Native to the Highlands of Scotland, this herb has feathery, aromatic, grayish-green leaves that are three to four times as long as they are wide. The flowers, tiny and daisy-like, are generally lilac or white, although they are occasionally found in yellows and reds. The flowers rest in heads 2 to 6 inches across and atop stems that can grow up to 5 feet tall, but generally are in the 2 to 3 foot range. This is a creeper and often considered a weed. Used by ancient soldiers in ointment form to treat wounds, a piece of the plant held against a cut will halt the bleeding. The leaves are said to stop the nose from bleeding. Yarrow will break a fever when used as an infusion and will relieve headaches when drank as a tea. This herb tea has also been used to treat mild depression or melancholy and to ease digestive disorders. Mixed with peppermint, yarrow tea will help in battling a cold. Although having a bitter astringent taste, yarrow was once consumed in salads.

These five herbs will be great starters for your first attempt at cold stratification. Even with all of the methods to control the stratification process, and as much fun as it can be to build a cold boxes, assemble containers into mini-greenhouses, and to have canisters of one type or another to look upon from the warmth of the kitchen, I find that natural cold stratification is the most exhilarating and freeing to employ. In my mind, nature's way is always best. This process helps me to better recognize the rhythms of nature and reminds me to work within those rhythms rather than against them.

This winter, take a chance, risk some seeds, give up control, and give natural cold stratification a try. The process is simple and fun. And while the seeds are breaking through their period of dormancy, you will have time to spend on other things.

Because we are all gardeners, I offer the hands-on, do-something method of natural cold stratification as a primer to slowly break out of the need to dabble. To start, one must have a garden place selected and prepared. Pick a spot in full sun, or what will be full sun once the sun shows itself, and fully exposed to the weather, including snows, wind, and frosts. The soil should be a mixture of compost and earth and be well-drained so that the seeds will not have to swim all winter. Sow your seeds in garden soil that has been amended with compost and cover with a thin layer of coarse sand to add a degree of protection. If you are still worried, build a protective wire mesh fortress to keep the critters away.

Finally, say a prayer, dance a ritual to ward off demons, and then wait.

# The Herb Way to Container Gardening

### ❧ by Misty Kuceris ❧

One of the joys of cooking is being able to infuse your food with herbs and spices that enhance the flavor and also add health to your life. Knowing that you can reach over your kitchen sink and pluck basil or walk out your door and bring in lemon verbena makes cooking so much easier. You don't have to drive to the store in case you forgot to purchase the herb. You don't have to worry about the quality or freshness of the product because you grew it. Nor do you have to purchase more than you need and let the rest of the herb just become compost for your yard.

The secret to this joy is found in the form of container gardening: using pots, hanging baskets, or trays lets you create a beautiful herb garden that can be used for cooking, potpourris, or healing. These various containers can be placed anywhere you have the right light or can create the right light: on your deck or porch, in your house, and even in your outdoor garden. Only your imagination limits your ability to create a garden. The reality is that if it grows in the ground, it will grow in a container as long as the soil content is right and the container size accommodates the roots.

Beginning an herb garden can be a lot of fun. You can create a theme for your garden or you can just plant the favorite herbs that you like to use. While herbs can be used for cooking, potpourri, or healing purposes, many of them actually serve more than one purpose. So, if you're new to herbs and container gardening, you might want to choose just a few of the standard herbs that serve more than just culinary purposes, such as basil or lemon verbena.

The first step in using containers is to decide where you want to place those containers. If you have a deck or patio, you could use any type of container. If you're limited to indoor plants, you might want to consider a hanging basket near your kitchen window or perhaps a planting tray on your dining room table that can also serve as a centerpiece. If you're worried about lighting, you might want to consider curly parsley or marjoram.

## Using Traditional Pots

If you decide that you want to use the traditional round pots, make certain that your pot has good drainage. It really doesn't matter whether you want to use plastic or terracotta pots. However, if you choose terracotta pots, remember to soak the pot thoroughly twenty-four hours before use, otherwise the silica in the pot will leach out the soil's nutrients. (And, a tip I learned from a friend of mine who is a gourmet cook: terracotta pots are wonderful for sharpening your very expensive knives.) The one thing about round pots is that they actually take up a lot of room. To save on space, you may want to consider square or rectangular pots. No matter what the final shape of the pot, the planting instructions are basically the same.

For your herbs to grow well, you need to have the right soil mix in your pot. For outdoor pots, you need a good organic potting soil made for outdoor use and either some cow manure or humus. The ratio for adding either manure or humus to your potting soil is 3:1. That means three parts soil to one part of the manure or humus. Make certain that you don't purchase the potting soil with fertilizer because pre-fertilized soil is often loaded with too much nitrogen that could actually burn your plants. You want to be able to add the right type of fertilizer or tea compost yourself.

When planting inside, the potting soil needs to be indoor potting soil with enough vermiculite or perlite to allow for proper moisture control. The cow manure will actually smell too much for an indoor pot, so you're better off adding fertilizer from seaweed or other organic products to make certain the mixture is correct. Again, avoid any indoor potting soil (if at all possible) that already has fertilizer in it. If you can't find any potting soil without fertilizer, go for the lowest first number you can find since that indicates the amount of nitrogen in the soil and you want to keep that low otherwise you might burn your plants.

The other thing that helps you decide on the specific pots you want to purchase is the type of herb you want to plant. Lemon verbena (*Aloysia triplylla*) and pineapple sage (*Salvia elegans*) are two of my favorite herbs. However, they are actually small shrubs that are perennials in Zones 8, higher but "iffy" in Zone 7, and annuals in Zones 2–6. What's exciting about these two herbs is that they can be grown indoors very successfully. But, because of their nature, they need to have at least 6 to 8 inches of soil depth and their own pot.

The fresh or dried leaves of lemon verbena make a wonderful substitute for an actual lemon. Rubbing the fresh or dried leaves relaxes the body and can be used in aromatherapy. It's ideal for potpourri and deters insects in the yard. You can also use it to make tea. Just remember that lemon verbena, as an actual essential oil, sensitizes the skin to sunlight.

Pineapple sage is a wonderful plant that puts out red flowers in late fall, giving hummingbirds that migrate through your yard a wonderful treat, since many other trumpet-like flowers are already done for the season. If you live in Zones 2–7, an early frost can kill the plant, so you may want to keep it in a sheltered location on your deck if you want those hummingbirds to enjoy this special treat. Of course, hummingbirds aren't the only living creatures to enjoy pineapple sage. Small amounts of the sage leaf can be used in cooking as well as an astringent. Just be careful with its use because it can be toxic in excessive doses, especially as an essential oil, and especially to pregnant women or epileptics.

In other cases, you can plant more than one herb in a pot and create a theme pot, such as herbs you would use for Italian cooking: oregano (*Origanum onites*), marjoram (*Origanum majorana*), sweet basil (*Ocinum basilicum*), and parsley (*Petroselinum crispum*). When you place more than one herb in a pot, think about the way each one grows.

Sweet basil is an annual that can provide you with culinary delights in your tomato sauce or the basis for your pesto. You can rub the leaves on insect bites to relieve itching. Initially weak-rooted, it grows tall and bold. You can place this in the back of the pot for greater structural emphasis. Or, you can keep your basil small and bushy by pinching back the top leaves as the plant grows. Not only can you use the fresh or dried leaves, but many people find the flowers a delicacy.

Parsley is often an understated herb, yet it has one of the highest levels of chlorophyll of any herb. You can use its leaves, seeds, or even roots. Not only is it a breath freshener but it is also a diuretic. It has an erect nature, yet it is also very gentle in its look. So, you may want to plant it in the row between the basil and marjoram or oregano.

Many people mistake marjoram for oregano. While all marjoram is also called oregano, not all oregano is marjoram. If you feel confused by that statement, think of marjoram as mild oregano. The leaves or flowers can be used in making various Italian dishes and tend to have a peppery and woodsy flavor. Marjoram soothes the digestive tract while oregano is a cough remedy and expectorant. Since both plants tend to be a little unruly, like hair on a windy day, place them at the side of the pot so they can also hang over the edge.

## Hanging Baskets

Hanging baskets are wonderful ways to increase any garden or home space. In a garden or on your deck, you can hang the basket on a shepherd's hook. Or, you can suspend the basket from the ceiling with a traditional hook. When choosing a basket, you need to consider its drainage needs and your watering abilities. The standard plastic hanging basket tends to collect water at the bottom. The moss hanging basket is a lot of fun because you can plant the herbs not only in the top portion of the basket, but also at the sides of the basket. However, the moss basket is not really for indoor use; water spills out from all sides. It also requires more watering, especially on hot or windy days, than the plastic hanging basket. The potting mixture requirements are similar as those for indoor pots, although you might want to add some moisture retaining mixture to the plastic hanging basket so you don't have to water it as often.

When creating a moss hanging basket, you can choose the theme of the Italian garden. Or, perhaps you'd love to have a breakfast garden with herbs that are known for their light flavors, such as chives (*Allium schoenoprasum*), thyme (*Thymus vulgaris*), or dill (*Anethum graveolens*).

As a perennial upright plant, chives produces beautiful flowers as the season comes close to its summer months. Its light onion flavor adds a hint of flavor to eggs or any dish. In addition, it's supposed to be good for your digestion. This would be a good plant to place in the center of the pot as a focal point.

Thyme comes in various varieties and the creeping version makes a nice statement in your pot as it cascades over the sides. Its flowers and leaves give a very light lemon flavor to your food. It's considered a cough remedy and expectorant by many healers.

Dill is a very finely textured plant and can actually "bolt" (go to seed) when the weather is hot and dry. So, if you use it in an outdoor pot, be prepared to cut it back as soon as it starts to grow too fast. Dill can add a flavor similar to caraway to your eggs or other dishes. You can use either its leaves or seeds. And, dill is best known for pickling and as a preservative. Its use as a healing herb goes back to biblical times and was believed to prevent infectious diarrhea and also work as a digestive aid.

But the real fun to using a moss hanging basket is that you can stick whatever herbs you want into the sides of the basket and just watch them grow together to create a lush statement.

### *Tray Containers*

Some people like to keep their herbs small by creating a tray container that is only about four inches in depth. A tray container can be the easiest of all to create. You can simply place the herbs you purchased in the tray. Just leave those herbs in their original containers. True, eventually they'll get root bound. At that time you'll want to find larger pots. But for several months you'll have a great centerpiece on your table.

If you want to plant into a tray, make certain that the tray has stones and a little bit of charcoal at the bottom before you put in indoor potting soil. Unlike other pots, trays really don't give you good drainage. The stones will help with the drainage and the charcoal will also act as a filtering process for the soil and water.

## A Few More Planting Tips

Unlike plants in the ground, container plants need to be fertilized on a regular basis. Herbs don't like a lot of nitrogen, but they do like more phosphate and potash, so always make certain the first number (nitrogen) is the lowest number. When you look at a fertilizer label, you'll see three numbers. The first number is nitrogen, which actually goes to the growth of flowers and leaves. The second number is phosphate, which goes to the development of the root structure. The last number is potash, which goes to the over all health of a plant. Usually a 10-20-20 fertilizer is good for herbs as is an organic 4-5-5 fertilizer. Herbs, especially basil, need to be fertilized on a regular basis, about every ten to fourteen days. If this is too much work for you, you can put in a slow-release fertilizer at the time you prepare the container. If you use a slow-release fertilizer, you probably won't find one where nitrogen is the lowest number, so use a balanced fertilizer with 10-10-10 or 5-5-5. The slow-release fertilizer will last between three to six months depending on the brand you purchase. Once that fertilizer is out of the soil, you will need to switch to the other fertilizer. All plants, including herbs, to go into dormancy in the winter months so only fertilize them between spring and late fall.

Compost tea is not really considered a fertilize but rather a soil enhancer that increases valuable microbes and other nutrients to the soil. As its name implies, it is compost brewed with various ingredients to increase the microbes. Users of compost tea have stated that it increases insect and disease resistance as well as promoting growth. Currently, scientific studies are being conducted to assess the benefits of compost tea and consider possible dangers, such as E. coli contamination. The National Organic Standards Board (www.ams.usda.gov) wrote in its "Compost Tea Task Force Report" (April 6, 2004) that there "have been no reported cases of food borne illness from the use of compost tea, but no epidemiological health/microbial studies done to evaluate this effect." If you are concerned about this possibility, pre-made compost tea, tested for safety, is available in many stores.

Most herbs are sun-loving plants and, when kept indoors, do best in a southern or western window. If you feel your home or apartment is too dark, you can still grow herbs with the use of a horticultural grow light or a fluorescent light. There are some herbs, such as French sorrel (*Rumex acetosa*) and curly gold marjoram (*Origanum vulgare aureum crispum*) that actually prefer shade.

If you live in Zone 7 and colder and grow your herbs in containers outside, you can bring them indoors for the winter months. Just make certain that you slowly move the plants inside. The best way to do this is to move the plants closer to the building over a period of a couple of weeks. You may also want to spray them with insecticidal soap to make certain that you don't bring in any insects or spider mites. When you spray your plants, you'll need to do it at least two times. The first time is to kill any insects or mites which are currently on the plants. The second spray, about fourteen days later, is to kill the eggs that hatched.

During winter months, homes get very dry and your herbs are in danger of getting overwatered (the number one killer of most houseplants). Although your herbs are in dormancy and don't grow very much, they really need humidity. You can increase humidity by creating a simple pebble dish. To create a pebble dish you take a tray, put pebbles in it, cover the pebbles about halfway with water, and place the plants on the tray. You don't want your plants sitting in the water. You just want the plants resting on the pebbles so they receive the moisture from the tray as the water evaporates.

### Other Containers

There are many types of containers in addition to those already mentioned. The traditional strawberry pot, which already has holes in its sides so you can combine different types of herbs. There are hanging baskets, called "upside down baskets," which were designed for tomato plants, but that work well for cascading herbs (oregano or marjoram) or creeping herbs (thyme). Or, an old wheel barrel can be filled with plants. The type of container you can use is limited only by your imagination.

### Herbs to Plant in Containers

Any herb, including rosemary or boxwood, can be planted in a container. Invasive herbs, such as lovage, catmint, spearmint, or peppermint, need to be in their own pots. Shrub herbs, such as lemon verbena, need to be in their own pots because of their size. Yet no matter what herbs you choose, you can create a garden either outside or in your home that can enhance your culinary delights, increase your health, and delight your senses.

# References

Bird, Richard and Jessica Houdret. *Kitchen and Herb Gardener* London: Lorenz Books.

Bonar, Ann. *The MacMillan Treasury of Herbs: A Complete Guide to the Cultivation and Use of Wild and Domesticated Herbs*. Houston, TX: MacMillan Publishing Company.

Castleman, Michael. *The Healing Herbs: The Ultimate Guide to the Curative Power of Nature's Medicine*. Emmaus, PA: Rodale Press.

McNair, James R. and James W. Wilson (Ed.). *All About Herbs*. San Ramon, CA: Ortho Books.

Rees, Yvonne and Rosemary Titterington. *A Creative Step-by-Step Guide to Growing Herbs*. Portland, OR: Graphic Arts Center Publishing.

# Culinary
# Herbs

# A Dash of Salt and Pepper

≈ by Chandra Moira Beal ≈

We take for granted the presence of salt and pepper at our dining table, but the products inside the shakers are the result of millennia of human experience. The development of civilization itself can be traced through the history of salt and pepper. Trade routes were established around their sources, cities grew up along these trails, and new worlds were discovered in a quest to find ever more salt and pepper.

Our ancestors knew about the importance of salt as they followed animal tracks to salt outcroppings, where they gathered the crystallized minerals and added them to their food, because they knew that salt allows flavors to blossom and unifies them in a dish.

People also valued salt as a preservative, knowing that it sealed in moisture, which allowed them to store foods long before refrigeration. In fact, salt is essential to our very survival as it regulates our bodily fluids. Even our blood contains the same salt content as the ocean.

# Pepper

True pepper (*Piper nigrum*) is made from berries harvested off the pepper vine and should not be confused with paprika, cayenne, or other fruits from the capiscum family. Pepper vine, which grows up to 10 feet tall, is commonly found in the tropical climate of India and Asia. When dried and crushed, the berries add a sharp and spicy heat or a warm smoky flavor, depending on which berry is used. There are three kinds of peppercorns—black, green, and white—and all are picked from the same vine at different stages of ripeness.

Black pepper is the most mature; it is picked at the peak of ripeness and dried in the sun. It has the fullest and strongest flavor of the varieties. Green peppercorns are picked while the berries are still soft and before they've ripened. They have a mild flavor and are often packed in brine for preservation. White pepper is ripened on the vine. The skin is removed before drying, which causes this pepper to lose its color. White pepper has a hot, wine-like flavor that makes it useful in light foods and in Asian cooking. The flavor fades quickly in green and white pepper so grind it just before using.

Pink peppercorns are becoming more popular. While technically not a pepper, these berries from a South American tree have a slightly acidic taste and a nice crunch, and lend a nice color to fish and cream sauces.

## *Lemon Herbal Pepper*

This blend makes an excellent all-purpose seasoning. Sprinkle over fish, chicken, vegetables, pasta, or just about anything else.

1   tablespoon black pepper

1   tablespoon lemon peel

1   teaspoon oregano

1   teaspoon marjoram

## *White Pepper Versatile Mix*

Here is another great all-rounder that adds depth of flavor to soups, pasta, and sauces. It also works well to season ground beef when browning, or mixed with olive oil and tossed with vegetables before roasting. It makes a great base for a marinade, and adds a kick to gravies and stocks. Pulse all ingredients about 30 seconds in a grinder until well combined.

1   teaspoon dried thyme

1   teaspoon dried basil

1   teaspoon dried parsley

1   teaspoon ground savory

1   teaspoon rubbed sage

1   teaspoon white pepper

1   teaspoon celery seed

1   teaspoon dried oregano

Garlic powder and onion powder to taste

### *Cumin, Salt, and Pepper Roasting Blend*

This is all you need for perfect fajitas or pot roast. Combine ingredients in a small bowl and mix well, then rub into meats before grilling.

- 1 tablespoon freshly ground black pepper
- 2 tablespoons cumin seed, toasted in a dry skillet until fragrant
- 1 tablespoon coarse sea salt

### *Green Pepper Curry Blend*

Blend the pepper and curry with a teaspoon of orange zest and a tablespoon of balsamic vinegar, and add to any curry dish.

- 2 tablespoons pickled green peppercorns
- 1 teaspoon curry powder

# Salt

There are even more varieties of salt than pepper available today, each with subtle differences in texture and taste. Salts are mined from the earth and the sea all over the globe.

A good salt pantry might include a fine sea salt for filling shakers, kosher salt for adding to foods in pinches, and at least one kind of *fleur de sel* (means "flower of the salt") for sprinkling on foods just before serving.

Sea salts have a fuller, more complex taste than table salt. Table salt can be slightly bitter, or taste of iodine. Sea salts also retain more minerals and can be slightly sweet. Salts harvested from different seas can have subtly different tastes. Because sea salts retain high moisture content, they are ideal for making herb blends that hold together. Kosher salt contains no additives. The large, coarse grains are easy to pinch together and add to a dish; it is also inexpensive and high quality, making it a favorite of chefs. *Fleur de sel* is the thin layer of crystallized salt that forms on the surface of salt ponds. Because it is gathered by hand, it tends to be the most expensive form of salt. It is usually served with the meal to sprinkle on food just before eating.

There are dozens of other types of salt, from pink Peruvian to Hawaiian black lava salt, and they are definitely worth experimenting with.

### Lavender Salt

Lavender adds a complex flavor component to foods. Try sprinkling this simple blend over fresh tomato wedges, rubbing it into beef before roasting, or seasoning any vegetables. It's sublime sprinkled over slices of melon. Mix together:

½ cup coarse sea salt

3 tablespoons dried lavender

### Rosemary Salt

Sprinkle this simple yet stunning blend over tomato slices placed on grilled bread, or dash it over a pizza before sliding the pizza into the oven.

½ cup coarse sea salt

2 tablespoons chopped dried rosemary

### Pink Peppercorn Herbal Tea

Never thought of adding pepper to tea? Try this lively caffeine-free blend and you'll love the deep, spicy taste.

1 teaspoon pink peppercorns

¼ teaspoon cinnamon

¼ teaspoon ginger

¼ teaspoon cardamom

¼ teaspoon chicory

### Fleur de Sel and Herbs de Provence

Mix one tablespoon each of finely chopped fresh oregano, savory, thyme, marjoram, and rosemary. Add to ¼ cup of *fleur de sel*. Try sprinkling this on hand-cut French fries for a gourmet touch.

# Salt and Pepper Blends

Combining salt and pepper is the ultimate marriage, bringing out the best in each and heightening the flavor of any food they season. Bringing herbs into this magical relationship opens the door to myriad combinations of flavors. Herbs add complexity and vibrancy, and can pull flavors together in an almost infinite number of ways.

You can also use herbal blends without the salt and pepper, without skimping on depth of flavor. This is great news for people watching their sodium intake or otherwise avoiding salt in their diets.

Herbal salt and pepper blends have a wide variety of applications. Add a few pinches to soft butter and mix well, then serve with bread. Stir some into soups just before serving. Add a few spoonfuls to potatoes, rice or pasta to jazz them up. Rub some onto your meat before roasting. Cut up vegetables into chunks, pour a little olive oil over them, and sprinkle with an herb mixture. Toss well to coat the vegetables evenly and then roast until tender. The possibilities are endless. The blends listed below should be stored in an airtight container in a dark place and used within six weeks.

Finally, if you happen to spill some of the precious salt crystals while preparing these blends, just throw a pinch over your left shoulder, where malevolent forces are said to gather, and make a happy wish!

### Rosemary Garlic Rub

This is one for the garlic lovers! Mix together black pepper, kosher salt, rosemary, and garlic. Gradually stir in enough olive oil to form a thick paste. Rub into meats before grilling, or use this on potatoes before roasting.

1 tablespoon ground black pepper

1 tablespoon kosher salt

3 tablespoons chopped fresh rosemary

8 cloves garlic, diced

⅓ cup olive oil

## No-salt Blends

If you want to avoid salt for health reasons, but not skimp on flavor, try mixing several herbs together for a tangy kick. Grind all ingredients together into a coarse blend.

### Herbal Salt Substitute One

¼ cup dried parsley

¼ cup dried savory

¼ cup dried thyme

2 tablespoons dried marjoram

### *Herbal Salt Substitute Two*

Grind all ingredients together into a coarse blend.

- 3 tablespoons dried basil
- 3 tablespoons dried marjoram
- 3 tablespoons dried parsley
- 3 tablespoons dried thyme
- 4½ teaspoons dried chives
- 2½ teaspoons dried paprika
- 1½ teaspoons dried rosemary
- 2½ teaspoons onion powder

# Wild World of Mustards

⪼ by Calantirniel ⪻

**M**ustard's common name comes from the Latin words *mustum*, "the must" (unfermented grape juice that could become wine), and *ardens* (means "burning") that describes the qualities of crushing and adding the spicy, pungent seeds to the must. Must and ardens together refer to the condiment we use today. The Romans were fond of this preparation on their meats and other foods, as it improved taste and aided digestion. Invading Romans may have carried it with them to England as early as 50 BC, and England quickly adopted mustard into its own cuisine.

Mustard is documented some 5,000 years ago in ancient Sanskrit writings,

mustard

and it has enjoyed extensive use from Asia to Europe as a plant with culinary as well as medicinal purposes. Ayurvedic medicine classifies this hot, dry herb for balancing scattered Vata and sluggish Kapha Dosha types. Culpeper placed the spicy, stimulating herb under the dominion of the planet Mars.

Even the Bible, particularly in Matthew 13:31–33, gives prominence to this plant. Jesus explained to a Palestinian farmer that mustard seeds were very small in size, yet each tiny seed contains a potential plant large enough to fit a bird's nest. Many scholars have speculated the story refers to black mustard (*Brassica nigra*), which can grow up to twelve feet tall. Maude Grieve said in her book, *A Modern Herbal*, that the plant was more likely khardal, an Arabic tree that has small seeds, numerous branches, and a flavor similar to mustard. Nevertheless, this story was intended as a parable to have faith in the potential or the unseen, and because of this, mustard seeds have become a Christian symbol representing the Kingdom of Heaven to those who trust it will arrive sometime in the future.

## Botanical and Cultivation Facts

Mustard is a "cruciferous" vegetable, in the Brassicaceae or Cruciferae family (known as the mustard, or the cabbage family), which includes cabbage, Brussel sprouts, Chinese cabbage (bok choy), kale, broccoli, cauliflower, turnips, kohlrabi, radishes, horseradish, and cress. It is also related to other medicinal herbs in the same family, one of which is known as shepherd's purse (*Capsella bursa-pastoris*), a midwife's staple that is used to stop hemorrhaging after birth. In Thomas J. Elpel's book, *Botany in a Day*, the mustard family is the first one he discusses after briefly describing introductory botany. One reason for this is that all mustard family plants, while not necessarily palatable, are edible—you can eat any mustard you find—and they are fairly easy to identify. The key words are: four petals and six stamens: four tall, and two short. The flowers are often white or yellow, and are arranged in an "X" or an "H" shape. At least 55 genera are in North America, and there are 375 genera worldwide, which include approximately 3,200 species. Many mustards are considered weeds and are often in the wild.

Mustard greens are usually grown from brown mustard seeds (*Brassica juncea*). These seeds are usually in Dijon mustard condiments as well. At this time, most of these seeds for commercial use come from Canada. However, the condiment that could be termed "American" mustard comes often from white mustard (*Brassica alba*). The mustard with a long recorded use in Western medicinal use is usually black mustard (*Brassica nigra*) and is also widely used in the commercial making of the condiment.

## Culinary Use and Nutrition

Besides having an appealing and rather spicy taste, mustard greens are an excellent source of antioxidant vitamins A (beta carotene), C, and E, as well as vitamin B6, niacin, and folic acid. They also contain calcium, magnesium, manganese, zinc, iron, monounsaturated fats, and are a great source of cancer-preventative phytochemicals.

What follows are some ideas about how to incorporate mustard greens, seeds, and sprouts into your diet for health and good taste.

## Basic Recipes

### *Healthy Mustard*

This is a wonderful condiment and healthier than store-bought, since whole foods are used. Use white or yellow seeds for the mild, American flavor, or brown or black seeds for the spicier Dijon-like flavor. The yellow color is provided by turmeric.

½ cup (125 ml) mustard seeds

2 teaspoons (10 ml) powdered turmeric (optional)

¼ cup (50 ml) ice cold water

¼ cup (50 ml) raw apple cider vinegar

2 tablespoons (30 ml) raw honey or agave (or other whole-food sweetener) to taste

Grind or crack mustard seeds, mix with turmeric. Add water to the ground mustard/turmeric and stir. Let sit 1 hour or more in the refrigerator. Add remaining ingredients and blend. Optional: add more herbs (or sea salt), or substitute wine for some of the vinegar. Pour into sterilized jars, seal, and keep refrigerated.

### *Sautéed Mustard Greens*

This is a basic recipe. You can also mix mustard greens with other greens, such as spinach, Swiss chard, turnip, or beet greens. Or if you have an unsprayed yard, pick and eat your weeds. Dandelion, lamb's quarters, plantain, comfrey, chickweed, malva, and young salsify greens can be used. Some may wish to add bacon, or if meat isn't desired, a tiny amount of liquid smoke helps here. You can also add cubed zucchini or tofu when stir-frying the garlic and onions. Enjoy!

1 teaspoon (5 ml) olive oil (more if tofu/zucchini is used)

1 clove garlic, minced

1 small onion, chopped

Small amount of cubed tofu, zucchini, or bacon (optional)

1 large bunch mustard greens

Optional seasonings: sea salt, fresh lemon juice, tamari (or soy) sauce, flavored vinegar, fresh or dried herbs (including fresh-ground pepper), and liquid smoke.

Wash and dry greens, and remove coarse stems. Chop remaining stems into small pieces and leaves into 3-inch pieces. In a large skillet, heat olive oil over medium heat, add onions and garlic (and other optional ingredients) and stir-fry until onions are transparent. Add stem pieces and a small amount of water. Cook covered for a few minutes until stems are slightly tender. Add leaves (and tiny bit of liquid smoke, if desired). Sauté until all liquid has evaporated and greens are tender. Season and serve.

### *Green Drinks*

If you have any greens left over from cooking or salads, juice them! Mustard greens add a whole lot of "kick" to your morning drink. If you are in the market for a juicer, the Power Juicer is an excellent value, quiet and easy to use—and clean.

Mustard greens are usually too strong to drink alone, so try mixing with milder tastes such as apples, carrots, and/or celery—and even some milder greens like spinach. It is a warm, spicy change from plain spinach green drinks that many may find welcome. Place the fibrous material in your compost, or find creative ways to greens add to your cooking, including soup stock, added nutrition in meat or nonmeat loaves—use your imagination.

### *Mustard Sprouts*

Sprouting is not only for raw-foodists. It is something everyone needs to look into while we are entering into uncertain times with our food supply. It is inexpensive, healthful, inspires self-sufficiency, and doesn't take up much room in your home. You can also have a fresh food supply anywhere you live, even in Alaska! Sprouting a seed will not only change the seed from acidic to alkaline (desirable for lessening all disease), it also increases the nutrition up to 1,200 times when sprouted! Your only investment would be a sprouting tray, which pays for itself very quickly.

To sprout mustard seeds, it is recommended that the mix be 20 percent mustard seeds with 80 percent of milder types, such as alfalfa and clover, that will have the same sprouting schedule because of their spicy quality (and a small amount of cabbage if desired). Start with a total of 2 to 3 tablespoons of seeds. Soak seeds in water for 4 to 6 hours (or overnight) and place in tray, in some sunlight to encourage chlorophyll. Water and drain once a day (preferably the same time of day). If you plan to be away, put the seed tray in the refrigerator until you return. The sprouted seeds will be ready in 4 to 6 days. Store your sprouts in a dry paper towel inside a plastic bag in the refrigerator, or in a special "green bag," to further extend their freshness. Eat them in salads, on sandwiches, or even by themselves as a snack. If you made too many and you can tell they will "turn," throw them in the juicer or compost them if it is too late.

# Parsley: Compliments of the Chef

### ❧ by Anne Sula ❧

When a chef is preparing a plate of food for a hungry customer, she often adds one last ingredient before sending it out. This final supplement tells the diner he is about to eat something classy. It says that though the chef may have toiled in the heat of a commercial kitchen to create this dish, she is offering it with her compliments. Not only does this little addition provide a welcome flavor, it adds a splash of color—whether sprinkled on top, or discreetly snuggled up next to the food. Humble yet ubiquitous, parsley can do all these things, as well as so much more.

Because of its perception as merely a garnish in most Western cuisines,

Parsley

parsley is not considered a flavor suitable to be the focus of a dish. Nonetheless, if a recipe calls for parsley, most of us are obliged to buy a bundle of the stuff at the store even when we only need a little. If we tried to find additional recipes in which to use up the rest, it could take forever if we stuck with only recipes from northern Europe. The countries surrounding the Mediterranean, however, hold parsley in higher esteem, and those are the recipes that we should turn to in order to use up our leftover parsley in a dignified manner.

This article includes several recipes that use parsley as an ingredient, but first, I'll share with you some facts, history, and lore about this complementary little herb.

There are three kinds of parsley: curly (*Petroselinum. crispum*), flat-leaf (*P. crispum neapolitanum*), and Hamburg parsley (*P. tuberosum*). They all send up segmented leaves on grassy stalks, but the Hamburg kind is grown more for its long taproot, which looks like a parsnip and can be boiled.

Parsley greens have a distinctive grassy flavor and an almost mentholated quality that carries the taste into the nasal passages. Flat-leaf parsley—also known as Italian or Neapolitan parsley—is thought to have the strongest flavor so is usually preferred for cooking. Curly parsley can also be used, but the leaves are often tougher.

Parsley's high chlorophyll content makes it a natural breath freshener, and it is a good source of vitamins A, B, C, as well as potassium, iron, and others. As a tea, it has diuretic qualities. It is sometimes used to bring on delayed menstruation. Thus, pregnant women should avoid ingesting large or concentrated amounts of this herb.

Parsley most likely originated somewhere in the Mediterranean, but its original homeland is unknown. Its botanical name comes from the Greek word, *petro*, which means "stone," and it can be found growing on the rocky slopes of that country to this day. The Greeks say parsley first grew up from the place where Archemorous (the forerunner of death) was killed and eaten by serpents. Because of this, parsley was an important herb used at funerals in their culture, but not as a culinary herb. Instead, they fed it to their horses to give them courage. The Romans, however, appreciated its breath-freshening effects and used it as a cure for indigestion and inebriation.

During the Middle Ages, from about AD 1000 to 1453, parsley began to take on some sinister attributes in the eyes of northern Europeans, which is perhaps why it plays such a minor culinary role in most of their cuisines. Notoriously difficult to grow, people believed they should sow this biennial's seeds while cursing it under their breath. They also believed the seeds had to go down to Hades seven to nine times before it would germinate. Its association with the devil meant it was unlucky to give parsley as a housewarming gift, or to transplant it at all.

This unfortunate myth should be abandoned. Whether fresh, dried, or cooked, parsley is a welcome addition to almost any recipe. It pairs well with eggs, butter, starches, grains, and vegetables. Would chicken soup be so medicinal if there were no flecks of parsley floating among the noodles? I hazard to say it wouldn't.

Note: Whenever any of my recipes call for tomatoes, know that I peel them. Peeling them is optional if your tomatoes have thin skins.

## Parsley Salad (Tabouleh)

This cool-tasting summer salad is a great showcase for parsley's bright flavor. Nearly all Arabic-speaking countries have their own version. The ratio of the ingredients can be adjusted to your taste. Bring it on a picnic and serve it as an outright salad or as a filling for a pita sandwich with cucumbers and chickpeas.

3 cups, packed fresh parsley, stems removed and chopped (about the amount from one commercially packaged bundle)

½ medium yellow onion, chopped fine

¾ cup couscous

Leaves from 2 sprigs fresh spearmint, chopped

Juice of two lemons

2 medium tomatoes, chopped

1 small jalapeno pepper, diced small

½ cup and 1 teaspoon extra virgin olive oil

1¼ cup water

Salt and pepper to taste

1. Place water in a saucepan on the stove over high heat. Add 1 teaspoon olive oil and a pinch of salt. When it boils, remove from heat, add couscous, cover, and let stand for at least 10 minutes. Fluff with a fork.

2. Combine the couscous with chopped parsley, onion, spearmint, chopped tomatoes, and diced jalapeno pepper. Mix gently with your hand or a spoon.

3. Add lemon juice, oil, and salt and mix well. (Serves 4–6)

## Moroccan Tomato Sauce (Chermoula)

This flavorful sauce goes well with anything you can put on the grill—beef, chicken, lamb, and vegetables. Serve with couscous cooked in chicken broth.

2  medium tomatoes, chopped

1  garlic clove, minced

½  onion, chopped

1  teaspoon cumin

1  tablespoon fresh lemon juice

½  cup packed parsley leaves, chopped

¼  cup packed cilantro leaves, chopped

Salt and fresh ground pepper

Olive oil

1. Coat the bottom of a saucepan with olive oil and place over medium heat. When the oil begins to ripple, add the onion and sauté until translucent.

2. Add the garlic and allow it to become fragrant before sprinkling with cumin. Next, stir in the tomatoes and lemon juice. Reduce heat, stirring occasionally, and continue cooking for about 15 minutes.

3. Just before taking the pan off the heat, throw in the cilantro and parsley. Add salt and pepper to your preference. Keep warm while you grill your meat or vegetables. (Serves 2)

## Parsley Squash Soup with Egg

This soup is reminiscent of the Greek egg and lemon soup, avgolemono, with the addition of late-season vegetables. It is a good way to use up summer squash and zucchini, and feel free to add more parsley, too, if you have a lot in your garden. Keep this soup in mind if you are stricken with a cold and looking for a quick chicken soup alternative.

¾  cup packed parsley leaves, chopped

2 to 4 summer squash or zucchini, shredded

1   onion, diced fine

⅛ cup rice

2   eggs

2   tablespoons fresh lemon juice

4   cups water

Olive oil

Salt and pepper to taste

1. Coat the bottom of a soup pot with olive oil and place over medium heat. Add onions and sauté until translucent. Add the rice and stir occasionally for about 3 minutes, so the grains become coated in oil.

2. Gently drop in the squash by the handful, dusting each layer with a pinch of salt. Let the mixture sit for about 1 minute, then begin to stir so the squash heats through and sweats. Add the parsley and continue stirring for about 4 minutes.

3. Add the water, increase the heat, and bring to a boil. Then reduce the heat and let simmer for 20 to 30 minutes.

4. Use a fork to beat the eggs with the lemon juice in a large heat-resistant bowl. Carefully—so not to curdle the egg—stir in a teaspoon of soup broth. Continue to add broth and stir until the mixture begins to feel hot, is lemony yellow, and smooth in texture.

5. Lower the heat and pour the egg mixture into the pot while stirring the soup. Add salt and pepper to taste. Feel free to add more lemon juice. (Serves 4)

My oven broke while researching recipes for this edition of the *Herbal Almanac*, so I was overjoyed to find myself drawn to Moroccan culture, where a lot of their cuisine was created for a nomadic way of life, and does not require an oven. This recipe uses steaming to cook the chicken, so it is necessary to own a steam basket that is large enough to hold one. Or, purchase a poussin (a young chicken), Cornish hens, partridge, or quail.

The proportions of the stuffing in this recipe makes more than will fit in the bird. I simply prepare the extra in a saucepan as I would regular rice, adding a ¼ cup of chicken broth and simmering for 15 minutes. If your bird is much larger than the one in the recipe, you might need to increase the stuffing's proportions. Save the leftover water in the steamer as a base for chicken broth. It is worth tracking down preserved lemons for this recipe. I have discovered that they make a great garnish for vodka martinis, and can be added to lots of savory dishes.

## Chicken with Parsley Stuffing

½  cup basmati rice, cooked and rinsed

2  celery ribs, chopped

2  medium tomatoes, chopped

1  cup packed parsley, stems removed and chopped

1  preserved lemon, chopped (or ¼ cup fresh lemon juice with 1 teaspoon salt)

1  jalapeno, minced

2  pound whole chicken

1  carrot

2  bay leaves

Salt

1. Combine cooked, rinsed, and drained rice with the one celery rib (chopped), tomatoes, parsley, one half of the preserved

lemon (or lemon juice and salt) and jalapeno. Place the stuffing in the cavity of the chicken.

2. Set the chicken into the top part of a steamer and cover with a damp cloth. In the bottom of the steamer, pour in at least 6 cups of water and add the carrot, bay leaves, three pinches of salt, and the remaining celery rib.

3. Set the bottom of the steamer over high heat and bring to a boil. Put steamer top and chicken into place and cover with the lid. Lower the heat slightly, so it is still bubbling, but not as vigorously. Let it steam for at least one hour. Occasionally, check the level of water in the bottom of the steamer and add more if necessary. The chicken is done when the meat falls off the bone. (Serves 2)

# Gremolata

A versatile parsley condiment, gremolata enlivens otherwise heavy foods, like *osso buco alla Milanese*, steak, and grilled hamburgers. Use liberally and often.

> 1 cup packed parsley leaves, with thick stems removed and chopped fine
>
> 1 head garlic (about 16 cloves), peeled and minced
>
> Zest of one lemon

Mix together all ingredients. (Makes about 1½ cups)

# Jade Splendor

After all those savory dishes, how does parsley fare in a sweet recipe? Honestly, I was having difficulty coming up with one on my own. Then one day, I stopped in for breakfast at Tao

Natural Foods, in Minneapolis, and saw a fresh juice recipe that showcased parsley and fruit. The green frothy drink smelled intensely of parsley, but when I took a sip, the herb's grassy flavor was hidden among the sweet notes of the apples and pears. My brain tried to come up with a logical association and I decided that it tasted like apple cider tastes like when made with green-skinned apples.

Kitchen manager Dan Relyea created the drink in 2006 and was gracious enough to share the recipe. He confessed that Jade Splendor was the answer to the question that most every person, who finds they're in possession of too much parsley, asks: "What am I going to do with all that stuff?"

This recipe requires a juicer that has the ability to grind greens. An alternative is to create a parsley and lemon puree to pour over the other fruit in the form of a salad. Also, if you ask nicely, your local juice bar may be willing to concoct this drink for you.

¾ cup parsley (about ¼ of a bunch)

2 pears, cored and chopped

2 apples, cored and chopped

1 lemon, juiced

1. Run the parsley through the juicer in small quantities so it will not overload the engine. Combine with the lemon juice in a glass.

2. Juice the pears and apples and add to the parsley and lemon.

3. Stir vigorously because the parsley has a tendency to coagulate.

4. Drink immediately. (Makes 12 ounces)

# For Further Reading

Bsisu, May S. *The Arab Table: Recipes and Culinary Traditions.* New York: William Morrow, 2005.

Callery, Emma. *The Complete Book of Herbs: A Practical Guide to Cultivating, Drying, and Cooking with more than 50 Herbs.* Philadelphia: Courage Books, 1994.

Hemphill, Ian. *The Spice and Herb Bible: A Cook's Guide.* Toronto, Ontario: Robert Rose, Inc., 2000.

Hemphill, John and Rosemary Hemphill. *What Herb is That? How to Grow and Use the Culinary Herbs.* Mechanicsburg, PA: Stackpole Books, 1990.

Hollis, Sarah. *The Country Diary Herbal.* New York: Henry Holt and Company, 1990.

M'Souli Hassan. *Moroccan Modern.* Northampton, MA: Interlink Books, 2004.

Roden, Claudia. *Arabesque: A Taste of Morocco, Turkey, & Lebanon.* New York: Alfred A. Knopf, 2006.

# Cordial Craft

## ⤞ Susan Pesznecker ⤝

Y ou've just finished the perfect
ritual. The stars are sparkling
overhead and your circle is
wrapped—and rapt—in fellowship.
It's time for cakes and ale, but you want
something extra special. Imagine the
impact created by a silver tray bearing
a crystal decanter of sparkling ruby
or deep purple cordial, a tasty and
magickal concoction of fruit, herbs,
spices, and alcohol. Life is good!

Cordial craft is one of those sleights
of hand that impresses the guests even
as the hostess gives a secret smile. For
all of its elegance, a homemade cordial is easy to make and satisfying to
enjoy. It's also sustainable—a great
way to use fruit that's a bit too ripe
for eating. With a little time and a few
simple tools, your larder can be filled

and your life spiced up by an array of cordials, shrubs, safts, and other enchanted libations.

## What is a Cordial?

A cordial is an alcoholic beverage made with fruit pulp and juice. Cordials differ from liqueurs in that liqueurs may not include fruit and often use herbs, barks, flowers, roots, seeds, and sometimes cream. Both cordials and liqueurs can include spices and flavorings and are traditionally consumed in small amounts after the evening meal.

Cordials and liqueurs are the offspring of medieval herbal remedies, whose makers found that high percentages of alcohol or sugar could prolong the life of any infusion. Cordials then were believed to be invigorating, stimulating, and even aphrodisiacal. One well-known example, the Royal Usquebaugh, was fortified with flecks of gold leaf, echoing the alchemical *Aureum potabile*, "drinkable gold." Usquebaugh comes from a Celtic word meaning "life-water," with the golden flecks symbolizing the power of the sun.

Today's cordials are simple blends of fruit, sugar, and alcohol left to infuse for several weeks before bottling. Most cordials have an alcohol content between 15 and 30 percent (30 to 60 proof).

## Making Fruit Cordials

Cordial craft is a matter of time, patience, and good ingredients. You'll need one-quart glass canning (Mason) jars; fresh fruit; sugar (organic if possible); and good quality alcohol or vinegar according to the recipe. Wash the jars and lids in hot water and air dry, or put through a dishwasher cycle. Rinse the fruit, drain on towels, and crush or chop as directed. Measure sugar before beginning.

### Berry Cordial (Base Recipe)

2   cups crushed raspberries, blackberries, or other cane berries

¾   cup sugar

½–¾ cup vodka (depending on desired strength)

Add sugar and vodka to crushed berries and spoon the mixture into a Mason jar. Screw on the lid and shake well. Leave the jar sitting on your kitchen counter—out of direct sunlight—three to four weeks. Shake vigorously twice a day.

The finished brew will have a rich, deep color and flavor. Strain through a fine sieve or cheesecloth into a clean bowl, then pour into a decorative bottle or decanter. Store in the refrigerator for up to a year, bringing to room temperature before drinking.

### Cherry Cordial

1½ pounds sweet cherries (pitted, stemmed, and chopped)

3   cups vodka

1   cup brandy

2¼ cups sugar

For a cherry cordial, combine the above ingredients. Cover tightly; shake every two days and age for two to three months.

### Cranberry Cordial

1   pound coarsely chopped cranberries

3   cups sugar

2   cups light rum

Combine ingredients. Cover tightly, shake daily, and age for six weeks. Finish as in the base recipe.

Begin with spring water and include organic flavorings or spices: use almond for prosperity; allspice for luck; anise for purification; cinnamon for success or power; cloves for protection; ginger for love; or vanilla for mental powers. For a special effect, add a crystal, pearl, or other precious item to the cordial bottle or decanter—just be sure not to drink it! Serve your cordials in a fine decanter for the perfect toast, or a quiet evening by the fire. Stir a spoonful into your favorite vinaigrette, pour over ice cream, or concoct a delicious milkshake. A bit of raspberry or cherry cordial stirred into a rich mug of hot chocolate is wicked!

## The Vinegar Shrub

Shrubs are the cordial's grandmother, replacing alcohol with vinegar for a splendidly sharp, refreshing drink that's perfect in hot weather. For a raspberry shrub, crush ripe raspberries and add one part cider vinegar to 6 parts fruit. Mix well, cover, and set aside. Leave undisturbed for 4 to 5 days; then skim off foam and strain through a sieve or cheesecloth. Measure again and add 1 part sugar to 2 parts juice. Boil to a syrupy consistency and pour into clean jars. Store in the refrigerator for up to a year; freeze or process in a water bath canner for longer storage. To serve, add 2 or 3 tablespoonfuls to a glass of chopped ice and water.

## Cordials and Safts
## Down Under and Up Over

In Aussie-speak, a cordial is fruit syrup that's mixed with sparkling water or soda before drinking. This refreshing, alcohol-free drink is served at meals and consumed by the tumbler. It begins with simple syrup, made by boiling 1 part water and 1 part sugar until the sugar dissolves. The syrup is then allowed to cool. Combine one part fruit juice with 1 part syrup; add lemon juice or finely grated peel if desired. Bottle in clean Mason jars and refrigerate for up to one week, or freeze for longer storage. To use, mix 1 part cordial with 10 parts sparkling water or soda and serve over ice.

Sweden's saft is much like the Australian cordial in that it involves an alcohol-free mixture of sugar and fruit juice. But unlike the Aussie version, saft is cooked.

### *Saft*

4   cups fresh berries (stone fruits may be added)
1   inch piece of peeled, sliced fresh ginger
2   cups water
1½ cups sugar

Crush fresh berries. Combine berries with fresh ginger and water in a saucepan. Bring to a simmer and cook until fruit is soft, about 10 minutes. Strain into a second saucepan, pressing gently. Discard fruit. Add sugar to the fruit liquid. Bring to a simmer and cook until liquid reduces to a light syrup, about 15 minutes. Cool and pour into clean bottles; refrigerate for three months or freeze for longer periods. To serve, pour ¼ cup saft into an 8–10 ounce tumbler, add ice, and fill with soda or ginger ale.

## Wonderful Waters

Interested in more? A search through old cookbooks might uncover the English bragget, a boiled, fermented cordial of beer, honey, peppercorns, cinnamon, cloves, and mace. Claretum was another English concoction of claret wine and honey, boiled down to a syrup and strained to clarity. You might discover *aqua mirabilis*—"wonderful water"—a richly spiced wine using whole spices and sliced fruits. Ireland's ancient *aqua composita* combines aniseed, molasses, dates, and cloves to make a rich, spicy cordial. Explore a hearth full of liquid experiments: may you sip well!

# Edible Flowers

### ❧ by Dallas Jennifer Cobb ❧

Looking for a delicious way to use herbs that is both brilliant and novel? Consider the use of edible flowers. Not only are they good for us, but herb flowers taste great and are appealing to the eye, adding sensual beauty to our food and culinary arrangements.

While we often focus on herbs for their medicinal or culinary qualities, edible herbal flowers also possess the power to uplift our emotions and spirit, bringing beauty and artistry to our food. Eating the flowers is also a novel way to introduce the medicinal benefits of herbs to people who are often reticent to eat what is good for them. It is, for example, especially easy to get children to eat flowers because they are so beautiful.

# Pretty and Powerful

Before eating herb flowers, be certain to correctly identify them, as many herbs and weeds can be irritating or toxic. When you dine out in restaurants, don't make the mistake of assuming that all flowers served with or on the food are edible. Many chefs use flowers as garnishes these days, but sometimes without sound knowledge of herbs and their flowers. Sadly, non-edible varieties of flowers are often used.

As with dining out, when you use herbal flowers at home in your culinary creations, be sure that what you are using is safe. Many people, your family and friends included, assume that if a flower is on their plate, it must be edible. This is not always true.

To ensure safety and the well-being of yourself, family and friends, always identify the flowers you are going to use before using them. Get a good guide book to herbs in your area, one that features accurate pictures and verbal descriptions.

Then, confirm that no pesticides were used on the flowers during their growing process. This is easier to do if you grow them yourself. Never eat flowers that have been commercially produced in nurseries or garden centers, or purchased from florists. These are commonly treated with pesticides and it is impossible to track their production. If you are gathering wild herbal flowers to eat, choose the ones that grow away from major roadways to avoid the toxic effect of products spilled or applied to roads, and the herbicides used along roadsides to control weed growth.

Always remove the pistils and stamens of flowers before eating them. With some varieties it is important to remove the hard, waxy bits at the bottom of the petals as well. With edible herbal flowers, the petals, usually the most colorful part, are the part recommended for eating. Be sure to thoroughly wash all flowers before eating them to remove any bugs or dirt that might be on them. This is best done just before consuming them, so they don't wilt or brown.

The following list of herbs with edible flowers is not exhaustive, but identifies species commonly found throughout many parts of North America and successfully used in culinary creations. With each herb flower are suggestions for use, but feel free to find your own, adding edible herbal flowers to your favorite recipes. Included are a few of my favorite edible herb flower recipes to start you off.

## *Allium*

Allium, a family containing almost 400 species, is popular for culinary purposes. Most commonly used are leeks, chives, garlic, and garlic chives. A pungently flavorful family, the herbs range from mildly onion and garlic flavored, to very powerful onion and garlic flavors. While all parts of the plants are edible, the flowers possess a stronger flavor than the leaves. The flower heads are removed on bulbous roots in order to focus the plant's energy on development of the roots, so for onions and garlic, this process of flower removal actually helps the development of the fruit. Use chive blossoms to add a mild onion flavor and aroma to soups, salads, and omelets. Garlic blossoms, or scapes, make great edible garnishes, their twisty shapes adding to the beauty of presentation. Garlic scapes are also great for adding to fresh basil to make a mild pesto sauce. Also add diced garlic scapes to salad and salad dressings for a mild garlic zing.

Use either garlic scape or chive blossoms to give a savory flavor to a simple omelet. Scape tastes like a mild version of garlic, and chives are a mild onion flavor. The recipe for the mild allium omelet that follows will serve two people.

# Mild Allium Omelet

4 eggs

4 tablespoons milk or soy milk

Salt and pepper to taste

2 tablespoons minced chives, or 1 tablespoon minced garlic scapes

1 tablespoon butter

6 chive blossoms, or two whole garlic scapes, washed and dried, for garnish

1. Melt the butter at a medium heat in a frying pan.

2. Combine eggs, milk, salt, pepper, and chives in a bowl and whisk briskly until well combined, then pour into the hot, buttered frying pan.

3. Watching the edges of the omelet, and get ready to turn the heat down a bit when the egg mixture begins to set. Use a spatula to gently press the cooked edges into the middle, letting the uncooked eggs ooze out, to the edges to cook.

4. When the eggs are mostly set, sprinkle the washed, minced herbs in, and fold the edges of the omelet over.

5. When you serve the omelet, garnish with the remaining whole blossoms and whole wheat toast.

## Grilled Asparagus and Chive Flowers

Early in the spring, these two arise out of the garden close together in time. The delicate taste of asparagus enhanced by the savory chive flowers is a treat to remember. The gentle garlicky taste of chives enhances the flavor of fresh asparagus, and purple and green look good together.

Drizzle asparagus and whole chive flowers with a simple combination of olive oil and balsamic vinegar. Grill lightly, being careful not to overcook the asparagus. Serve the asparagus spears laying side by side, and place the chive blossoms on top.

## Angelica

Angelica flowers range from pale lavender to deep rose and taste similar to licorice. Angelica blossoms can be used for tea, to add a mild licorice flavor to baked goods, or for grilling fish. Another mildly licorice tasting flower is anise hyssop. A commonly used herb in Chinese cooking and traditional root beer making, the flower is a tasty addition to stir fry.

## Basil

There are many varieties of basil, all with edible flowers ranging in color from white to pink and light purple. Because of the different varieties, each basil has a distinct flavor. The flowers have a similar, though milder flavor, to the plant leaves. Basil is ideal for use in salad, pasta dishes, tomato sauces, and salad dressings.

## Bee Balm

Bee balm is part of the Monarda family, and is also called wild bergamot. With many different varieties bee balm comes in a pallet of colors, and tastes—lemony, orange or minty. Traditionally used in Earl Gray tea, you will recognize the amazing aroma and taste of bee balm. Use the colorful blossoms in fruit salad, teas, and as an edible garnish for desserts.

## Borage

You've seen the lovely blue of borage growing along the side of the road. Also known as cornflower, the blue star-shaped flowers are common throughout North America. Borage is commonly used to flavor drinks and fruit salads, and mixed with cream cheese to make a lovely blue spread for bagels. Similar in taste to borage, burnet can be used as well.

### *Calendula*

Calendula is one of the most versatile flowering herbs. Also called pot marigold, it is bright orange, to bright yellow, and has a mild peppery flavor. Used in salads to add startling color, or in pasta, rice, quinoa or other grains to suffuse them with a pleasantly yellow color, it is similar to saffron, but much more affordable.

### Summer Satisfaction Salad Recipe

Garnish your mixed salad greens with the colorful brilliance of calendula flowers and chive flowers. Not just gorgeous, they add a peppery zing to salad that enhances vinegrette dressings. The visual impact of green, purple, and two shades of orange is stunning, and the combined flavors of the peppery cabbage, spicy calendula, and sweet carrots is wonderful.

1. Combine 3 parts mixed greens, 1 part shredded red cabbage, and 1 part shredded carrot in a bowl.

2. Toss lightly. Before serving, sprinkle the top with calendula petals.

3. Serve with a light balsamic vinaigrette dressing.

### *Chamomile*

Chamomile flowers are commonly used in herbal teas that promote calm and sleep. These small, daisy-like flowers often grow along roadsides. They taste and smell sweet.

## Clover and Dandelion

Common weeds, clover and dandelion flowers can both be eaten. Clover blossoms have a sweet, licorice-like flavor, while dandelions are sweet like honey when they are young, and get bitter as they mature. Pick both of these when they are young and small. Both can be added to salads, eaten raw, or steamed.

## Coriander

Coriander is also known as cilantro, and the flowers have a taste similar to the leaves and seeds. Because cooking subdues the flavor, always use coriander flowers raw. Coriander is a tasty addition to bean dishes, salads, Vietnamese cooking, and cold vegetables.

## Dill

The flowers of the dill plant taste a lot like the leaves, but stronger. They can be used in vinegars, soups, seafood dishes, and salad dressing, or to make tangy dips.

## Lavender

We all love lavender for its unique flavor, scent, and color. Lavender can be used in baking, or to flavor sugars; and a sprig can be added to lemonade. It combines well with lemon and orange, and is a delicate taste to use with flan, custard, or crème brûlée. Try this recipe.

### Lavender Shortbread Recipe

An old-time recipe, this one makes a delicate shortbread that will melt in your mouth. Perfect for tea parties, kids' treats, and grown-up pleasures, lavender shortbread is delicate, savory and sweet.

1   tablespoon lavender flowers, stems removed
    and finely ground

1   cup butter

½   cup sugar

2¼ cups flour (use oat for a tasty traditional ver-
    sion, or rice for a gluten-free treat)

1. Powder lavender flowers in a coffee grinder, or mortar and pestle.

2. Cream together with cold butter and sugar. I often use a food processor to do this, keeping the dough cool. The cool temperature produces the exquisite texture.

3. Add flour and work into a dough, keeping the mixture cold. If you used your hands to mix the dough, refrigerate for 20 minutes to cool.

4. Quickly roll dough into a log shape, then slice in rounds ⅛ to ¼ inch in thickness.

5. Place these on a nonstick cooking sheet. Bake at 350°F for 12 to 15 minutes, or until golden brown.

6. Cool on rack before serving.

### Lemon Verbena

Lemon verbena is commonly used as a tea herb and has tiny, cream-colored flowers with a heady citrus scent. Lemon verbena can also be used to flavor custard, flan, and crème brûlée, or successfully used in oils and vinegars.

### Mint

Mint is widely used in North African and Mediterranean cooking, but here in North America, it is most commonly used as a tea herb. You can use mint in vinegars, oils, chopped finely in spring salads, or made into sauces for pork or lamb.

### Oregano

Oregano flowers can be eaten, and they are similar in taste to the oregano leaf, only milder. With high antioxidant properties oregano is considered one of the great healers. Use the flowers on gourmet pizza, to accompany Italian food or pasta dishes, or in vinegars and oils.

### Rosemary

When rosemary is happy, it flowers. The blossoms taste like the leaves, only milder. They are often used to accent meat dishes, make lemon rosemary chicken, rosemary bread, or shortbread, or to season Mediterranean dishes. Don't forget to add rosemary flowers to vinegars or oils for flavor and beauty.

### Sage

Like rosemary, the flowers of the sage plant taste like the leaf, only milder. They are a gorgeous blue and can be used in baking, salads, and as a garnish. You can also use the blossoms anywhere you would usually use the leafy sage—in bean dishes, with chicken, or as part of a Provençal herb mixture.

### Thyme

Like rosemary and sage, thyme flowers have a milder taste than the leaf. Thyme tastes great with chicken, and in Caribbean cooking, so use the flowers as you would the herb, or use them to garnish, or finish, the plate.

## Edible Flowers

While not classified as herbs, there are many common ornamental flowers, common to our gardens, that are also edible.

Like with the herbal flowers, always take time to properly identify the species before eating it.

### Carnation

Carnations have sweet petals, but they need to be cut away from the bitter base of the flower before using them in baking and desserts. Bright in color, the petals are ideal for adding to salads, stir fry, or bottled vinegars and oils. The liqueur chartreuse contains carnation petals.

### Chrysanthemum

Used throughout the world in teas and cooking, chrysanthemums are edible too. With colors ranging from white, to pink, red, and orange, their taste varies from tangy to bitter. Most people blanch these petals before eating them to remove some of the bitterness, then scatter them in salads or on plates as a garnish.

### Daylily

The petals of daylilies possess a slightly sweet vegetable flavor so long as the bitter white base is cut off of the flower. With such a wide variety of colors, this is a versatile flower for visual presentation on a veggie or fruit tray, or sprinkled in a mixed greens salad.

### Fuchsia

We love fuchsia at my house. The ornamental flowers have a slightly acidic taste and are commonly used as a garnish. Their vibrant colors make a focal point for the plate. Dipped in sugar and dried, the blossoms make a lovely after-dinner treat.

### Hibiscus

Hibiscus flowers have been long used in herbal teas. With a sour, cranberry-like flavor, they combine well with citrus, and add zing to salads. The gorgeous trumpet-like shape is also a versatile garnish.

### Hollyhock

While they grow abundantly, hollyhock flowers have a very bland taste. They are edible though, so use them freely to garnish plates or float in punch. Their wide bell-shape comes is a huge variety of summer colors.

### Johnny-Jump-up

Johnny-jump-ups, with their yellow, white, and purple flowers have a mild wintergreen flavor. They can be added to baking, used to decorate cakes, or sprinkled on salads; it can be added to summer drinks, used to garnish pates, or sprinkled on top of soups—wherever a mild, minty taste would be welcome.

### Nasturtium

Nasturtiums are commonly used by chefs to garnish food, adding bright color and zingy taste. They hold their shape nicely and do not easily wilt. Nasturtiums come in colors ranging from pale yellow to bright orange and brilliant red and are one of the most commonly used edible flowers. Similar to watercress in taste—a little peppery and spicy—they make wonderful addition to salads, floating on top of soup or gazpacho, or garnishing any serving plate or tray.

### Pansy

The common garden pansy has a sweet alfalfa flavor. Historically, sugared and served with tea, you can use them in fruit salads, green salad, desserts, or soups. The brilliant purple and yellow colors add a focal point to the plate when used as a garnish.

### Peony

Peonies are known as a plant for prosperity in China. Include some peony petals in a summer salad, or to color lemonade or summer ice tea.

### Rose

Historically, rose petals were used to flavor chocolate, ice cream, and desserts, and to make rose petal jelly. With a wide range of colors, they add a wonderful accent to a plate or dish, with the darker colors possessing the stronger taste. Sweet, fruity, and tasting like the flower smells, rose petals can also be scattered on a plate to dress it, or tossed in a salad.

### Violet

Violets are related to Johnny-jump-ups, violas, and pansies. They come in colors ranging from vivid purples and yellow to soft pastels. Candied violets were common in the Victorian era, and are still widely used to decorate cakes and desserts.

## Vegetable Flowers

Certain vining plants flower prolifically and the blossoms are edible. Broccoli and cauliflower are actually the flower buds of the plant that, when left too long in the garden, burst into bright flowers.

### Peas

Pea blossoms taste a lot like peas. Remember that you don't want to eat all your blossoms or your plants will never yield vegetables. But often they are abundant and you can eat some of them in their flower states without hurting the harvest. Be sure you eat only the blooms of edible peas, as ornamental pea blossoms are toxic.

## Radish

You have probably had radish sprouts and eaten the radish itself, but have you ever eaten the flowers from a radish plant? Like the sprouts, they have a delicious radish flavor, with a bit of bite. Use these pretty pink blossoms in salads or Asian-type stir fry to add some spice.

## Squash and More

Flowers from vining plants are commonly eaten in many parts of the world. The most common are squash, zucchini and pumpkin. If you grow your own vines, you can harvest a few flowers to eat or cook with, leaving some to mature into vegetables. Taking the flowers off will actually help the plant focus its energy on fruit production.

In Mexico fried squash blossoms is a delicacy often found in the market cafes. They are also common to Spain and Italy. You can use either squash, zucchini, or pumpkin blossoms for this recipe.

### Fried Squash Blossoms

12  squash (pumpkin or zucchini) blossoms

1  egg, scrambled

5  tablespoons bread crumbs

4  tablespoons vegetable oil

Garlic scapes to garnish

Remove squash blossoms from their stems. Press them to flatten, then open them into nice flower shapes. Heat oil in frying pan over medium heat. Dip blossoms into egg mixture, then into bread crumbs and place them into the fry pan, frying 6 flowers at a time until crispy. Drain on paper towels before serving.

# Create an Edible-flower Garden

Planning and planting a theme garden is great fun. Creating an edible-flower herb garden will give structure and purpose to the garden, and pleasure to the gardener. It gathers together the herbs with edible flowers, so you know where in the garden to look when you are preparing culinary delights requiring interesting color, taste, and texture. Having your own garden assures you a source of pesticide-free, quality edible-herbal flowers.

Because many of the herbs that have edible flowers are so easy to grow, an edible flower garden is one that returns again year after year, and thrives with little intervention.

The best edible-flower herb garden is comprised primarily of perennial herbs and requires the reseeding (or self-seeding) of some favorite annuals. Choosing a few of the most common herbs to start with will get you off to a good start. Chives, parsley, sage, rosemary, thyme, chamomile, calendula, and a few different flavored basils make a great selection of flavors, colors, and fragrances.

With your own edible-herbal flower garden you can enjoy the beauty, taste, and medicinal qualities of herbs year-round.

# Indian Herbs for Curries

### ❧ by Chandra Moira Beal ❧

India's cuisine is a swirl of textures and flavors that evolved from a flourishing spice trade over centuries. The exotic ingredients of this continent are making their way into supermarkets everywhere, making the creation of authentic Indian food easy. Dishes are as varied as the many states making up this land, and every Indian dish is created with a distinct blend of spices, sometimes combining over a dozen herbs for a complex flavor. In Indian homes, spice blends, or "masalas," are made up ahead of time. They can be stored from three to six months if kept in a jar in a cool, dark place.

Following are some of the commonly used herbs in masalas, with instructions for mixing up your own blends and cooking with them.

# Asafoetida

Asafoetida isn't native to India, but it has been an essential part of the cookery there for ages. The name comes from *aza*, which means "resin," and *foetidus* or "stinking." It has an offensive smell and is sometimes called "devil's dung." Asafoetida comes from the rhizome of a giant species of fennel. Just before flowering, the stalks are cut and a milky liquid oozes out. When dried, it forms asafoetida. The commercial product is a pale yellow powder that smells somewhat like pickled eggs due to the presence of sulphur. It tastes horrible on its own, but don't be put off. When it's added to savory dishes, asafoetida can complete the complexity of flavors, especially with lentils, vegetables, and pickles. Always use sparingly—just a tiny pinch will do. Toasting it will also calm the pungent taste.

# Cardamom

If pepper is the king of spices, then cardamom is the queen. Cardamom is the dried fruit of an herbaceous perennial in the ginger family which can grow up to 15 feet tall! The fruit pods are picked just before they ripen and then dried in the sun. Each pod contains several dark brown, sticky seeds. The seeds are sweet and mild smelling, but when crushed they release a strong, camphor-like fragrance. The taste is bittersweet. To get the most flavor, buy the whole pods and release the seeds as you need them.

# Coriander

Coriander, also called cilantro, is used prolifically in almost every Indian dish, usually with the bright green leaves scattered across the plate as a vibrant garnish. The leaves are fragile and bruise easily, giving a fresh and fruity taste, while the seeds are sweet and peppery. A powder made from the roasted and ground seeds is indispensible in the kitchen and can be used in virtually every savory dish, in curries, chutneys, soups, and drinks.

## Cumin

Cumin is another of the ancient herbs, found in almost every Indian dish. The seed is actually the fruit of a small annual herb related to coriander, native to the Nile valley. The seeds can range from light green to dark brown and have a very distinctive smell—some say bitter. Like coriander, you either love it or hate it. Cumin is commonly available as whole seed or powder. You can make your own powder by toasting the seeds in a skillet until they change color, then grinding them into a fine powder. Roasting cumin releases and enhances its earthy flavor.

## Curry Leaves

Essential to any south Indian dish, these fresh green leaves are often grown on a windowsill and used as needed. Dried leaves and powders can be used in place of the fresh leaves.

## Fennel

Fresh stalks of fennel are sold outside Indian schools, where children chew on the juicy sweet leaves. The roasted seeds are commonly served after a meal as a digestive. The seeds, which are the dried ripe fruit of the perennial herb, have a sweet flavor that turns mellow and bitter when toasted. The fresh plant has feathery leaves and clusters of tiny yellow flowers. You can buy the fresh bulb and use the whole plant, or buy the dried whole seeds or ground powder. Fennel adds richness to gravies, sweetness to desserts, and zest to vegetables.

# Fenugreek

Fenugreek is an essential ingredient in most curry powders. Use the fresh leaves and stalks, or the seeds, which come whole, crushed, or powdered. It has a powerful taste and aroma with strong curry overtones. Cooking the plant subdues its flavor.

# Nigella

Nigella is the dried seed-like fruit of a small herb with wispy leaves and white flowers that ripen into seedpods. Like cardamom, the pods that nigella produces are dried and crushed to release the tiny seeds. It has a faintly nutty taste but can also be bitter. Buy the seeds whole and grind them at home for the best flavor.

# Turmeric

A very traditional and versatile Indian spice, turmeric is at the heart and soul of any curry. Its vivid yellow-orange color is associated with purification and cleansing. Even today Indian brides and grooms are ritually anointed with turmeric before their wedding. Turmeric has an earthy, musky flavor on its own but has a way of enhancing and balancing other flavors when used in combination. Add it to a dish for color or taste, or to thicken liquids. Added to oils before other ingredients, turmeric gives the whole dish a deep saffron color and pungency; when added after the main ingredients, it imparts a more subtle flavor and gives the dish a soft yellow hue. Be judicious when using it with green vegetables, as it can turn them grey and bitter. Also be careful when handling turmeric as it can stain skin and clothes.

Other ingredients you may want to have on hand, and which should be readily available at the supermarket, are: cloves, cinnamon, black peppercorns, bay leaves, mace, dried red chilies, sesame seeds, flaked coconut, cayenne pepper, ginger powder, garlic, and salt. Tamarind pulp and mango powder are frequently used in Indian cooking, and should be available in ethnic shops.

# Make Your Own Spice Blends
## *Garam Masala*

Used in the north, where the winters are bitter and cold, garam masala is a warming blend.

| | |
|---|---|
| 1 | teaspoon black peppercorns |
| 2 | teaspoons cumin seeds |
| 1 | stick cinnamon |
| 1 | teaspoon cardamom seeds |
| 1 | teaspoon cloves |
| 3 | bay leaves |

Grind everything in a dedicated coffee grinder, or with a mortar and pestle, and store in a jar.

## *Sambhar Powder*

Sambhar is named for a lentil dish created in the mostly vegetarian region of Tamil Nadu. It is eaten every day to provide protein in the meat-free diet. The masala is rust-colored and has an earthy smell with a warm and acidic taste. Sambhar is always used with lentils and is best added before the legumes so the flavors can develop. It also thickens the dish.

1 teaspoon black mustard seeds

1 teaspoon fenugreek seeds

2 teaspoons cumin seeds

12 red chilies, de-seeded (or number to your taste)

1 teaspoon black peppercorns

1 teaspoon coriander seeds

1 teaspoon turmeric powder

¼ teaspoon asafoetida

3 teaspoons corn oil

3 tablespoons lentils

Dry roast all the whole spices in a heavy skillet over low heat. The seeds will crackle and pop. Add the turmeric and asafoetida, stir and remove from heat. Remove to a bowl. In the same pan, heat the oil and sauté the lentils. When they turn dark brown, add the mixture to other roasted spices. Cool and grind until fine.

## *Goda Masala*

Goda masala comes from Mumbai, on the west coast of India. It's an area that is infused with foods from the lush tropical climate. Dishes tend to be hot and use coconut sauces. This mixture flavors lentil and vegetable dishes, and can be added before or after the main ingredients, depending on whether a subtle or strong flavor is desired.

5 cardamom pods

1 stick cinnamon

5 cloves

2 bay leaves

1 teaspoon corn oil

2 teaspoons sesame seeds

2 teaspoons coriander seeds

4 teaspoons flaked coconut

10 black peppercorns

2 tablespoons poppy seeds

Release the cardamom seeds from the pods and sauté with cinnamon, cloves, and bay leaves in oil until the cloves swell. Dry roast the remaining ingredients until the coconut turns dark brown. Cool and grind with the other spices into a fine powder.

### Tandoori Masala

Tandoori cooking comes from Punjab, where large earthen or clay ovens are half buried in the ground and made red hot with a coal fire. Marinated meats or cheeses are skewered and cooked in the tandoor until juicy and done. Breads and rotis are also cooked this way. Food cooked in a tandoor comes out with a blend of spice and charcoal flavors. Adding tandoori powder to a skillet at home can impart the same flavors without the tandoor. This masala is fragrant and spicy, with hot, salty and sour flavors dominated by the cumin and coriander. Use it in marinades or add to the dish with or after the oil. You can even dry roast it and add to mayonnaise or sour cream for a spicy dip. Commercial tandoori masala is bright red due to a coloring agent. Your homemade masala will have a more earthen, amber color, or you can add red food coloring for a more authentic look.

2 teaspoons cumin seeds

2 teaspoons coriander seeds

1 stick cinnamon

1 teaspoon cloves

1   teaspoon cayenne powder

1   teaspoon ginger powder

1   teaspoon turmeric powder

1   teaspoon garlic powder

1   teaspoon mace powder

1   teaspoon salt

¼   teaspoon red food coloring (optional)

Dry roast all the whole spices until they begin to smoke. Cool and grind with the powdered spices, salt, and food coloring.

### Panch Phoron

Panch phoron comes from Bengali in the northeast of India. The people here favor fish and rice dishes made with clotted milk, rose water, and saffron. Panch phoron has a bittersweet flavor and a powerful aroma that works well with lentils and vegetables. Add it to the oil before any other ingredients or sauté it in butter and pour over the top of a dish to liven it up.

Mix equal amounts of cumin seeds, fennel seeds, fenugreek seeds, black mustard seeds, and nigella seeds. Grind in a mortar and pestle by hand for a fine powder.

### Kholombo Powder

This masala comes from the western coast of India where fragrant dishes are made up of fish, coconut, rice, and mangoes. The aroma of this blend is like wood smoke and complements the flavor of food the way grilling does with barbecue. The taste is hot and slightly bitter, so it is usually combined with tamarind to balance it out. Use it with beans, rice, and vegetables, and add it to the dish along with the main ingredients.

2   teaspoons coriander seeds

8  dried curry leaves

2  teaspoons cumin seeds

4  whole cloves

1  teaspoon black peppercorns

1  stick cinnamon

3  tablespoons flaked coconut

4  tablespoons split lentils

1  tablespoon corn oil

Cook everything in the hot oil until the lentils turn dark brown and the mixture releases the fragrance of wood smoke. Cool and grind to a powder.

🌾 🌾 🌾

Now that you have several masalas stocked in your kitchen, try them in these recipes. All dishes serve 4.

### *Green Pepper Stir Fry*

4  tablespoons chickpea flour

4  tablespoons corn oil

1  teaspoon cumin seeds

1  pinch asafoetida

2  onions, chopped

3  green peppers, de-seeded and chopped

4  tablespoons unsalted peanuts, crushed

1  teaspoon cayenne powder

1  teaspoon turmeric powder

1  teaspoon coriander powder

1  teaspoon garam masala

Dry roast the chickpea flour until it is brown and fragrant. Heat the oil in another pan. Add the cumin and asafoetida. Add the onion and stir until golden. Add the green peppers, peanuts and spices. Cook until the peppers are just tender. Sprinkle the chickpea flour over and stir well. Cook another 5 minutes and remove from heat.

### *South Indian Tamarind Soup*

4   tablespoons lentils, soaked for 15 minutes and drained

3⅓ cups water

2   tablespoons corn oil

1   teaspoon black mustard seeds

1   teaspoon cumin seeds

1   pinch asafoetida

10 curry leaves

4   cloves garlic

1   teaspoon tamarind paste, diluted in 2 table-spoons water

1   teaspoon sambhar powder

1   teaspoon turmeric powder

1   teaspoon cayenne powder

2   tablespoons coriander leaves

Boil the lentils in water until soft. In another pan, heat oil, and add mustard seeds. When they being to pop, add the cumin, asafoetida, curry leaves, and the whole cloves of garlic. Sauté 1 minute. Add the tamarind and cook until thick and bubbly. Stir in the spices. Pour the lentils into the tamarind mixture and heat through. Serve hot with fresh coriander.

## String Bean Stir Fry

3 tablespoons corn oil

1 teaspoon black mustard seeds

1 teaspoon cumin seeds

1 pinch asafoetida

1 onion, chopped

1 potato, cut into cubes

10 ounces string beans, chopped

1 teaspoon turmeric powder

1 teaspoon cayenne powder

1 teaspoon goda masala

1 teaspoon coriander powder

Heat oil in a wok. Add mustard seeds and when they crackle, add cumin and asafoetida. Add onion and stir until translucent. Add potatoes and cook 1 minute. Add string beans and the spices. Add a teaspoon of water and cover, letting the vegetables cook in their own steam until the potatoes and beans are cooked through.

## Spiced Cottage Cheese

3 tablespoons corn oil

1 teaspoon minced ginger

1 teaspoon minced garlic

2 onions, chopped, boiled, and ground to a paste

10 tablespoons tomato purée

1 teaspoon cayenne powder

1 teaspoon turmeric powder

1 teaspoon cumin powder

1 teaspoon tandoori masala

1 teaspoon sugar

2 cups paneer cheese (available in most Indian groceries)

6 tablespoons heavy cream (lightly whipped)

Heat oil and sauté the ginger and garlic for one minute. Add the onion paste and the tomato purée along with all the spices. Stir well. Add the sugar and simmer for 5 minutes. Drop in the paneer gently and simmer for 1 minute. Serve with a dollop of cream on top.

## *Sweet and Sour Bengali Lentils*

1¾ cups lentils

3⅓ cups water

1 teaspoon turmeric powder

2 teaspoons sugar

3 tablespoons corn oil

2 tablespoons panch phoron

4 dried red chilies, deseeded

2 bay leaves

1 teaspoon mango powder

2 teaspoons raisins

Simmer the lentils in water until soft. Add the turmeric and sugar. Heat the oil in another pan and add the Panch phoron. When it crackles, add the chilies, bay leaves, mango powder, and raisins. Sauté for 1 minute and pour the oil and spices over the lentils. Add water if necessary to make it the consistency of a thick soup.

# Ginger's Cousins in the Zingiberaceae Family

### ⁂ by James Kambos ⁂

J ust the mention of the word *ginger* conjures a myriad of sensory remembrances involving taste and smell—from fragrant, freshly baked ginger cookies to icy-cold ginger beer or ginger ale on a summer's sweltering afternoon, to fiery Sichuan stir-fries, Mongolian hot-pots, and blissfully searing Indian curries. But the well-known, beloved, and indispensable herb ginger (*Zingiber officinale*), whose scientific name lends itself to the Zingiberaceae family, is related to dozens of gastronomically and medicinally important herbs. But here we will explore some of the better known of its lesser-known cousins, namely greater galangal, Chinese keys, tumeric, and cardamom.

# Descriptions, Cultural Requirements, and Harvesting of Zingiberaceae

Because these herbs all belong to the Zingiberaceae family, there are similarities in both physical appearance and cultural requirements. Whether we choose to use it or not, most of us would recognize a piece of fresh ginger root that we encounter at our local supermarket or green grocer. It is tan-colored, thickened, knobby, often branched, and it looks like a root. Botanists call this type of root a rhizome and all of the herbs we will discuss are rhizomatous, that is, rhizome bearing. They are technically not roots but modified horizontally growing stems designed for the storage of water and nutrients the plant can draw upon during times of drought or environmental duress. It is the rhizomes of ginger and its cousins that we rely upon in our kitchens for flavoring, coloring, and scenting our foods. In the case of cardamom, however, it the small, fragrant seeds that we use. The rhizomes are subterranean in nature and the shoots arise vertically from them, bearing medium-green, lance-shaped leaves that vary in size, depending on the species. The flower spikes emerge directly from the ground as well.

All of these ginger cousins grow outdoors in subtropical climes of USDA Zones 10–11: Hawaii, southern Florida, as well as the United States territories of Guam, Puerto Rico, and the U. S. Virgin Islands. They prefer humus-rich, water-retentive but well-drained soil, and lightly dappled shade. Regular applications of water are a must. They dislike scorching sun, drying winds, and seaside properties because these plants resent the relentless salt spray and desiccating winds associated with beachfront life. During summertime, the herb tumeric goes dormant (as well as its cousin true ginger), and becomes leafless in a dismal display of withered stems. No matter how much water or fertilizer is dispensed, that is tumeric's natural life cycle. Simply cut off (do not rip out) the dying stems and add them to the compost pile. They will begin to sprout anew in early autumn. Chinese keys, greater galangal, and cardamom will grow throughout the calendar year.

In northern locales, these herbs will grow as houseplants. They require the largest containers you have room for in an unobstructed east window, or a bay window, sunroom, or greenhouse. If possible, give apartment- or indoor-bound specimens a summer vacation outdoors under the cover of trees, or on the shadiest—usually the northern—side of the house. The fresh, circulating air and natural environment will quickly revive lackluster specimens. Watch housebound plants for mealybugs and spider mites, and use your favorite biological control (predatory insects) or organic insecticide for eradication. Even indoor tumeric will become dormant. During that period, the forlorn, leafless specimen can be tucked away out of sight. But remember that even a dormant plant still requires weekly watering to keep the rhizomes alive until it begins to sprout again.

Home gardeners rarely propagate ginger's cousins from seed. Mail order suppliers vend small potted examples, but portions of the branching rhizomes may be easily cut off, dusted with fungicide (which is available at most garden centers and nurseries), and replanted in small pots to create new plantlets. Division can be accomplished at any time of year. Simply use a sharp knife to cut through the soil and remove the desired portion. The plant will not notice the minor surgery. For home gardeners and cooks, the rhizomes are only used fresh and will keep for a couple of months in a ventilated bag in the produce drawer of the refrigerator. For longer cold storage (up to a year), the pieces of rhizome may be kept in glass jars and covered with quality sherry or vodka, which will become infused with the particular aromatics. The enhanced spirits will make a flavorful addition to your sauces, stews, and soups (meat, seafood, vegetable, or vegan). In fact, between you and me, a little glass of greater galangal sherry enjoyed with a homemade cardamom cookie, of course, makes a great afternoon pick-me-up!

## Greater Galangal

Greater galangal (*Alpinia galanga*) has medium-green, lanceolate (lance-shaped) leaves 20 inches long that are borne on upright stems that may grow as tall as six feet under ideal conditions. Containerized indoor specimens will make a fine 3-foot-tall houseplant. Unlike true ginger, greater galangal does not have a dormant period; its Y-shaped, branching, ginger-scented rhizomes grow at or just below the surface of the soil. The rhizomes look like true ginger; they are thinner, however, and the shoots and stem bases are bright pink. The skin of the rhizome is pale tan or white and the interior is pinkish-white. When cultivated outdoors in frost-free locales, it will produce spikes of pale-green, orchid-like flowers with a white and pink-striped lip throughout the year. Upon pollination, typically by insects, they produce red, three-lobed, spherical capsules.

This ginger cousin is native to tropical Asia, mainly Indonesia, which may not be surprising because the herb's name in Indonesian is "laos," as in the landlocked country, Laos, which is the major commercial source of the root. It is also produced commercially in Malaysia (where it is called "lengkuas"), Thailand (where it is known as "kha"); and to a lesser extent, Southern China (where it is referred to as "dà gao jiang").

European cooks have known greater galangal since the time of Marco Polo. The slightly pungent rhizomes are employed as a flavoring for masaman and other curries, soups, meat, and fish dishes. It is also combined with other seasoning mixtures. I simmer a little of the chopped rhizome with minced lemon grass (tender inner part only), shallot, garlic, a splash of nuac nam (fish sauce), and some unsweetened coconut milk, to make a sauce for grilled extra-firm tofu or tempeh. It is the source of an essential oil used to flavor liqueurs such as Chartreuse, and digestive bitters, including Angostura, as well as soft drinks. In southeast Asia, the young shoots are eaten raw or steamed as a vegetable or side dish. The flowers and flower buds are also eaten raw or steamed, but they may be pickled, added to soups, or mixed with chili paste as a condiment for plain rice. The red berries are also consumed. In Russia it is used to flavor teas, vinegars, and spirits, and a liqueur nastoika.

## Chinese Keys

Chinese keys (*Boesenbergia rotunda*) bears large, medium-green to bluish-green, elliptic, prominently veined leaves that emanate from a distinctive, subterranean, short, rounded rhizome. The leaves grow to about 2½ feet tall. The rhizome bears downward-growing, finger-like, fleshy, orange-brown skinned roots. The underground structure is supposedly reminiscent of a set of Chinese keys. The rhizomes and roots are bright yellow on the inside and have an aromatic, spicy flavor.

In August garden-grown plants will produce twin, zygomorphic (bilaterally symmetrical) spikes, with pale-pink outer lobes and a darker rose-pink lip that are borne on erect stems held close to the ground well below the foliage. Chinese keys are thought to be indigenous to Java and Sumatra, but they are now widely cultivated all over southeast Asia, from India and Sri Lanka to Thailand, Vietnam, Malaysia, Indonesia, and

Indochina. It is often eaten in April—the hottest month of the year—for its cooling, refreshing properties, and as accompaniment for ice-cold rice. It has become an important food and spice plant in Thailand, Vietnam, central Asian countries, Russia, and even Hungary! The roots are used medicinally through Southeast Asia and China.

The rhizomes and roots are consumed in soups and stews, in *sambals* (a condiment), or made into pickles. Both the rhizomes and the hearts of the stems are eaten raw as a side dish with rice. Young leaves and shoots, along with the rhizomes, are finely chopped and mixed with grated, fresh coconut, herbs, and spices (such as minced ginger, shallots, and chopped coriander leaf), and wrapped in a banana leaf and steamed. I do this at home. To make this side dish: First, form small "pillows" of the mixture and wrap them in banana leaves (I grow my own). Steam them for 45 minutes in a bamboo Chinese steamer basket. Serving them is easy. Have people unwrap the packages on their plate (the banana leaves are not consumed) and eat the mixture with a helping of steamed jasmine rice.

Cooks in northern regions can find packaged frozen banana leaves in Asian and Latino markets. Parchment paper may be used instead. In Thailand, fresh rhizomes and roots are eaten raw in salads or *khao chae* (the dish gives its name to the whole course) and they are added to fish curries, soups, and pickles. They are paired with boiled rice noodles in Khanom chine. As a spice, small amounts are added to curries, mixed vegetable soups and other savory dishes. Nowadays, it is commonly used as an ingredient in instant packaged soups produced in China.

# Turmeric

Turmeric (*Curcuma longa*) bears medium-green, oblong-elliptic (like a long stretched circle), 20-inch-long leaves on 3-foot-tall stems. With its tan skin, the rhizome looks like those of ginger. Tumeric rhizomes are larger, however, and brilliant carrot-orange on the inside. During summer, in-ground plants will produce dense spikes of yellow flowers with green bracts that are held well below the foliage. Potted windowsill specimens rarely bloom but make beautiful foliage plants. The leaves are cut as required when needed fresh, but the rhizomes are harvested only during the dormant period.

In Sanskrit, *tumeric* means "yellow," which is a sacred color used by Hindus. It is the colorant for the robes of Buddhist monks. Called "haldi," it is also used for body painting during rites connected with birth, marriage, and death. Not surprisingly, India seems to be the country of origin of this spice, although botanists have not discovered examples growing in the wild. It has been employed as a spice and dye plant (for wool, cotton, and silk) for centuries. From India, the plant spread to Southeast Asia and the Far East, but India remains the most important producer of tumeric, producing nearly 350,000 tons per year. Smaller amounts are grown in Bangladesh, Pakistan, and various southeast Asian countries.

The powdered rhizomes are used as a yellow colorant (thanks to a pigment known as curcumin) and flavoring agent in store-bought, prepared curry powders, mustards, cheeses, butter-type spreads, gravies, sauces (including Worcestershire sauce), packaged rice dishes, bottled pickles, and other things. It lends its extraordinarily vibrant color to nasi kunyit, the Malaysian yellow rice dish that is consumed at ceremonial and festive occasions.

I sauté some finely chopped tumeric rhizome in a little oil for a few minutes and add it to rice prior to cooking to impart its flavor and color. I guarantee that once you use your own home-grown tumeric root, you will never want to use the commercially dried and powdered form again. Tumeric was once touted as a wonderful substitute for saffron for more economical food coloration, but because of the rhizomes' aromatic flavor, that is quite untrue. Saffron rice is distinctively different from tumeric rice in both taste and ultimate color. This herb is also a constituent of krary powder from Thailand. The leaves are used as a flavor-imparting wrapper for roasting fish, and they are an ingredient in rendang, a traditional water buffalo meat dish of Sumatra. I also use the leaves as food wrappers. I skewer leaf-swathed, uncooked, shelled shrimp, bits of fish, or cubes of extra-firm tofu, and grill or broil them a few minutes until the leaves are charred and the seafood is done. The young shoots and rhizome tips are consumed raw. I find they are quite crunchy and tasty and add a welcome kick to humdrum mid-winter salads, when all I can find is tedious iceberg lettuce at our local markets.

In Chinese folk medicine, tumeric rhizome is used to treat biliousness (remove excessive gas), to increase menstrual flow, and to treat liver and stomach diseases, abdominal pains, convulsions, delirium, and jaundice. Traditionally, it is used to treat stomach ailments and to stimulate bile secretion. This herb may reduce the chances of strokes and heart attacks and lower cholesterol. It also has proven anti-inflammatory properties.

## Cardamom

Cardamom (*Elettaria cardamomum*) is the largest of the lesser-known ginger cousins. It may grow as tall as 20 feet and its gracefully arching stems bear 2-foot-long linear lanceolate, dark-green leaves. It has thick, sturdy rhizomes that produce 3-foot-tall spikes of greenish-white blossoms with a mauve lip during summer. Upon pollination, pea-sized, three-chambered oval pale green to beige capsules are produced, with each chamber bearing fifteen to twenty hard, angular, aromatic, dark-brown seeds. Although it is the seeds that are employed as the major flavoring agent, the leaves may be used as well, which is a boon because greenhouse- or windowsill-grown plants will rarely, if ever, flower.

Cardamom is indigenous to peninsular India. Once known as "queen of spices," it was one of the three major spices (along with black pepper and dried ginger) of the Oriental spice trade as long ago as the third century BC. Guatemala has become the number one producer of cardamom, where annual production is about 5,000 tons, closely followed by India, where annual production is about 4,000 tons. Small amounts are also grown in Sri Lanka, Tanzania, and Papua New Guinea.

Essential oil made from store-bought ground cardamom or whole cardamom pods loses its vitality quickly upon opening the jar and subsequent room temperature storage in the pantry. It is better to purchase whole seeds (or pods) and store them in the freezer to retain their freshness. Grind the small, perfumed seeds as needed in a spice grinder. The ground seeds can be added to curry powders, cakes, sausages, meatballs, drinks, cordials, digestive bitters, European and American gingerbread, and pickles. Scandinavian cooks use cardamom liberally in their savory cooking, Danish pastries, confectionary work, mulled wines, and stewed fruits. It is a principal ingredient of the Ethiopian hot pepper mélange, as well as that country's berbere spice mixture (see the recipe below) and its qahwah coffee blend. In India the seeds are chewed after meals to sweeten the breath. The young shoots are eaten raw, steamed, or roasted as a vegetable, and the foliage is utilized as flavor-imparting wrappers for roasting, steaming, or braising meats and seafood. As a vegetarian, I wrap extra-firm tofu or tempeh in cardamom leaves, using toothpicks to secure the foliage before steaming, grilling, or broiling to add a certain *je ne sais quoi* to the final dish. And when I prepare jasmine or basmati rice, I put a few fresh leaves in the pot to impart their exotic perfume. I remove the leaves prior to serving. I also line steamer trays with the leaves to add a fragrance and flavor to steamed buns and dim sum.

Cardamom seeds have numerous medical applications as well in Chinese traditional medicine. They are used to stimulate gastric activity, to increase menstrual flow, to treat premature ejaculation, decrease involuntary discharge of urine, and to alleviate stomach pains. The rhizomes are used as a tonic and a laxative. Cardamom is also used in Ayurvedic medicine for bronchial and digestive complaints.

# Recipes

## Thailand: Nam Ya Pa (Thai Seafood Soup)

Use a clear measuring device with marked fluid ounces. This is a spicy, stew-like soup.

- 5 cups unsweetened coconut milk
- ½ cup each of sliced garlic and shallot
- 8 ounces finely shredded Chinese keys
- 2 tablespoons shrimp paste
- 1 tablespoon finely shredded greater galangal root
- 1 tablespoon salt
- ½ cup flaked smoked fish (kipper, codfish, haddock) boned and skinned
- 6 ounces thick coconut cream (unsweetened)
- 3 pounds large shrimp, shelled and deveined
- ½ cup red and green chilies, seeded and sliced thin

1. Simmer the first seven ingredients until tender.

2. Add the shrimp or prawns and cook several minutes until heated through. Remove the pan from the heat.

3. Add the coconut cream and the chilies and heat to warm through, but do not boil.

4. Add extra salt if desired or a dash of nuac nam (Thai fish sauce).

5. Serve over plenty of hot boiled or steamed white rice and accompany with quartered hardboiled eggs, fresh Thai basil leaves, and lightly cooked bean sprouts. Serves 4 to 6.

### North Africa: Berbere (Ethiopian Spice Mix)

This is a hot and spicy mixture essential to many Ethiopian dishes. Use 2 tablespoons per 1 cup of dried Old World legumes (lentils, garbanzos, pigeon peas, or split peas) when cooking them up.

| | |
|---|---|
| 2 | teaspoons coriander seeds |
| 1 | teaspoon fenugreek seeds |
| ½ | teaspoon black peppercorns |
| ¼ | teaspoon whole allspice |
| ½ | teaspoon cardamom seeds |
| 4 | whole cloves |
| ½ | cup dried onion flakes |
| 5 | stemmed and seeded dried red chilies, broken into pieces |
| 3 | tablespoons paprika |
| 2 | teaspoons kosher salt |
| ½ | teaspoon ground nutmeg |

½  teaspoon ground ginger

½  teaspoon ground cinnamon

1. Combine spices in a small dry skillet. With heat set to medium, swirl skillet constantly until spices are fragrant (about 4 minutes). Let cool slightly.

2. Transfer spices to a spice grinder along with dried onion flakes and dried red chilies. Grind until fine.

3. Transfer mixture to a bowl and stir in remaining spices.

4. Store in airtight container for up to six months. Makes about ¾ cup.

# References

Grigson, J. and C. Knox. *Cooking with Exotic Fruits and Vegetables.* New York: Henry Holt and Company, 1986.

Morris, S. *Oriental Cookery: Every Cook's Guide to the Cuisines of Malaysia, Singapore, Indonesia, China, The Philippines, Thailand, Korea, Burma, Japan and Indochina.* Secaucus, NJ: Chartwell Books, Inc., 1984.

Van Wyk, Ben-Erik. *Food Plants of the World.* Portland, OR: Timber Press, 2005.

# Herbs
## for
## Health

# Quit Smoking with Herbal Support

⇜ by Lisa McSherry ⇝

Introduced to Western culture by one of Christopher Columbus's traveling companions, tobacco was first thought to cure colic, nephritis, hysteria, hernias, and dysentery. By the early 1600s, stern warnings were being written about this "devil weed" or "Indie poison," but it wasn't until the mid-1900s that tobacco use was condemned as a health hazard. Nowadays, smoking is banned from public places all over the world—even in countries where smoking is nearly inextricable from the nation's image (France, for example, or Hong Kong).

For those of us caught by the devil weed, the hazards are clear; the warnings are on every pack we smoke. Smoking tobacco causes lung cancer and greatly

increases the risk of cardiovascular disease and many other forms of cancer. We aren't stupid, nor do we lack willpower, but smoking is a very tough habit and addiction to break. Numerous studies have shown that nicotine impacts the brain like cocaine or heroin, producing pleasure from increased dopamine activity. Cigarettes relieve minor depression, suppress anger, mildly enhance concentration, and strengthen a sense of well-being.

There are lots of ways to quit, and many products to help. This article will focus on herbal allies to combat the challenges of quitting smoking, the foremost of which are ginseng to increase stamina and combat stress, St. John's wort to help balance the mood swings, and milk thistle to support the liver as you flush the pollutants from your body. There also several less-researched but oft-recommended herbs: vervain, valerian, skullcap, and licorice. All of these herbs combat various side effects of nicotine withdrawal, making the process easier.

## Ginseng

One factor of smoking is that it makes us feel more alert, and research shows that smoking is a mild stimulant, along the lines of a strong cup of coffee. Replacing the smoke stimulant with something else is a key component in managing our withdrawal.

Ginseng (American: *Panax quinquefolius* and Asian: *Panax ginseng*) is considered by the Chinese as a sovereign remedy for many diseases, which is reflected in the genus name *Panax* that is derived from the Greek *panakeia*, which means "universal remedy." Ginseng is particularly useful in relieving fatigue and increasing vitality—duplicating the "hit" smokers get from their cigarettes. It helps aid the body in withstanding mental and nervous exhaustion.

The American Academy of Family Physicians (AAFP) notes that the main active components of ginseng "have been shown to have a variety of beneficial effects including anti-inflammatory, antioxidant, and anticancer effects. Results of clinical research studies demonstrate . . . ginseng may improve psychological function, immune function, and conditions associated with diabetes." In other words, drinking ginseng tea helps us feel alert and helps fight the fatigue of processing the smoke's toxins out of our bodies.

The recommended dosage for ginseng extract is 200 mg per day, or 0.5 g to 2 g of dried root when brewed into a tea or chewed. The standardized extract is the safest and most predictable way to get ginseng's benefits, but nibbling on one end of the whole root (often found at health food stores) can give you the standard dose while easing the desire to put something in your mouth.

Ginseng's side effects include nausea, diarrhea, euphoria, insomnia, headaches, hypertension, hypotension, and vaginal bleeding. People with diabetes are discouraged from using ginseng as it interacts badly with insulin. As usual, it is not recommended for children and pregnant or lactating women.

## St. John's Wort

Fairly recent smoking research (2003) indicates that quitting smoking is easier when taking a mild antidepressant, such as Wellbutrin (Bupropion Hcl), which reduces the severity of nicotine cravings. An herbal alternative is St. John's wort (*Hypericum perforatum*), although the effects have not been proven by American researchers (notably, the National Institute of Health). In Germany, St. John's wort is commonly prescribed for mild depression in children and adolescents.

The AAFP notes that the main active components of St. John's wort act "via inhibition of the reuptake of serotonin, dopamine, and noradrenaline, along with activation of gamma-aminobutyrate and glutamate receptors. . . . The data continue to support the overall conclusions . . . that St. John's wort is more effective than placebo and as effective as standard anti-depressants for the treatment of mild to moderate depression." For smokers, St. John's wort can help keep a positive mental attitude, which is especially important in the first days of becoming non-smokers, when the cravings are the most intense, as is the psychological addiction.

Findings suggest that 900 mg of St. John's wort (ideally, 300 mg three times daily) is needed to reduce symptoms of depression and that the full effect may take two to four weeks to manifest. Although the side effects of this herb are very mild (stomach upset, increased anxiety, minor palpitations, photosensitivity, fatigue, restlessness, dry mouth, headache, and increased depression) it is not recommended for pregnant women. It also interacts with a number of common medications, including antidepressants, birth control pills, and anticoagulants. Because a specific dosage is particularly needed, the standardized pill form is the recommended method of delivery.

## Milk Thistle

Quitting an addiction means that we need to help our body flush toxins from our system at a higher rate than usual, which means the liver and associated organs are going to be under a lot of additional stress. Once we quit smoking, toxins are released from our fat deposits and eliminated through the liver. Milk thistle (*Silybum marianum*) has been reported to have protective effects on the liver and to greatly improve its function. The active part of the plant is the seeds (fruit) which contain silymarin (a flavinoid complex).

It is important to note that studies of milk thistle's effectiveness are contradictory, and focus mainly on "curing" liver disease arising from alcohol abuse, hepatitis, and cancer. Studies focusing on milk thistle's protective effect on the liver were more positive. People with allergies to plants in the aster family or to ragweed, marigolds, daisies, artichokes, or kiwi may have allergic reactions to milk thistle. Aside from allergic reactions, serious adverse effects are virtually unheard of (the most common side effect is an upset stomach). And there are no significant drug interactions, making this a safe herb worth using to support the liver function. Recommended dosage of the seed extract is a 150 to 175 mg capsule, standardized to 80 percent silymarin, three times daily.

The following herbs have little or no scientific evidence to support their use, but many respected herbalists recommend them for various ailments that apply to quitting smoking, such as nervousness, anxiety, and the quick detoxification of the body.

## Burdock

Burdock root (*Arctium lappa*), a traditional blood purifier, is often combined with dandelion. Used as another way to flush toxins from the body, burdock root also acts as a diuretic (helping rid the body of excess water by increasing urine output).

Recommended dosage for the root is as a decoction. To make the decoction, place 1.5 ounces dried root in 3¼ cups cold water. Bring to a boil, reduce heat and simmer for about one hour until water is reduced by one-third. Strain and keep in a cool pace. Drink ½ cup, three times daily.

# Dandelion

Historically, dandelion (*Taraxacum officinale*) was used to treat liver diseases, kidney diseases, and spleen problems; its use today continues as a liver or kidney "tonic" although there is no compelling scientific evidence for using dandelion as a treatment for any medical condition. Dandelion leaves aid in the flushing of excess fluid from the body, because the root is a liver stimulant.

The recommended dosage for this herb is as a decoction. Place 1.5 ounces dried root in 3¼ cups cold water; bring to a boil, reduce heat and simmer for about an hour until water is reduced by one-third. Strain and keep in a cool place. Drink ½ cup, three times daily.

# Licorice

Licorice root (*Glycyrrhiza glabra* and *Glycyrrhiza uralensis*) contains glycyrrhizin, which is fifty times sweeter than sucrose and encourages hormone production. In doing so it acts as a natural anti-inflammatory and restimulates the adrenal cortex. Dosage in tincture form is recommended. Its cousin, *G. uralensis*, is an energy tonic, particularly for the spleen and stomach. Dosage is best as a daily tonic drink with ginseng. Chewing licorice root can help to reduce food cravings. What's more, licorice sticks—the natural twigs at a health food store—work as an oral substitute for a cigarette.

# Skullcap

The aerial parts of skullcap (*Scutellaria lateriflora*) are calming for many nervous conditions and may actually renew and revive the central nervous system. Few studies have been done on American skullcap, but one of its compounds, scutellarin, has been shown to have mild sedative and antispasmodic properties. Dosage is best as a tincture of ¾ ounce taken up to four times a day.

## Valerian

Valerian (*Valeriana officinalis*) is nature's tranquilizer. It calms the nerves and is a mild muscle relaxant. It is not recommended as a daily dose for longer than two weeks (take a week off before resuming use). The recommended dose is 1.5 ounces dried herbs steeped in 2 cups hot water for 10 minutes and then strained. Drink a single cup just before bed.

## Vervain

An effective nerve tonic and liver stimulant, vervain (*Verbena officinalis*) is best taken as an infusion of 1.5 ounces dried herbs steeped in 2 cups hot water for 10 minutes, strained. Drink ½ cup three times a day.

## Good News for Smokers

There's good news for us smokers. Within 245 hours after that last smoke, our blood pressure and pulse lower to a more normal rate. Within a week, the level of oxygen and carbon monoxide in the blood stream normalizes, and we can smell and taste better than we have since we started smoking. If we can quit for 10 to 20 days, the chemical dependence on nicotine is gone, and if we can go for three months, we are extremely unlikely to take up the habit again. Use your herbal allies to quit and give yourself the gift of health.

# References

Fegert, J. M., Kölch, M., Zito, J. M., Glaeske, G., and Janhsen, K. "Antidepressant use in children and adolescents in Germany." *Journal of Child and Adolescent Psychopharmacology*, 2006. 16(1-2): 197–206.

National Cancer Institute. "Quitting Smoking: Why to Quit and How to Get Help," Retrieved on September 13, 2008, online at http://www.cancer.gov/cancertopics/factsheet/Tobacco/cessation.

Ody, Penelope and Dorling Kindersley. *Home Herbal*. New York: Dorling Kindersley Publishing, 1995.

Ody, Penelope and Dorling Kindersley. *The Complete Medicinal Herbal*. New York: Dorling Kindersley Publishing, 1993.

Tonnesen, P., S.Tonstad, A. Hjalmarson, et al. "A multicentre, randomized, double-blind, placebo-controlled, 1-year study of bupropion SR for smoking cessation." *Journal of Internal Medicine*, 2003. 254(2): 184–192.

# Blessed Bitters

### ⁓ by jim mcdonald ⁓

In medicinal herbcraft, we sometimes speak of the "actions" of herbs. Most herb books will have a section listing such properties as anti-inflammatory, antispasmodic, hepatic, alterative, diuretic, tonic and a plethora of other words both familiar and obscure. But while these terms are all grouped together, some actions are far more telling than others. For example, saying that an herb is "anti-inflammatory" seems useful, since it indicates what the herb is used for. But it tells us nothing of how the plant achieves this end; it tells us nothing of the herb's essential nature.

Why is the plant anti-inflammatory? Is it aromatic, containing volatile oils? Is it rich in antioxidant flavinoids?

In soothing mucilage? Is it astringent? It is these actions that provide a foundational understanding of traditional herbcraft, for in these properties the plants speak to us of their virtues. A plant's scent is its language. Its color communicates. In its flavor it speaks to us; not in our language, but in its.

Among the most pervasive flavors found in healing herbs is that of bitterness. Isn't it interesting that this flavor, so widespread and variant in so many of our most trusted remedies, is an unfamiliar one to us? One that people often claim deters them from plant medicines? If plants' tongues speak to our tongues, then what do we not hear when we taste no bitterness?

## Bitter Deficiency Syndrome

Bitters are imperative; everyone needs some bitters in their diet. No traditional culture could have imagined a diet virtually (if not absolutely) devoid of any bitter foods—as we seem to have established in most modern diets. This is not to say that one should force themselves to eat a bowl of raw dandelion roots, but to posit that the "medicinal" actions associated with bitters might be viewed in an entirely different light.

I am a firm believer in Bitter Deficiency Syndrome; a notion that posits that much of the health woes faced by modern folk has at its root a lack of bitter flavor in the diet; and that many of the digestive problems for which we see bitters as a "remedy" are actually symptoms of deficiency of this flavor. Perhaps it is not right to think that bitters should be used to *treat* sluggish digestion, but that a lack of bitter flavor in one's diet can be a *cause* of sluggish digestion. Perhaps many of the conditions calling for bitters as a remedy arise from their omission, not unlike rickets arises from a lack of vitamin D.

I was first introduced to the idea of bitter deficiency syndrome by James Green, who wrote in *The Male Herbal:*

It is my opinion that the nearly complete lack of bitter flavored foods in the overall U.S. and Canadian diet is a major contributing factor to common cultural health imbalances such as PMS, other female and male sexual organ dysfunctions, hormonal imbalances, migraine headache, indigestion, liver and gall bladder dysfunction, abnormal metabolism, hypoglycemia, diabetes, etc.

As the years have passed since I initially read this, I have come to agree more and more fervently with this notion, seeing firsthand the restorative actions of dietary bitters. To better understand the notion of bitter deficiency syndrome, let us look at the scope of bitter's virtues.

## A Flavor and an Action

One cannot separate the taste of bitterness from its medicine. Though as with all things there are exceptions, it can be broadly stated that by simply tasting bitterness in an herb, one can immediately know a number of the plant's virtues. Should one not taste the plant's bitterness (perhaps the plant is trapped inside a capsule), the actions of the plant will not fully manifest. Its potential is masked with its flavor.

What is it that bitters do? It is often summarized that bitters stimulate digestive secretions and the metabolism as a whole, and in so doing increase appetite, relieve constipation, and generally ease the heavy glumness of sluggish digestion. But, this is really too simple and cursory a summation, and a deeper look into the actions of bitters is not only theoretically insightful but practically invaluable.

## The Scope of Bitters

Bitters stimulate all digestive secretions: saliva, acids, enzymes, hormones, bile, and so forth. Each of these acts as a solvent to break down food for absorption, and the quantity and quality of these fluids ensure proper nutrition. Inadequate production of these secretions is common in modern cultures (i.e. cultures lacking bitters in their diet), and the implications of such deficiencies are myriad.

When first tasted, bitters promote salivation, which begins the process of digestion by breaking down starches and beginning to work on fats. Taste receptors in the mouth (there are over twenty-five different bitter taste receptors) recognize the presence of bitters, and trigger a system-wide reaction throughout the digestive tract.

In the stomach, sufficient hormones, acids, and enzymes are needed to help break down proteins and carbohydrates, and to free up minerals for assimilation. Bitters stimulate the secretion of the hormone gastrin, which regulates the production of gastric acid. Inadequate stomach acid will prevent the uptake of minerals, which will in turn rob the body of essential nutrition needed for wellness (even if those nutrients are being consumed as foods or supplements). Low acid also weakens stomach tissues, and is often the foundational cause of esophageal reflux (though most people mistakenly believe they have too much acid). It is well known that as people pass into their elder years, they produce less stomach acid. This is sometimes remedied by taking supplemental hydrochloric acid, but it makes far more sense to restore bitters to the diet, which will allow the body to produce its own acid, rather than relying on a supplement and allowing bitter deficiency to continue. Bitters also increase production of the enzymes pepsin, which helps break down proteins, and intrinsic factor, which is essential for the absorption of vitamin B12, which has far-reaching effects ranging from blood building to neurological function.

Bitters act on both the pancreas and liver/gall bladder, helping to normalize blood sugar and promote the production and release of pancreatic enzymes and bile, which ensure good digestion of fats and oils. A healthy flow of bile helps rid the liver of waste products, prevents the formation of gallstones, and emulsifies lipids, which the pancreatic enzymes then break down along with proteins and carbohydrates for absorption in the small intestine. Bile also provides lubrication for the intestines, helping to facilitate the passage of digested food. Deficient bile and sluggish liver/gall bladder function can lead to dryness in the intestines, which is often a cause of chronic constipation. Bitters also promote secretion of digestive juices within the small intestine, further aiding bowel transit and nutrient assimilation. New Mexican herbalist Kiva Rose adds:

> In close relationship to the effects on both the liver and pancreas, bitter herbs and foods can often dramatically help the irritability, bloating, moodiness, and digestive upset of PMS.

In addition to the action of bitters on digestive secretions, they also strengthen the tone of tissues throughout the digestive tract, as well as aid in the healing of damaged mucous membranes. This helps resolve conditions ranging from gastroesophageal reflux to ulcers to leaky gut syndrome. Peristalsis, the wavelike contractions of muscles lining the digestive organs is likewise enhanced, helping move digestate through and out of the body.

All these actions, taken together, can have a net result of restoring appetite, indicating bitters for loss of appetite resulting from causes ranging from chronic indigestion to illness to anorexia nervosa. On the other end of the spectrum, bitters also seem to be very useful when addressing cravings, particularly of sweets. I believe the craving our minds feel for sweets is literally the craving our bodies have for bitters. In their natural form, most sweet flavors are associated with some degree of bitterness (sweet foods and herbs such as pure sugarcane, licorice root, and stevia all possess some bitterness). Any bitter flavor, though, is removed entirely when sugars are refined. Our bodies evolved with this association and they still remember it; hence, sweet cravings are a way our bodies have of asking us for bitters, and they can often be sated by tasting things that are bitter. Cravings need not be relegated to food, however. Small doses of many bitter herbs can be very helpful for cravings associated with many addictions, due to their calming affect on mood (elaborated on below). An example of this is the chewing of calamus root to ease the cravings for tobacco.

Traditional herbalism in cultures throughout the world consider bitters to have a "downward" action. This refers not only to bitters more readily perceived digestive actions (including their admirable efficacy in resolving bad breath arising from the gut), but also to their more esoteric virtues.

Bitters tend to be grounding, helping to strengthen one's connection to instinct. They help to shift people from intellectual "brain" energy (which looks at things, takes them apart, and sees the pieces) to gut energy (which reacts to things instinctually, independent of intellectual consideration). An example of this might be when a person meets someone, and initially gets a bad vibe for them, but then goes on a head trip about how they're being judgmental and how they're probably projecting and they're going to let go of their preconceptions . . . only to discover (time and again) after doing so that their gut was right in the first place.

Bitters also help people return to present moment reality. In "not here" situations, bitters will help bring someone from wherever they're "at" back to the present. This has to do with the head/gut dynamic as well. Head energy is notoriously "not present;" rather, the person's consciousness exists where their thoughts are. A taste of bitter helps to reground a person to the present.

British herbalist Sarah Head has called the bitter flavor of bitters "releasing." Reaching beyond the physiological release of gastrointestinal (GI) fluids, we can see that they help one let go of stuck energy—particularly anger and frustration—emotions often viewed in traditional medicine as being tied to stagnant/sluggish liver energy. Bitters, in addition to releasing bile, also help people let go of the emotional energies housed in different organs.

This correlation between bitters and mood may seem to some speculative or even spurious, but here there is abundant rational evidence to support the assertions (for those who are stuck in their head energy). The gastrointestinal system, as a whole, houses the enteric nervous system (ENS), a part of the autonomic nervous system that controls the involuntary goings-on of digestion. But this isn't the only role played by the ENS. Many people are surprised to discover that the brunt of mood-related hormones and neurotransmitters, including serotonin, dopamine, endorphins, and benzodiazepines, are produced not primarily in the brain, but in the gut by the enteric nervous system. So, if your metabolism is deficient, and the GI tract has to deal with the problems that come along with deficiency, wouldn't it seem reasonable that something we know perks up GI functions (bitters) might perk up the production of mood-related hormones as well? This seems especially likely when we consider that we know bitters stimulate the production of the hormone gastrin, and the action of serotonin in the gut, which is to calm irritation, and promote peristalsis and digestive secretions. Practically speaking, bitters do indeed serve as excellent calmatives and often can banish depression correlated with digestive deficiencies.

So, to summarize, we see that bitters possess a corrective influence over sluggish metabolism, deficient stomach acid, and bile secretion resulting in difficulty digesting fats, oils, and proteins, nutrient deficiency, loss of appetite, cravings, addictions, ungroundedness, anxiety, depression, and other conditions that are rampant in our culture. That these conditions are among the most frequently medicated, using both over the counter and prescription drugs, underscores the merit of using bitter plants.

## Contraindications and Considerations

Bitters are considered "cold" in energy in traditional herbcraft, and long-term or heavy use is said to "cool the digestion," something not seen as desirable. This doesn't mean their use should be avoided, but that they can benefit from combining them with a warming herb (ginger, for example), or by the use of bitters that are also warming (like calamus or angelica).

Another consideration is that if a person is frequently bothered by intestinal gas, pungent, aromatic, "carminative" herbs (such as fennel, orange peel, chamomile, or anise) should be added, as the volatile oils they contain possess a dispersive effect and their use helps to expel gas.

Bitters are also said to be drying, because the increased secretions they stimulate remove fluids from the body. Constitutional dryness is often associated with nervous anxiety, and again our friend Kiva Rose offers an insightful observation:

> I have observed bitters having the ability to space out already airy people. This seems to be because of the drying

qualities, and these vata-ish airy people need extra moisture to keep them grounded and present, when they dry up, they have a tendency to blow away.

This isn't really a contraindication for bitters, but it does present a need to complement them with something moistening—licorice being an exemplary consideration. Some bitters, such as fenugreek, also provide moisture to address this aspect.

These considerations regarding bitters are easily addressed by combining bitters with other herbs in a formula, or by using those bitters that are also warming, aromatic, or moistening. Also, such issues are most pertinent when using more overtly medicinal bitters, as opposed to nutrient-rich foods which possess a bitter flavor.

## Bitter Foods and Bitter Medicines

The quality of a plant's bitterness is widely variable in both character and degree. Many bitter herbs are more accurately referred to as foods, while others are decidedly medicinal in their action. Bitter foods should be considered essential to good nutrition, whereas bitters of a more medicinal nature should be reserved to address specific concerns not remedied by dietary bitters.

How can you discern between dietary and medicinal bitters? Primarily by whether the plant can be considered a food you can easily eat. Dietary bitters consist of many incredibly nutritious leafy greens. The very notion of having salad before a meal originates from the role of the bitter greens that were once the mainstay of salads. Indeed, salad wasn't always chopped iceberg lettuce and fatty dressings, but used to be made from wild leafy herbs such as dandelion and chicory, or many of the common weeds that naturally spring up around human habitations. These nutrient-rich herbs were complemented by vinegar dressings, which also serve to extract their minerals for optimal absorption. A salad of this nature not only serves as a nutritious appetizer, but also aids in the digestion of heavier foods, which often make up the "main course" of meals.

Medicinal bitters are too powerful in flavor to make useful foods. Few indeed (even me) would care to sit down to a soufflé of gentian roots, or replace their tarragon (*Artemisia dracunculus*) with wormwood (*Artemisia absinthium*). Such herbs are appropriately used to address a particular need, be it chronic indigestion or that heavy, stuffed feeling that often follows liberal holiday feasting.

## Using Bitters in Food and Medicine

So how does one go about introducing bitters into their diet? Initially, by the gradual inclusion of bitter foods, which include a slew of immensely nutritious greens, high in vitamins, minerals and other nutrients we don't yet value enough. When making your next salad, try adding some of the many bitter greens, available either from your own healthily neglected lawn or even many supermarkets. Arugula, watercress, endive, radicchio, and various mustard greens can be found at many groceries these days, either on their own or in herb or "spring mixes." Even better, dandelion, chicory, and other weedy plants will grow of their own accord in your yard (without any work from you) if you let them—wild bitter greens abound.

Likewise, such greens can be used to top sandwiches or garnish familiar dishes. I often top pasta with a blend of slivered dandelion leaves and sesame and ground flax seeds, and have been known to bring in a small bag of bitter leaves to replace the sad looking lettuce restaurants place atop a sandwich.

Stir fries are spruced up by such greens, thrown in shortly before serving, and pestos can even be made more nutritious and palatable by blending such plants as garlic mustard in with the basil.

A few considerations are worthy of mentioning. If the bitter flavor is new to you, and seems more agreeable to your brain than your palate, ease bitters into your dietary repertoire. Taste different bitters individually to see which one's you like best, and blend them into a salad consisting of milder or sweeter greens (including other wild plants, such as chickweed or violet leaves). You needn't clobber yourself over the tongue with their flavor; just add enough to sense their bite.

Acids generally complement both the flavor and effects of bitters. As mentioned above, vinegar can be used as a dressing on salads, and will both mellow the flavor and aid in the assimilation of minerals. Ginger in a dressing will also "warm up" the flavor. A splash of lemon juice, or the addition of sun-dried tomatoes, can likewise make bitter greens more palatable. Fats, spices, and a bit of sea salt also help balance and enhance the bitters' bite.

Although initially an unfamiliar taste you may feel an aversion to, you'll probably find that the body quickly recognizes the essential nature of bitters. After using them a bit, the brain registers that the body is reacting to them in an "Oh, finally" manner. Once we feel them satiate a craving we've long nursed and tried unsuccessfully to fill with something else, it clicks.

The use of medicinal bitters often requires more consideration, though there are a number of simple indications for their use. Most simple, acute indigestion can be allayed by a small dose of bitters; 15 to 30 drops of a bitter tincture will relieve the slow, stuffed, stagnant feeling that comes with too-liberal feasting. In fact, the addition of Angostura bitters to champagne is intended to do just that. For more developed or chronic health concerns, greater discernment is required when choosing which herbs to use, and further study or the insights of a knowledgeable herbalist are likely warranted.

Bitter tinctures can be made simply by soaking chopped dandelion or yellow dock roots in vodka in a mason jar for a few weeks, or they can be formulated from several plants for a broader action. I make a tincture blend of gentian and orange peel spiced with a bit of ginger, which tastes quite nice and works equally well. A blend of roasted and raw dandelion root could be used as a more readily available substitution for the gentian. Small quantities of tea can also be used; and, in fact, the familiar and tasty chamomile, if made by steeping an ounce of the dried flowers in a quart of water just off the boil overnight, yields a potent brew, both bitter and aromatic. Such a strong infusion can be taken in an ounce or so as a dose, with the excess frozen in ice cube trays and thawed as needed to lessen the task of daily tea making. It's worth noting that bitters that are also diaphoretic, such as chamomile, will favor sweating over GI effects when drunk hot, and so best consumed lukewarm, cool, or cold.

## The Bitter End

*What seems to us as bitter trials are often blessings in disguise.*
~Oscar Wilde

While not referring to the taste of plants, this sentiment holds true when applied to them. People associated bitterness with negative virtues such as spite and resentment, and yet, what emotional bitterness really originates from is stagnation; the inability to release a belief or feeling that no longer serves, but rather hinders, our wellness, development, and growth. The bitter person is oppressed by avoidance of the very thing they cannot let go. Only by embracing bitterness can we learn what it has to offer—to teach us. In this embrace we find it rich in medicine.

As it applies to herbs, these same factors resonate. We avoid bitterness because its taste seems uncomfortable; it challenges us. And yet when embraced, we find what it offers us is an abundance of medicine, which allows us to escape from a state of stagnation and release those things, both physiological and emotional, that hinder the blossoming of our wellness.

# References

Breakspear, Ian. "The Bitters." Client Handout. 2005.

Garner-Wizard, Mariann. "HerbClip™ Bitters: Their History, Conceptual Context, and Health Benefits." Retrieved online at http://content.herbalgram.org/wholefoodsmarket/HerbClip/pdfs/020442-258.pdf on September 10, 2008.

Green, James. *The Male Herbal: Health Care for Men and Boys.* California: The Crossing Press, 1991.

Hardin, Kiva Rose. "The Medicine Woman's Roots Terms of the Trade 4: Bitters." Retrieved on September 10, 2008, online at http://bearmedicineherbals.com/?p=404.

Head, Sarah. "Bitters: Herbs which promote release?" Retrieved on September 13, 2008, online at http://kitchenherbwife.blogspot.com/2008/07/bitters-herbs-which-promote-release.html.

Hoffmann, David. *Medical Herbalism: The Science and Practice of Herbal Medicine.* Vermont: Healing Arts Press, 2003.

Hoffmann, David. *Healthy Digestion: A Natural Approach to Relieving Indigestion, Gas, Heartburn, Constipation, Colitis & More*. Massachusetts: Storey Publishing, LLC, 2000.

"Herbwifery Forum: Bitters." Retrieved online at http://herbwifery.org/forum/viewtopic.php?t=272 on September 14, 2008.

King, Dr. Rosalyn M. "The Enteric Nervous System: The Brain in the Gut." Retrieved on September 8, 2008, online at http://www.psyking.net/id36.htm.

# Metabolic Herb Boost

≈ by Kaaren Christ ≈

Think of your metabolic system like a furnace. Your metabolism is responsible for taking fuel, in the form of food, and turning it into energy. What we want is a high-efficiency furnace; a metabolic system that burns clean and runs smoothly all the time. We want it to be in good repair. When our home's furnace doesn't operate properly, we can become uncomfortable. Similarly, when our metabolic system doesn't operate properly, our bodies become uncomfortable, too. Other systems start to get sluggish. Our digestive system slows, our circulatory system gets lazy. When our metabolic "furnace" doesn't run well over a period of time, we also gain

weight and have difficulty taking it off. This is because our body accumulates toxins and waste products our sluggish metabolism is unable to get rid of, and the process of converting food into usable energy becomes slower and slower.

This is a little owner's manual for those who wish to use natural metabolic approaches to maintaining a healthy body weight. Taking care of your metabolic system can be accomplished using a whole body approach, and using as many strategies as possible will give best results. The benefits are countless. Not only will you more effectively turn your food into energy, but your body's other systems will also thank you for your efforts, too. Your skin will have a healthy glow, your bowels, liver, and kidneys will be squeaky clean, and better circulation will help keep you warm in the winter and nice and cool in the summer.

## Feed the Furnace

Paying attention to what we eat is the first step toward enjoying a vigorous metabolism. The most basic approach is to eat organic foods in their simplest forms. Typically, this means eating raw food or food that has not been highly processed. Raw food is good for us because it adds fibre and enzymes that processing sometimes destroys. The simpler food is, the easier it is for our bodies to do exactly what we need them to do, which is burn food as fuel. This is because your body won't need to expend extra energy to filter out the bad stuff, or flush it out. Nor will it need to find a place to store it, like in your liver or your colon. Don't expect to be able to make all of these changes at once. At first, try only one or two, or try them just a couple days a week. Just start thinking about simple food as fuel, and regularly fuel up.

When you begin to add organic food, start with fruits and veggies. The first thing you will notice is their superior taste. I don't know if this is a scientific fact, but you may also notice that they are often heavier than their non-organic counter-parts. I like to imagine this is because they are more dense with all the good vitamins, minerals and enzymes our bodies need to thrive. Many people find that although the cost of organic food may be a little higher, they do not seem to need to eat as much to feel satisfied because the added vitamins and minerals satisfy our hunger more quickly.

After you have added some organic produce and real-ize what you have been missing in taste, the next part comes naturally: add more organic produce! Stop thinking of fruits and vegetables as side dishes and think of them as the main attraction. Invest in a good vegetarian cookbook or find some good vegetarian Web sites online. Ask your friends and family members for their favorite vegetable dishes. Prepare fruits and vegetables with every meal and notice how your system begins to thank you. The first organ to thank you will be your bowels. The natural-occurring fiber in fruits and vegetables is abso-lutely crucial for a healthy body. Remember that elimination is a sign of efficient burning, so when our bowels regularly rid us of waste, this is our metabolic system doing its job faster! If you are not having one to two bowel movements a day, you are not eating enough fiber.

## Timing is Everything

When we sleep, our metabolic engine rests. The best thing we can do is give it a jump-start in the morning with break-fast. It needn't be a large breakfast, but it should be substantial, and free of refined sugars and highly processed food. It is also good for the metabolism, if breakfast includes a small amount of lean protein such as cheese, fish, beans, and peanut or other nut butters. Fruits and vegetables are also a natural choice for breakfast, as are whole grains like oatmeal, seven-grain cereal, or brown rice. One of my favorite breakfasts consists of an organic grapefruit and apple chopped and put over organic salad greens, with the grapefruit juice as dressing. I sprinkle a few toasted pumpkin seeds on top, too. It is also essential you eat a number of small meals each day instead of three large ones. This keeps your metabolic system from entering a resting state, or becoming overwhelmed with large amounts of food to process at one time. If you want to have a healthy metabolism, it is counterproductive to severely restrict calories. This form of strict dieting is extremely ineffective for achieving a stable, healthy body weight. Essentially, our metabolic system is smart. When we do not have enough fuel in our systems, our body reads this as starvation and immediately kicks into preservation mode, slowing the whole metabolic process down until refuelling has been resumed. Never starve your metabolism!

## Feisty Metabolic Foods

There are certain foods that have special abilities to jump start a sluggish metabolic rate. These include foods with "bite" such as ginger and hot peppers. This is because spicy food increases your body's adrenal reaction and elevates your heart rate slightly. This in turn positively affects your circulation system. Other foods that work to jump start metabolism are grapefruits and blueberries. Both have natural sugars—an immediate source of energy, and blueberries have wonderful antioxidant qualities, as well. Dark green veggies like spinach, beet greens and kale are known for the same qualities. Seaweed and kelp contain iodine and are said to stimulate the thyroid, also giving the metabolism a boost. Grapefruit and other citrus fruits also have multiple metabolic benefits. They are high in vitamin C and appear to be able to stabilize insulin levels, leading to weight loss for many people.

Green tea is also wonderful for boosting metabolism, as it has antioxidant qualities. Not only that, but drinking green tea also increases the amount of water you take in and it is a relaxing ritual, giving you triple benefits.

## Water Your Metabolism

Given that adult bodies are made up of up to 75 percent water, it shouldn't be much of a surprise that water is absolutely essential to keeping our metabolic engine running smoothly. One of the primary functions of water in our bodies is to carry away toxins and waste from our kidneys and liver. It is also responsible for aiding digestion, which we know is directly related to metabolism. Additionally, without water your body is unable to absorb the vitamins and minerals necessary for survival. Think of water as the lubricant for your metabolic system. Water is essential for the health of your whole self, but particularly for the digestive system. A lack of fiber in our bodies, combined with a lack of water, leaves our poor colons full of waste that is not able to move through our system. A constant flow of pure water through our systems helps to avoid this. Never begin your day without enjoying a big glass of water to start. Carrying a water bottle with you as you go about your activities or making a point of drinking a glass of water before each meal are also habits that will help you get the water your body needs to stay hydrated.

Here's an interesting thought. Many health and nutrition experts believe we often misinterpret our body's cry for water as a feeling of hunger. You might try an experiment for a week, and drink a glass of water each time your body says "eat" and see if the feeling of hunger goes away. If so, you will not only be lubricating and jump-starting your metabolism, but you will be eliminating unnecessary calories, which will also assist with achieving a healthy body weight. Remember that water is particularly essential when we are doing activities that make us sweat—another sign of an active metabolism.

# Herbs

One could spend a lot of money and a tremendous amount of time exploring all the available herbal weight loss products and metabolism boosters. You want to exercise caution using such products, given their potential side effects, such as bloating and cramping. I prefer to use everyday herbs to help me along. Just about everything we need can be found on our supermarket shelves. As mentioned earlier, spicy herbs and foods may be just the thing to perk up your metabolic function.

# Walk Your Way to a Healthy Metabolic Rate!

Another completely natural way to boost metabolism is through regular aerobic and strength training exercise. A brisk twenty-minute walk each day will get your heart rate up as well as stimulate your circulatory and digestive system. Muscle building exercise such as weight training or yoga are even more effective at boosting metabolism because muscle actually increases the number of calories your body burns while it is at rest. Even ten minutes a day will make a difference.

Remember that your metabolism is a whole body system and every step you take to boost it will help you reach and remain at your healthy body weight. Eat organic foods as often as you can. Keep your body well hydrated with pure water. Add some herbs and spices known to boost metabolism, and take time every day to exercise your body.

# All About Plantain

≈ by Calantirniel ≈

O f the ten species of plantain located in the United States, the two most common are the broadleaf variety (*Plantago major*) and the lanceleaf variety (*Plantago lanceolata*), both of which originate in Europe. Common names for plantain include: blackjacks, broadleaf, cat's cradles, chimney sweeps, clock, cocks, cuckoo's bread, dog's ribs, Englishman's foot, headsman, healing blade, hen plant, Jackstraws, Kemps, Kempseed, lamb's foot, the leaf of Patrick, leechwort, Patrick's dock, ram's tongue, rattail, ripple grass, salt and pepper plant, St. Patrick's leaf, silk plant, snakebite, snakeweed, waybread, waybroad, weybroed (Anglo-Saxon), white man's foot, and windles.

The *Plantago major* species can be either an annual or perennial plant; it is a low-growing rosette of egg-shaped, broad leaves (for the *P. lanceolata*, narrow pointed leaves), with tough, fibery veins that distinctly follow the outline of the leaf shape, and all of the veins meet at the point of the leaf, which is sort of rounded. The flowers arise on a stalk that resembles a "spike." They are very small, even inconspicuous, and of the same green color, only slightly darker, and are arranged up and down the stalk in tiny "sausage" shapes. They feel scaly to the touch. There are slight variations between the species, but once you recognize one, you will easily recognize others.

Many species of the *Plantago* genus can be found around the world, and are often considered pesky garden weeds because people do not know the miracles of this plant. It seems no matter what part of the world it grows in, it is usually found in meadows and in almost any type of soil, even dry soil that is disturbed. They also are found more often in temperate to cool areas, and less often found in the tropics or deserts.

## History of Plantain

Plantain has a long record of medicinal use, widespread availability, and an expansive variety of internal and external healing applications, dating from Hippocrates and Dioscorides to the modern herbalist doctors, from ancient China to the Native Americas and ancient Anglo-Saxons to Maude Grieve's *A Modern Herbal*.

Historically, external uses for plantain have been noted for wounds of nearly every cause and even in a toxic state. Plantain has been used for war wounds, snakebite, mad-dog bite, spider bite, bee sting, and for any infected or puncture wounds; as well as for skin rashes, ulcerations, poison oak/ivy, eczema, burning eyes, earaches, and to drawing out splinters. It is also theorized to be a part of the proprietary blend in the soap brand-named Cuticura. Documentation of internal use includes treatment for loss of male sexual potency, ulcers, asthma, epilepsy, rheumatism, ulcerated lungs or glands and related cough, stomach pain, leucorrhea, fever, laxative, diarrhea, hemorrhoids, cholera infantum, dysentery, female disorders involving passive hemorrhage, de-worming, scrofula, syphilis, glandular disease, mercurial and other metal poisoning, bladder and urinary difficulties, and clearing mucous from the respiratory system.

# How You Can Use Plantain

Once you learn to identify it (and don't be surprised if it is in your yard), keep some on hand for emergencies like snake or spider bites, bee stings, poison oak/ivy rash, or any wound. Plantain is well known for its drawing qualities. Pick two to four leaves and stick them in your pocket before hiking. Chew the leaf or leaves and apply directly to the wound if needed (it is best if the victim does the chewing, since there is a relationship with the saliva and the body). Secure to the area with a bandage or whatever is on hand, then change the leaves when the drawing qualities are not felt (which varies from one to twelve hours). Eat the leaves or drink the tea to enhance internal healing properties. Since plantain's medicinal qualities cannot stay in the dried herbal form, you can tincture the fresh leaves.

### *Plantain Tincture*

Place torn up fresh plantain leaves in a glass jar (try filling toward the top). Fill the jar with brandy or vodka that is 40 to 50 percent alcohol and keep on the kitchen counter, away from sunlight, for at least two weeks (it can be longer, too). Twice a day, shake the jar around to evenly distribute the mixture. After two weeks, strain out the leaves in an unbleached coffee filter and place the tincture into a dark glass bottle that has a glass dropper. Don't forget to label it.

This is excellent to keep when the fresh plant material is not available. For external use, soak a cotton ball or cloth with tincture and apply. For internal use, add 20 to 30 drops of tincture to 8 ounces of water (using hot water will "boil" some of the alcohol off). Raw honey, agave juice, or stevia can be added to the drink, but sweetener is optional.

## *Plantain Tea*

To make fresh tea that actually tastes good, gather approximately 2 teaspoons of fresh leaves, tear them, and drop pieces into a cup. Add 8 ounces hot water. Cover and steep away from heat for 15 minutes. Filter out leaves and drink. Sweeten as directed above.

Whether you use the tincture or the fresh plant, drink two cups a day for chronic issues or long-term cleansing (try for two to three months), or five cups a day if you are fighting off poisons or infection, or otherwise have acute issues. If using for the latter, you can combine with other helpful herbs like Echinacea or yarrow.

Not only is plantain readily available, it is extremely versatile and it can clean the entire system: digestive/colon, kidney/bladder, respiratory/lungs and even cleans the blood—and it is safe. Enjoy the tremendous benefits of plantain!

# Tea Time Herbs

### ❧ by Dallas Jennifer Cobb ❧

Tea time was an event in our household as I grew up. Raised by a British mother and grandmother, for me tea was both a ritual and a right. Midmorning we would gather in the kitchen for tea and toast, or tea and a "bickie" (biscuit). Midafternoon everything stopped for a more formal tea, which included sandwiches, scones, and jam. Not just a midafternoon meal, when body or feelings were hurt, a "cuppa" tea was the healing balm.

Tea time is still infused with all the memories and associations of my youth. While I know the medicinal benefits of herbs, I find that tea time is a spiritual time when I can experience peace, calm, and soothing emotions that inspire me to recall feelings of comfort and well-being from my childhood. Step into the kitchen with me while we put the pot on the stove, prepare a delightful snack, and dish up a helping of sweet comfort, savory care, and herbal calm with herbal tea time.

## The History of Tea

Long before British colonists tried tea, people in southeast Asia and Africa had been enjoying teas made from leaves that were gathered from various bushes, prepared in the traditional way of adding hot water to dried leaves, and then consumed as a hot drink. It wasn't until the 1600s that British aristocracy started to imported teas from British outposts such as Ceylon (modern day Sri Lanka). When they tried the brew, they were attracted to the tastes and stimulating qualities of the teas.

Initially, a custom of the upper class who could afford the specialty imports, tea time eventually spread throughout the classes, becoming a widespread British custom. As the British Empire grew and its citizens emigrated, the custom of tea time was exported with them.

While a midmorning tea break is very common, it was the afternoon tea time that gained renown. High tea is the small meal served midafternoon. It traditionally included tea, sandwiches, pastries, or scones served with jam and clotted cream. Today, high tea is served around three o'clock in England, and to date, many shops, banks, and government offices still close for the hour-long period to observe the ritual. In Scotland, tea time eventually replaced dinner. It is customarily served in the late afternoon, between five o'clock and six o'clock, and includes a variety of more substantial foods.

While many of the teas originally consumed contained caffeine, tea time has changed. More herbal and caffeine-free teas are served today, which appeals to people with particular dietary preferences and choices. These days, herbal teas are widely available in loose leaf and individual tea bag format. The shelves of grocery stores and health food stores are rich with the variety of tea mixes available. You can purchase teas for flavor, healing qualities, or spiritual energy. You can grow herbs and make your own loose leaf teas according to your own tastes and preferences. While many different herbs and spices are now used in commercial tea blends, a number of common herbs are used over and over in many of the culinary and healing tea blends.

## Plant Your Own Tea Garden

Planting a small tea-themed garden is a great way to ensure you always have the herbs you desire, and that the herbs are free from pesticides. The best herbs to include in a tea garden are easy to grow and primarily perennial. Herbs that can be used in a variety of teas include chamomile, lemon balm, mint, catnip, spearmint, sage, rosemary, red raspberry leaf, fennel, and lemon thyme. Although it is suited to a very warm climate and is therefore an annual in many areas, stevia is a great herb to grow because the sweetness of its leaves adds considerable appeal to many tea blends.

Some herbs are not suited for general introduction into a garden. Because they send out runners and spread wildly to potentially overtake other plants, mint, spearmint, and lemon balm are best planted in pots to contain them. Beware of letting these go to seed, as the wind can then spread the seeds throughout the garden, making for a busy spring of weeding Start small. Select a few herbs to add to the tea garden each year. Build the garden close to the kitchen door so you can easily gather fresh herbs to put in the tea pot. Some annual herbs, like rosemary, can be brought inside each winter to extend their use.

Plan to vary the heights, colors, and textures of herbs to give the tea garden visual appeal. And remember to plant lots of what you like to drink so you have it on hand, and so you can consume it fresh in season or dry it for use in the winter months.

## Uplifting Herbs

Many stressors can be overcome with herbs. We hear so much about the calming effects of chamomile, but herbs can also trigger olfactory responses and emotional associations. When I smell the combination of chamomile, mint, and lemon balm, I am transported back to my grandmother's kitchen where everything was orderly, safe, and comforting. These three herbs were combined and administered to sick children by my grandmother, who also said they were good for promoting sleep, relieving fever, and calming a bad tummy.

Herbs contain very high levels of polyphenols, vitamins A, C, and E, and known antioxidants. As a result, herbs can be uplifting and have deep-rooted healing properties. An antioxidant protects key cell components from the damaging effects of free radicals, a natural byproduct of metabolism formed when oxygen metabolizes or burns. Free radicals can disrupt the structure of other molecules and cause cellular damage that contributes to aging, and cell mutations, like cancer. The antioxidants contained in herbs (and fruits and vegetables) play a role in the maintenance of healthy cells and the prevention of cancer and other cell mutation because they counter the negative effect of oxygen metabolic process, hence the name antioxidant.

Many herbs are reported to contain higher levels of phenols, the active antioxidant ingredient, than berries, fruit, and vegetables. Listed in decreasing order of antioxidant activity, these herbs include the oregano family of herbs, sweet marjoram, rose geranium, sweet bay, dill, thyme, rosemary, and sage. Other herbs known to be high in antioxidants include borage, lemon balm, and peppermint.

## Making a Perfect Pot of Tea

Most tea drinkers prefer a teapot made of clay or ceramic. It holds the heat well, and doesn't affect the taste or qualities of the herbs. Put a kettle of water on and heat to boiling. The hot water temperature provides the optimum catalyst for the herbs to release their oils, flavor, and potent power. When water is merely warm, the herbs do not release their maximum flavor or potency. While you're waiting for it to boil, rinse your tea pot. A clean teapot ensures that the tea will taste pure. Place herbs inside the pot, either loose or in a tea egg (a special metal ball for containing the leaves).

Use 2 tablespoons of fresh herbs, or 1 tablespoon of dried herbs, for each cup of water you will put in the pot. Traditionally, the British would add an extra spoon "for the pot" when making more than one cup. So a five-cup pot of tea would have 6 tablespoons of herb added. Cover and allow to steep for 5 to 10 minutes. Many tea drinkers use a tea cozy to keep the pot warm and better steep the tea.

## Herbal Tea Recipes

There are so many herbs and so many combinations that there are herbal teas for almost any complaint. The following recipes are ones I have used for common ailments, like an upset stomach, and are not intended to replace a trip to the doctor for more serious problems.

### *Tummy Tea*

Whether you have a touch of the flu, have eaten too much, or have motion sickness, this tea can help settle your stomach and relieve nausea. Mint actively relieves nausea and cleanses the palate after vomiting, leaving a pleasant taste in the mouth. Chamomile calms and promotes sleep, and lemon balm actively promotes sweating and can lower a fever. All these herbs are pleasant tasting alone and, when combined, they make something delicious that even children will drink.

Combine equal parts of chamomile, lemon balm, and peppermint together. You can also use spearmint for a variation of flavor. For children, less mint and more chamomile is preferred, focusing the flavor on sweet rather than minty.

### Mama's Milk Tea

New mothers who nurse their babies cannot drink caffeine because caffeine is one of the substances that passes directly to the baby through the breast milk. Since infants need their sleep to satisfy the growing their body is doing, most mothers switch to caffeine-free beverages while nursing. There is one tea that actually promotes greater milk production in the mother. It tastes great, nourishes the growing infant, and provides optimum nutrients and immunity.

Combine 2 parts fennel with 1 part each of nettle, vervain, or borage. Not only is there a galactagogue effect (increased breast milk production), but nettle is high in calcium, making it nourishing for both babe and mother. When I was nursing, I found that even the scent of the fennel brewing in the pot seemed to stimulate a let-down of breast milk.

### Winter Wonder Tea

This aromatic blend will warm both your hands and tummy. It actually increases the metabolism, producing a feeling of warmth and well-being.

Save and dry orange peel. Use a blender to chop the dried peel nice and small.

In a saucepan, simmer 1½ to 2 cups water with a teaspoon of dried orange peel with about 2 ounces of fresh ginger, coarsely chopped. Just before serving, squeeze juice from half a lemon into the mix and add honey to taste.

### *Bone-building Tea*

As we age, many of us face osteoporosis. Bone-building tea provides lots of usable calcium in a tasty and easy to consume format. Get in the habit of drinking it regularly and forget about the "it's good for me" part.

Combine 3 parts of red raspberry leaf with 1 part of nettle. Mix well and use a heaping tablespoon per cup of tea. It is tasty and calming, and goes great with citrus, which provides the needed vitamin C to help your body assimilate calcium.

## Tea Time Nibbles

Because the British tradition always includes something to eat with tea, I have included a few simple recipes for nibbles to accompany your tea.

### *Scones*

3   cups flour (try oat flour for taste, or rice flour for gluten-free baking)

⅓   cup sugar

2½ teaspoons baking powder

½   teaspoon baking soda

½   teaspoon salt

¾   cup cold unsalted butter, cut into pea-size pieces

1   cup buttermilk (or use regular milk and add a tablespoon of lemon juice to sour it)

1   tablespoon grated orange or lemon peel as zest

1. Preheat oven to 425°F.

2. Mix all the dry ingredients together.

3. Add butter pieces and mix with fingers.

4. Add milk and zest and mix well. Work the dough quickly and do not overmix.

5. Roll dough on a lightly floured surface and cut it into desired shapes, leaving the edges of the dough sharp so they rise in layers.

6. Bake on an oiled baking sheet for 12 to 15 minutes.

7. Serve with jam, whipped cream, or custard, and your own choice of delicious tea-time tea. Yields 12 to 14 scones.

This is a recipe with many variations. If you love herbs, try adding ½ cup of minced lemon balm, or ¼ cup of rosemary to the recipe for a savory biscuit. If you prefer sweet, add raisins, currants, or nuts. A really yummy scone is made when you add ½ cup of shredded cheddar cheese. (Skip the citrus zest if you make cheese scones.)

# Herbal Love Potions

### ≈ by Lisa McSherry ≈

Love potions have a long history in herbalism, although they mostly have a dark side involving manipulating another's will and forcing the imbiber to fall in love. Modern love potions focus on the more ethical practice of working to make their creator more attractive and lovable—thereby allowing natural attraction to play its part. This article is about ways a couple can use herbal potions, lotions, balms, and infusions to ignite their desire for one another as well as to increase their physical attraction for one another.

## Mellifluous Mask

I often spend "spa days" with my partner. It's a day of nurturing for both of us as we take care of one another, spreading delicious concoctions over our bodies and helping to clean one another off afterward. Such intimate contact often leads naturally to the obvious (and enjoyable!) conclusion. Honey is a delicious, sweet way to soften and hydrate skin. It's a pleasure to gently smooth over your partner's face, and to be soothed in return.

Before starting the massage, cleanse your face thoroughly. Using about 2 teaspoons of raw honey, gently spread it over your partner's entire face, neck, and chest following this pattern:

Start by stroking the whole face. Use both hands and work up the neck, out across the cheeks, then glide gently inward and work up and out over the forehead. Finish by applying gentle pressure to the temples. (Be careful not to get any in the hair. We usually wrap our hair in slightly damp towels.)

Stimulate the skin by loosely rolling your fingers up the cheek. This is also nice on the neck and under the chin.

For tension in the neck and shoulders make firm circular movements, working up either side of the neck then out across the shoulders.

Be careful to avoid the delicate area around the eyes. Leave the honey on for about 15 minutes. Finish by tapping your fingers across the face as if you are playing rapidly on a piano. This further stimulates the flow of blood to the face and feels fantastic. Rinse with warm water, or use a soft washcloth rinsed in warm water and wrung out until it's just damp.

## Beautifying Body Butter

In a double boiler (you can use a small metal bowl over water in a saucepan), warm 5 tablespoons sesame oil and 3 tablespoons shea butter until just melted. Remove from heat and gently stir to blend. Cool to body temperature and then add 10 drops each of cardamom, ginger, and sweet orange essential oil. Then stir again. (This smells incredibly good.) Pour into a storage container (I use a wide mouth glass jar; it's easier to get my hands into) and let "set up" for about twenty-four hours.

If you care about potentially staining your bed sheets, place a large towel (or several) underneath before applying. Use this butter to massage all over the body, about 1 teaspoon at a time (it really spreads out a lot).

Start on your partner's back. Grip both of the shoulders and begin massaging with a bread-kneading motion. Glide palms down to the back region (NEVER apply pressure directly to the spine). Apply some pressure in a circular motion on the lower back and work your way up to the area around the shoulder blades. Run your hands up the neck using an oval-shaped motion with your fingers around the sides of the neck. Focus on the base of the skull where some headaches begin. Move to the buttocks and down the legs, replicating the basic strokes and movements you used on the back and neck.

When it feels appropriate, take your fingertips and run them gently down your partner's back. Don't apply pressure, but gently rub them like feathers across the skin. Repeat as desired, and see what happens from there.

The butter has a slight warming effect, and makes you smell (and feel) good enough to eat.

## Sweet and Spicy Sugar Scrub

For several years now my partner and I have visited a spa as part of our annual vacation. We spend time soaking in a tub big enough for us both, have a sugar scrub and side by side massage, and finish in a steam shower. It's a bit of romantic luxury that we both love. I developed this scrub for us to re-create a piece of the romance with at home. (Alas! Our tub isn't even big enough for one. But we make do.)

1 cup brown sugar (the kind that isn't too granular)

1 cup white sugar (you can use turbinado sugar)

¾ cup almond oil

2 teaspoons each of ground cinnamon, ginger, and nutmeg

40 drops cardamom essential oil

1. In a medium bowl, combine all ingredients except the essential oil. Use a whisk to thoroughly mix them. Make sure there are no lumps of sugar.

2. Add the cardamom oil, drop by drop, blending after each drop.

3. Spoon into a well-sealed storage container (I use a canning jar with a rubber seal).

Take a shower and pat dry (so much fun being dried by your partner!). Using about one-fourth of the scrub at a time, massage into skin using a circular motion. On the long muscles of the thighs and arms, and on the back, long strokes feel fantastic. You will want to avoid the genitals (no surprise), face, and breasts. The skin is very delicate there. Rinse again when done.

Herbal concoctions are fun to make and a delicious way to reaffirm your love for one another. Go ahead, try one today and see how easy it is to fall in love all over again.

# Herbs
# for
# Beauty

# Herbal Beauty Baths

### ➤ by Kaaren Christ ➤

If we could recall our earliest memory, it would be of bathing—suspended weightless in warm amniotic fluid, safely cradled in our mother's womb. This memory is so primitive, so deeply etched in our collective consciousness, that humankind has a natural longing to return regularly to this experience for health, peace of mind, and spiritual growth.

But we have lost touch with the many benefits that come with the bath. With the pace of our lives and multiple demands on our time, many of us forfeit bathing for a rushed morning shower instead, scrubbing quickly with commercial products while our coffee drips and children await our attention.

With one eye on the clock, our minds race ahead into the day. We hardly notice the sensation of the water on our skin and the scents of the products we use are simply familiar fragrances we pay little attention to. Our relationship with water and cleansing has become a ritual of rushing instead of relaxation. A return to a ritual of tranquility is as simple as drawing a bath. It's a pleasure worth contemplating and remembering.

## Nature's Bathtubs

The earliest baths were found in nature. People traveled for miles to visit warm rivers, or small bodies of naturally heated water, to submerge themselves with other like-minded bathers. Naturally occurring thermal hot springs and geysers were given spiritual or health significance, and were often the location of ceremonies, healings, and rituals. They were also common destinations for pilgrims seeking spiritual wisdom. Turns out, early people were on to something.

*Balneology* is a study of the therapeutic benefits of natural hot spring therapy. Although not a well-known body of knowledge in North America, it is popular throughout Europe and Japan, where physicians routinely prescribe hot spring immersion to treat a variety of conditions. It is slowly gaining popularity in the West as people return to the simple pleasures of bathing to treat various conditions and improve health and wellness.

Essentially, there are two kinds of hot springs: filtration springs and primary springs. Filtration springs begin as rain water that seeps into cracks and crevices in Earth's crust, which is then carried through long passages deep beneath the earth and heated. As this happens, the water absorbs minerals through leaching. It then returns to the earth's surface, where lucky bathers are able to enjoy its benefits.

Primary hot springs are created when direct volcanic action and magma chambers beneath the earth heat underground water, changing its mineral and gas content. Balneotologists have found that mineral water from both kinds of springs has therapeutic qualities, depending on the type and concentration of minerals found in the water.

Water rich in bicarbonates, such as calcium bicarbonate, bicarbonate, or carbon dioxide, have been found helpful in opening blood vessels and improving circulation to arms, legs, and feet. It has also been found helpful in the treatment of hypertension. Hot springs rich in sulphur and sulphates are said to be helpful in the treatment of swelling, respiratory problems, and infections. Springs rich with chlorides are considered by some to be helpful in alleviating pain associated with arthritis, gynecological problems, and trauma. When boron is present in the water, one can hope for increased brain activity and stronger bones. Magnesium converts blood sugar to energy and clears skin. Sodium is well-known for its soothing effect on the symptoms of arthritis. These are all helpful things to remember when you are contemplating bath additives for your home, or if you are planning a journey to a hot spring.

## Temperature Therapy

The temperature of bathing water is also a factor to consider. Use very hot water for bathing (using common sense), and seek the advice of your health care provider if you have specific medical conditions. Health concerns such as hypertension and heart disease can make hot-water bathing unadvisable. That said, hot water therapy, when used carefully, is associated with increased body metabolism, improved digestion, and detoxification.

Cold-water baths are often used after hot-water baths to constrict blood vessels, reduce swelling, and bring blood to the capillaries to increase circulation throughout the body. They are also known for their ability to reduce blood pressure on internal organs, strengthen the nervous system, contract the muscles (which helps to eliminate toxins), and strengthen mucus membranes. This helps us fight off allergies and colds.

## Communal Bathing

Not only does bathing offer benefits associated with the mineral content of the water, or water temperature, there appear to be significant social benefits as well. Although we are unlikely to invite a large number of people into our bathroom for social gatherings, many of us do enjoy going to a local health club or recreation center to soak in the hot tub and visit with others who regularly drop in. Throughout history, people around the world have ritualized the practice of bathing in the same way, often developing subcultures and communities around the practices. The popularity of the private hot tub is also rising, with more and more families choosing to install in their homes soaking and jet tubs that seat five to ten people. These tubs are often outside, or in a room designated for their use.

The ancient Romans certainly loved their baths. Although indoor plumbing was available in some private homes, most Romans traveled to a public bathhouse, where people gathered at scheduled times each day to exercise and bathe. These daily rituals were as much for entertainment and social connection as for hygiene and relaxation. The large bathhouses contained a courtyard in the center where Roman bathers lifted weights, exercised, or played competitive games with others. They had an interesting practice of applying thick oil to their entire bodies prior to working up a sweat, which would be scraped off before going into the baths. After exercising and removing the oil, they traveled through a series of connected rooms heated to differing temperatures, which housed baths that ranged from ice cold to very hot.

The Japanese are well known for public bathing, as well. The *sento* (a large communal bathhouse) has a common pool divided into two sections by a tall barrier to segregate men and women. Shoes are removed upon entry and stored in a separate room. Bathers enter into the large room, where small stools and buckets are placed around the walls next to faucets to allow bathers to wash thoroughly before entering the water. Washing and bathing are separate activities. Washing is about becoming clean, while bathing is a way of connecting to others and relaxing. Although these are two of the most commonly known cultures to have developed social conventions around the act of bathing, many other cultures have developed similar rituals and customs. When you think about the many benefits of bathing, don't forget about our public pools and saunas. They are a wonderful resource for all.

## The Royal Treatment

Aside from the simple pleasure of sinking into a tub full of warm water, other pleasures similar to those associated with bathing in hot springs can be experienced with the addition of milk, salts, and herbs, for example, to our private baths. The tradition of adding ingredients to the bath has been around for centuries.

Cleopatra was renowned for her enjoyment of milk baths. Her prized beauty secret was in the lactic acid found in milk, which naturally exfoliates the skin. For a milk bath at home, use 2 to 5 cups of milk in a full tub. You can use more or less depending on your preference. You can use fresh or powdered milk, as either works wonderfully. If you find your skin a little oily after a fresh milk bath, you may want to switch to a skim variety, although there are some benefits to allowing the oils to stay on the skin and be absorbed.

Many people like to add a couple tablespoons of honey to a milk bath. This adds a lovely sweet fragrance that is almost intoxicating. In order to ensure that is fully dissolved, mix the honey in a cup of very hot water first, and then pour into the bath. Wrap yourself in a warm terry cloth robe when you are finished, and you will feel like royalty.

## Salts

Bathing in the sea has long been thought to have healing properties. In Greece, this is called "tallassotherapy" and the benefits include increased circulation, rejuvenation of cells, and relaxation. It seems that salt water has a way of activating the body's healing abilities. The Dead Sea has been known for centuries as Mother Nature's spa. Salts taken from the Dead Sea, when rubbed into the skin or used as a soak, are believed to draw out toxins and purify the body.

You need not rush out to find salt from the Dead Sea to reap the benefits of bath salts, because Epsom salts has many of the same qualities. Epsom salts is made up of magnesium sulphite, which has the ability to soothe the body's nervous system. Not only can you add a couple cups directly to your bath, they also make an effective exfolient. To do this, rub the salts over your wet skin, starting at your toes and working up. Rub in small circles. When complete, immerse yourself in warm water and enjoy the fresh silkiness of your baby soft skin. Mixing a half teaspoon of Epsom salts into your regular facial-washing cream will also give a healthy glow.

## Herbal Additions

No discussion about the art of bathing would be complete without an exploration of herbal infusions. Infusions are made by pouring a specified amount of boiling water (usually 1 to 2 liters) over a mixture of herbs chosen for their healing properties. This mixture is then left to steep. After it is strained, it can be added to a bath. Almost any herb can be used in the bath, but here are some potential combinations you may enjoy.

Lavender, calendula, thyme, rosemary, marjoram, rose petals, peppermint, and chamomile all make wonderful additions. You might consider adding a couple drops of an essential oil to enhance the scent, as well. Make sure you add the herbs and oils after the bath has finished running so that steam does not carry away some of the benefits.

## Finishing Touches

Whether you choose salts, milk, or herbs to enhance your bath, take time to make your ritual meaningful to you. Choose a time with the least likelihood of distractions or interruptions. Make a point of telling family members that your time in the bath is special time, and insist they learn to manage without you while you indulge. Keep a special towel or slippers on a top shelf for use when you bathe. Add scented candles or soft music, and remember to keep your window sealed during your bath to ensure scents do not escape.

Although communal bathing has fallen out of fashion, many couples enjoy bathing together at home, and look forward to sharing a tub together to unwind and create a quiet space to share their days. If you are in a position to make changes to your bathroom, there is a wide range of tub sizes and styles to suit all purposes and styles that facilitate couple or family bathing practices.

Although taking a bath is a familiar idea, many of us have simply forgotten both the benefits and the pleasures of this simple, and fundamental pleasure. It has the power to take us back to a place of utter contentment and safety and to experience the simple joy of relaxation. It's time to remember the bath.

# Craft Your Own Organic Body Lotions

≈ by Sue J. Morris ≈

Have you ever read an article in a magazine, newsletter, or journal that made such an impact on the way you thought about things that it caused you to change the choices you make forever? That happened to me a few years ago, when I received a newsletter from The Breast Cancer Fund. I read an article about the harmful chemicals in cosmetics and learned how many of these chemicals we put on our bodies in our daily ritual to stay beautiful.

The article was titled: "Not So Pretty," and it focused on a survey completed in 2004 by the Campaign for Safe Cosmetics. I learned that the average adult uses nine personal care products each day, containing 126

unique chemical ingredients that are known or probable human carcinogens. According to the survey, more that 25 percent of women use at least fifteen products daily, thus exposing themselves to toxicants that have been associated with reproductive and developmental harm to fetuses, and which pose a potential link to breast cancer. As one who strives to live organically and uses very little make-up and as few commercial beauty care products as possible, I thought my own list would be short. But as I added up the products I use each morning, the list was not as short as I'd imagined it would be. Let's see—shampoo, conditioner, body wash, deodorant, moisturizer, body lotion, hair product, toothpaste, and mascara just to start my day. There were my nine products. In comparison to many women, I think my list is comparatively short.

As the owner of a natural skin care company, Sue's Salves, crafting organic, healing skin salves and herbal massage oils has become my life's work. I had never considered making body lotions until I started to understand what was in the lotions and creams stocking the shelves in the beauty care aisles. I became even more troubled when friends and coworkers were being diagnosed with breast cancer. Women shouldn't have to die to be beautiful. That became my motto.

We think we are protecting our skin and somehow fighting the war on aging, as if it is a threat in itself, when we use products such as anti-aging creams. The real threat, though, is the very creams we are putting on our skin. Preservatives in lotions and creams aren't preserving us; they are contributing to our demise. No one should unwittingly cause themselves harm because they do not understand the extent of the danger that comes from using chemicals on their bodies—chemicals that are common ingredients in all commercially made non-organic products!

Once I started to scrutinize the ingredient labels on hundreds of beauty care products, it became very clear that there was not one single product I could find that did not contain the most ubiquitous chemical of them all—parabens. There are six types of parabens found in over 13,000 cosmetic products, with methylparaben being the most common. This group of chemicals is used as preservatives in cosmetics and is an antibacterial agent in some toothpastes. Four main parabens are in use: methyl-, ethyl-, propyl- and butylparabens. Many products will have two or more of these chemicals as part of a preservative system. Retailers of high-priced cosmetics with beautiful packaging are selling lotions and creams that have more than three types of parabens included in the ingredient list. Chemicals from cosmetics can build up inside the body, and there are tens of thousands of synthetic chemicals in common everyday cosmetic products!

The cosmetics industry insists the chemicals, which are used as preservatives and are approved for use by regulators, are safe. But these parabens preserve the shelf life of cosmetic products from now to eternity. Many of these lotions are going to be around a lot longer than the women who are covering their bodies with them. This realization sparked my lotion-making operation.

Why is it so important to protect our skin? Our skin is made up of connective tissues. These tissues give our skin strength and elasticity. The approximately six pounds of skin each human carries around is a porous membrane through which numerous environmental toxins enter the body. As we age, connective tissues become hardened and lose both elasticity and strength. The ideal lotion is one that is made from an oil that not only softens the skin, but protects it against damage. Coconut oil fits that description. Having done some research, I learned that pure-virgin coconut oil is the best natural ingredient for skin lotion. It prevents destructive free-radical formation and provides protection against them. Coconut oil will absorb easily and keep the skin soft without feeling greasy. Virgin organic coconut oil is especially useful in fighting free radicals, as it is unrefined and hasn't been stripped of any of its natural components through the refining process.

So after reading one article and doing more research, I signed the Compact for Safe Cosmetics and began my search for the best lotion recipe I could find. I found many recipes online by searching for natural beauty care recipes.

## Recipe for Body Lotion

At first I thought lotions would be fairly easy to make, but I have a preference for using plants in the products I craft for the skin. In the end, I created my own recipe using fresh aloe vera and organic coconut oil.

When you choose to make an organic lotion, you must determine what ingredients you want to use. I chose organic, virgin coconut oil as a base because it hasn't been stripped of any of its natural components through the refining process. I soon learned that although this natural oil makes a heavenly lotion when it is warm and freshly made, it reverts to its solid consistency once it cools (coconut oil is solid at 65°F or below). The addition of sweet almond oil solved this problem.

As a plant person, I chose to include freshly pureed aloe as the next ingredient. I carefully peel the skin from the plant's leaves and puree the juicy part of the plant—the aloe gel—and add it to the melted oils. Lanolin, vitamin E oil, emulsifying wax, and essential oils are added next. After melting and then mixing up the ingredients in the blender, voilá, a lotion is born!

Preservative free and divine smelling, this rich, creamy lotion is not only safe, it is a truly healing lotion for dry skin.

## *Organic Lotions Are Perishable*

The reality of making organic lotions is that they are perishable. I liken them to buying fresh, organic vegetables from the farmers' market. You don't want to take them home and leave them in the fridge. You want to eat them while they're fresh. Preservative-free body lotions are the same. Use them, delight in them, nourish your skin with them, and buy more when you run out.

Here is a simple body lotion recipe:

1 cup aloe vera gel (use either fresh aloe or bottled pure aloe vera gel)

1 teaspoon lanolin

1 teaspoon vitamin E oil

⅓ cup organic coconut oil

½ ounce beeswax

¾ cup sweet almond oil (or grapeseed, jojoba, apricot, or sunflower oil)

2 teaspoons of essential oils of your choice (do not use fragrance oils)

1. Melt the oils and the beeswax gently in a saucepan or a double boiler.

2. Use a blender to puree together the aloe gel and the essential oils.

3. While the blender is running, pour the melted oils in a steady stream, using a medium speed. Blend until smooth and creamy, or about 5 minutes.

4. Pour into sterilized containers.

This recipe makes approximately 2 cups of lotion. If you use only coconut oil it will become body butter, and be solid and fabulous as it melts into your skin.

Use Google or another Web search engine to locate other recipes. Enter "make your own cosmetics," or "natural beauty care recipes," or "organic body lotion recipes" for an endless array of recipe ideas.

Avoid the synthetic chemicals found in commercial beauty care products by making your own lotions or by choosing to buy organic products. It is definitely worth the time it takes to make your own. A homemade lotion is as delicious for your skin as a meal made with fresh produce straight from the garden is for your belly! Experiment and enjoy!

# Head to Toe Beauty with Herbs

### ➤ by Elizabeth Barrette ➤

Everyone wants to look good. Store shelves bulge with products for skin care, hair color, fragrance, and more. Unfortunately, most of those products contain harsh chemicals that can harm the body and the environment. Many also undergo testing on live animals, which some consumers prefer to avoid. The end result makes commercial beauty products unappealing to many shoppers.

Herbal preparations are an excellent alternative. Herbal beauty supply shops will also have organic liquid, solid, or powdered soap bases to enhance with herbs. Alternatively, you can make your own beauty supplies from herbs you've gathered and dried.

# Fragrant Herbs

Many herbs bear a potent scent, either in their flowers or other parts. Natural techniques for capturing these scents include using fresh or dried herbs and essential oils. Beware of synthetic "fragrance oils," however, that mimic the real thing. They lack the benefits of true essential oils and may contain undesirable chemicals. Real herbs deliver a more complex and natural scent than synthetics. These scents have a positive effect on the mind and body. Beauty products should have a harmonious blend of ingredients and fragrances that work well together and support each other's effects.

### Bergamot

Bergamot belongs to the mint family and grows to about 2 feet tall, often with scarlet trumpet flowers that attract bees and hummingbirds. Although some fragrance can be obtained from the leaves, essential oil is better and not too expensive. It has minty, green, and floral notes, which make it an excellent choice for blending other herbal scents together.

### Lavender

Lavender grows from 1 to 3 feet tall, putting out tall stems of blue or purple flowers. Dried, they impart their fragrance to soaps, bath bombs, salt scrubs, and many other preparations. Essential oil of lavender is widely available. The scent may be sweet and cool, or sharp and almost medicinal. It soothes headaches and stress, relieves sexual tension, and promotes relaxation. Lavender is a feminine fragrance, often favored by women.

### Lemon Balm

Lemon balm is a bushy green plant in the mint family, reaching 1 to 2 feet tall. Fresh or dried, it readily releases its fragrance in warm water. It exudes a bright, strong lemon smell with a fainter green note. Like other citrus scents, it uplifts the spirit and invigorates the body, making it ideal for a "wake-up" blend. Children enjoy the perky smell of lemon balm.

### Mint

Mint spreads aggressively, growing up to 2 feet tall. Different varieties have different scents, but the most potent are the cool smell of peppermint and the brighter smell of spearmint. Fresh leaves impart good fragrance, although dried may work. Best of all is mint water, a by-product of making the expensive essential oil. Mint water makes a fine base for body care products.

### Pikake

Pikake is a tropical vine that can reach 10 feet tall in the wild; it may also be grown as a houseplant. It bears white flowers with a sweet, intense fragrance. The essential oil soothes emotions, promotes optimism, and encourages romantic feelings. It blends well with floral or spicy scents.

### Rose

Rose is a small to medium bush, and the antique or wild varieties serve better than modern ones. Bourbon, damask, gallica, Portland, and rugosa roses give off intense perfume. Fresh petals make lovely rose-flower water, but you can also buy rose-flower water in ethnic grocery stores. Rose essences, especially attar of roses, tend to be ruinously expensive, but they are luxurious ingredients if you can afford them. Rose is the quintessential feminine perfume.

### Rosemary

Rosemary grows as a bushy or prostrate plant with long stems and needle-shaped leaves. It bears a strong resinous smell similar to pine—especially in the pine-scented rosemary, an excellent scent for men's products. This herb purifies and invigorates; it also mutes body odor, making it a favorite of hunters. Rosemary can be used fresh, dried, or as essential oil. Run the dried leaves through a spice grinder to make exfoliating granules.

# Cleansing Herbs

People have long used herbs for personal cleansing. Herbs aid cleansing in two ways. First, they can add texture to soaps and scrubs, so that the grit helps pry loose the dirt. This works well for stubborn stains on less-sensitive areas. It also removes dead skin and calluses. Second, some herbs have active ingredients that break down oils, open or close skin pores, and kill germs. These clean by dissolving grime and purifying the skin. Some are gentle enough for use on sensitive areas such as the face; others are especially good for the hair.

### *Calendula*

Calendula is a bright yellow to orange daisy-like flower. Its petals add a sunny color to herbal preparations. Calendula has antiseptic and antifungal properties, but it is also soothing to skin damaged by sunburn, rashes, or bug bites. It softens and heals the skin.

### *Corn*

Corn is a grain from a very specialized giant grass. The corn used in soap making is called "field corn" or "dent corn," and it's different from the sweet corn that we eat fresh. Field corn dries hard and is ground into cornmeal, which makes a moderate exfoliator for use in soaps or body scrubs. It helps unclog the pores and remove excess oil from the skin.

### Oats

Oats are the grains produced by a grass. They can be powdered, rolled, or ground for use in soaps, body scrubs, and bath salts. Oats provide a very gentle exfoliating effect and soften the skin.

### Olive Oil

Olive oil is produced from the fruit of the olive tree. For beauty care, choose olive oil that is nearly clear, with minimal flavor or odor. It cleans by diluting natural oil on skin or hair, so that dirt may be lifted away. Olive oil makes an excellent "carrier" for essential oils and herbs with other properties, and leaves skin and hair feeling soft.

### Poppy Seeds

Poppy seeds come from the poppy flower, which produces a large pod full of tiny dark seeds. Poppy seeds make a strong exfoliator in soap or scrubs, useful for reducing calluses and removing stubborn dirt or stains.

### Tea Tree

Tea tree, an essential oil, is produced from the leaves of the Australian tea tree. This oil has strong antiseptic and antifungal properties and a sharp medicinal smell. It is used in shampoos, soaps, and many other beauty products.

### Witch Hazel

Witch hazel is a medium bush with bright yellow flowers. Essential oil of witch hazel has strong astringent properties. It is good for oily skin and hair, often used in aftershave.

### *Yarrow*

Yarrow is an upright herb with finely divided foliage and flat panicles of tiny colorful flowers. It has soothing and astringent qualities.

## Coloring Herbs

Artificial hair dyes rank among the most noxious of commercial beauty products. They can damage the hair and the environment. Herbal hair coloring is far safer and less obnoxious. It also yields more natural-looking colors. Some of the methods change color gradually rather than suddenly—a useful trick if you don't want anyone to notice! Furthermore, you can mix and match herbal ingredients to create the shade you want. (Commercial dyes discourage mixing because each is a complex chemical solution; they don't all go together.) By combining different herbs, you can control the emphasis of tawny, ruddy, and dark tones in your hair. This is especially handy if you're trying to restore your hair's natural color.

### *Alfalfa*

Alfalfa is an annual plant most often grown for hay. When dried and ground, it yields a beautiful green powder full of mineral and other nutrients. Alfalfa powder gives a fresh green color to soaps, scrubs, and other things.

### *Bay*

Bay is a small Mediterranean tree with glossy dark green leaves. When dried and boiled, the leaves produce a rinse that enhances the color of dark hair.

### Chamomile

Chamomile is a lush green herb with very finely divided leaves and daisy-like flowers. Dry the flowers and boil them to create a rinse. When poured over light brown to blond hair, chamomile brightens the natural color and brings out highlights. It can also shift strawberry blond hair more to the blond side of the spectrum. Chamomile can be mixed with henna to create reddish-gold streaks in darker hair.

### Cinnamon

Cinnamon is a large bush or small tree. The bark is peeled, dried, and sold in sticks or as powder. Cinnamon powder may be added generously to damp hair and left on overnight. It lightens the color and adds reddish tones, along with a strong spicy fragrance. It can brighten hair along the red spectrum, from auburn to red to strawberry blond. In soap or other preparations, it gives a tan to red-brown color.

### Clove

Clove is a bush whose flower buds are harvested and dried to make the familiar spice. Steep whole or powdered clove to make a strong tea, then pour repeatedly over hair as a rinse. This strengthens reddish tones. In soap or other preparations, it gives a tan to red-brown color.

### Henna

Henna, a Middle Eastern shrub, has fragrant flowers and small evergreen leaves. The leaves yield a potent reddish-brown dye, the brightest red of natural colorants. Henna can be used to color skin or hair.

### Lemon

Lemon peel and lemon oil are often used for fragrance. Lemon juice lightens hair; however, it should be used sparingly because the strong acid can damage hair. Add small amounts to abundant water to create a rinse, especially in combination with other suitable herbs.

### Marigold

Marigold is a small plant with ferny leaves and bold yellow to red flowers. Yellow petals yield a lighter dye good for brightening blond hair. Orange or red flowers yield deeper colors suitable for dark blond, reddish, or light brown hair. Marigold can bring out the red tones in strawberry-blond hair. In lotions or other preparations, it gives a golden to orange color.

### Sage

Sage is a woody herb with leathery gray-green leaves. Dry the leaves and boil them in water to make a rinse. This enriches the color of dark hair and helps cover any gray or faded parts.

### Walnut

Walnut is a large tree that bears round nuts encased in a thick fleshy hull. The hull creates a strong dye in shades of dark brown to black. It will color skin as well as hair.

## Herbal Recipes for Your Hair

Conventional hair care products can leave hair feeling dry and brittle. Some shampoos and conditioners are okay, but hair dyes and blow dryers take a toll. You can make herbal formulas that are gentler and leave your hair smelling delicious. Some herbs are for color, some are for cleansing, and some are for conditioning. Here are a couple of recipes to get you started.

### *Sunshine Brightening Rinse*

Combine ½ cup dried chamomile flowers, ½ cup orange marigold petals, and 1 cinnamon stick. Add 2 quarts of water; bring to a boil, then remove from heat and allow to steep for half an hour. Strain and discard the solids. Add 1 teaspoon of lemon juice to the liquid.

Wash hair normally and towel off excess water. Place a basin or bucket to catch the runoff, then pour the rinse over your head, making sure to wet all of your hair with it. Pick up the catch basin and repeat the process fifteen to twenty times. Carefully squeeze out extra moisture, wrap your hair in a towel, and wait half an hour. Finally, rinse hair with plain cool water. This preparation brightens medium to light hair, bringing out golden and reddish highlights. Reapply once a week until desired coloration is achieved.

### *Herbal Oil Conditioner*

Combine ½ cup dried rosemary, ½ cup dried bergamot, and ½ cup lemon balm. Add 1 cup olive oil. Heat gently until warm. Remove from heat; strain and discard solids. Add 2 drops tea tree oil.

Wash hair and towel dry. Massage the warm oil into scalp and damp hair, making sure to coat the ends of the hair. Wrap hair in towel for 15 to 20 minutes. Then wash hair to remove oil, and dry as usual. Use once a month to condition dry or damaged hair.

## Herbal Recipes for Your Hands

Hands do hard work around the house and yard. Most "hand soap" sold in grocery stores is actually a detergent in bar form, which does more to dry out the skin than does true soap. Commercial lotions tend to use synthetic fragrances and other ingredients. Homemade preparations with real essential oils and herbs will do more to soften rough skin. Pamper your hands with recipes such as these.

### Healing Hands Soft Scrub

Combine 1 cup organic castile soap powder, ½ cup calendula petals, ½ cup ground oatmeal, ½ cup alfalfa powder, 2 tablespoons crushed dried bergamot, and 1 tablespoon comfrey root powder. This loose scrub has a fresh yellow-green color. Put about a teaspoon of it in your palm, then wet your hands and rub gently. It's good for cleaning and soothing hands that are chapped or scratched and dirty from hard work.

### Tropical Butter Rub

Combine 3 ounces cocoa butter, 2 ounces shea butter, and 2 ounces mango butter. Melt gently until liquid. Stir in 1 ounce almond oil. Add 3 drops tea tree essential oil and ½ teaspoon pikake essential oil. Pour into a jar and allow to cool completely before sealing. Rub on dry skin after washing.

## Herbal Recipes for Your Feet

Your feet carry you wherever you want to go all day. There are fewer commercial products for foot care, mostly aimed at making feet less tough or smelly. Herbs can soften thick, dead skin for easier removal. They can also wipe out some of the fungi and bacteria that create foot odor. (Plain or herb-scented baking soda in your shoes will help too.) Give your feet something special with these herbal treats.

### *Lemon-poppyseed Foot Soap*

Combine 1 tablespoon ground dried rosemary and 1 table-spoon poppy seeds. Chop 1 pound of organic glycerin soap base into cubes and microwave for short periods until they begin to melt. Stir in 10 drops of lemon essential oil. When the soap is fully melted, stir in the rosemary and poppy seeds.

Carefully spoon the melted soap into soap molds or muffin tins. Allow to cool for about four hours before unmolding the bars. Then let the bars dry overnight. In the morning, they're ready to use! After washing yourself normally in a bath or shower, use this exfoliating soap to scrub the soles of your feet.

### *Floral Foot Bath*

Combine 2 tablespoons dried lavender flowers, 2 tablespoons dried rose petals, and 2 tablespoons oatmeal. Place in a muslin bag and cover with 2 cups boiling water. Allow to steep for five minutes. Add enough cool water to reach a comfortable temperature. Squeeze water from bag and remove. Add 2 drops essential oil of witch hazel. Soak feet until the foot bath gets cold. Finally, rinse feet in plain water and pat dry. This soothing foot bath aids relaxation and sleep.

## Conclusion

Taking care of your body uses a lot of different materials, each with its own cleaning or revitalizing qualities. Herbal preparations offer more variety in performance and more control over contents than what you find in a typical supermarket. Learning to make them yourself, or at least learning what to look for when buying them from an herbal supplier, gives you more influence over your appearance and well-being. If you can't use herbal versions for everything, that's okay too; every little bit helps, and most herbal beauty supplies interface well with more conventional ones.

# References

"Ayurvedic Beauty Care" by IndiaMART, 1996-2009. Supplier of herbs and herbal beauty care products. Retrieved from http://www.ayurveda-herbal-remedy.com/beauty-care/

Cunningham, Scott. *Cunningham's Encyclopedia of Magical Herbs*. St. Paul, MN: Llewellyn Publications, 1991.

Griggs, Barbara. *Helpful Herbs for Health and Beauty: Look and Feel Great, Naturally*. Infinite Ideas Limited, 2008.

Kowalchik, Claire and William H. Hylton (editors). *Rodale's Illustrated Encyclopedia of Herbs*. Rodale Press, 1987.

"Mountain Rose Herbs," no author listed, 2000–2009. Supplier of organic herbs, essential oils, beauty care products, and more. Retrieved from http://www.mountainroseherbs.com/index2.html/

"Natural Herbal Beauty" blog, no author listed, 2008–2009. Many articles on herbal beauty preparations, ingredients, and uses. Retrieved from http://herbalbeauty.blogtells.com/

Yan, Qing. "Herbs for Beauty: Imperial and Secret Herbal Formulas from Ancient China." Retrieved from http://www.Lulu.com/

# Herb
# Crafts

# The Art of Making Infusions

≈ by Susan Pesznecker ≈

What is an herb? The word refers to a group of aromatic plants used medicinally or for cooking. In scientific terms, an herb is a plant that doesn't produce woody, persistent tissue and that dies back after each growing season. Herbalism is the lore and art of understanding and using the various properties of plants, a study sometimes called by its ancient name, wortcunning, which means "skill with herbs."

Healers brew medicinal draughts and tonics, alchemists harness the power of the heavens through spagyrics (alchemy), and students of meditation improve their focus with relaxing potions. Whatever your forte, learning the basics of wortcunning will increase your craft confidence and make your experiences richer and more fun. Read on as we explore the basics of infusions.

# Herbal Safety

Let's begin with a few reminders.

1. Just because herbs are natural doesn't mean they're safe. Many substances are natural and harmful—radioactive uranium, poisonous plants—you get the idea. Herbs can be harmful, too, so be sure of what you're using and how you're using it.

2. Herbs may interact with each other and with other non-herbal medications. If you're already using herbs or taking medication, don't use new herbs without verifying their compatibility.

3. Store your herbs in well-marked containers and out of children's reach. See #1, above.

4. Label and date your herbs. This will help you identify them and will remind you when an herb is outdated.

# Materials

Every herbalist needs a few basic materials:

- Lidded saucepans (avoid aluminum and copper)

- Measuring cups and spoons

- Mortar and pestle for crushing herbs and spices; use a heavy tablespoon and a small bowl as a cheaper version

- Infusers

- Medium and fine strainers

- Honey or turbinado sugar

- Clean jars with screw lids. Use canning jars or save jars from jarred foods. Wash in hot soapy water or put through a dishwasher cycle to "sterilize."

- Water. Spring, bottled, or filtered water are best. Most tap water contains toxins, and rainwater may contain impurities from air pollution.

- Plain white or clear teacups and saucers; these help you see your results and make tasseomancy (tealeaf reading) easy.

- A means of keeping your herbal records and recipes. Writing down the details will allow you reproduce a brilliant result or "tweak" one that went awry.

It's possible to assemble inexpensive equipment, but if you want "high end," look up herbal suppliers. They'll sell you all manner of herbal gear, including amber and blue glass bottles, marble mortars and pestles, beakers, and more. Find a place to keep your materials together and reserve them for herbal workings.

## Handling and Preparing Your Herbs

The the herbs themselves are the most important part of your materials, and there are at least four ways to obtain a ready supply. First, grow them yourself—they flourish in gardens or containers. Second, find a friend who grows herbs and beg or barter with him or her. Third, try wildcrafting—gathering herbs in the wild. Always follow ethical gathering practices and work in areas that aren't sprayed or polluted. Fourth, purchase herbs from a reputable organic supplier or grocer.

While fresh herbs are more potent than dried herbs, even the best herbalist doesn't have access to fresh herbs all the time, and dried herbs are a simple solution. Fresh herbs contain more water than dried, which increases their bulk; when using fresh herbs you'll need more of them to get the right concentration in the brew. A general rule is to use twice as much fresh herb by weight or volume as one would use of the dried version.

Because herbal potency deteriorates with drying and storing, always start with the best quality available. Harvest herbs at the peak of potency, wrap in paper toweling, place in plastic bags, and store in the refrigerator. Most will last for several days. If they wilt, smell funny, or change color, toss them out. Herbs with heavier stems (e.g., basil and rosemary) do well refrigerated in small water-filled vases.

To dry herbs, spread on flat trays lined with dry toweling or newspaper. Place trays in a warm room out of direct light; turn and "fluff" daily and the herbs should be dry in a few days. Store in airtight glass or plastic jars in a dark drawer or cupboard.

Whether using fresh or dried herbs, all must be broken down to release their essence. Fresh leafy herbs may be chopped with a sharp blade on a cutting board or snipped into small pieces with kitchen scissors. Dried herbs can be crumbled with the fingers. Use a mortar and pestle to bruise or crush hard or fibrous material. Most dried aerial parts (leaves and flowers) will keep for one year in a cool, dark, dry place, while heavier parts (roots, bark, stems, berries, wood) may last for two to three years. Check regularly for evidence of mold or discoloration. A few herbs—notably calendula blossoms, ginger, and aloe stems—can be frozen whole and used in herbal preparations without thawing.

Think of each herbal session as an experiment. Assemble and prepare the materials before beginning, then work through the process one step at a time. Take notes throughout and include your sensory observations: what did the mixture look/smell/taste like? Evaluate the results and make notes on what to change next time.

# Infusions 101

To infuse is to soak plant material in liquid (called the solvent or menstruum) to extract flavors or essences. If you've ever had a cup of tea, you've sipped an infusion. In fact, water-based infusions are commonly called "teas." A "simple" is an infusion using a single kind of plant material, while a "potion" combines two or more components. A potion with medicinal qualities is sometimes called a "tisane." One with mostly magickal qualities is referred to as an "elixir," while a "philter" (philtre) is a brew designed to work as a love potion. An infusion that supports health and vigor is known as a "tonic," and a cleansing potion is one that removes toxins from the system.

Most infusions are water based, that is, soaked, brewed, steeped, simmered, or coaxed using water. Infusions can also be made with oil, alcohol, honey, fruit juice, vinegar, or any potable liquid. They're simple and quick to make; however, they must be refrigerated and will only keep for two to three days.

### *Hot Water-based Infusion*

To make a hot water-based infusion, place 1 to 1½ teaspoons crushed dried herbs (2 to 3 teaspoons fresh) in a heatproof cup or mug, or an infuser. Pour 1 cup freshly boiled water over the herbs. Cover the mug and steep 5 to 10 minutes. Strain and sweeten if desired. Drink warm or cool.

### *Cold Water-based Infusion*

For extremely aromatic herbs in which the volatile oils might be destroyed by hot water, cold water-based infusions are ideal

Cold infusing also extracts the largest amount of minerals from the plant material. For a cold infusion, place 1 to 1½ teaspoons crushed dried herbs (2 to 3 teaspoons fresh) in a jar. Add 1 cup cool water. Cover tightly, shake for one minute, and infuse four to six hours before using.

## Decoctions

Simple infusions work well for extracting essences from a plant's delicate aerial parts: its leaves and flowers. For tougher, heavier types of plant materials—roots, bark, stems, twigs, berries, and seeds—decocting is necessary. The word decoction comes from a Latin root meaning "boil down," and a Latin root *coquere*, meaning "to cook, boil, bake, or ripen." In a decoction, you combine plant materials with a quantity of water, bring it to a boil, and then simmer the mixture for a period of time, allowing a more vigorous extraction than does simple infusion. The decocted mixture is strained before using.

To make a water-based decoction, place 1 tablespoon chopped roots, seeds, stems, and/or bark in a medium saucepan. Cover with 3 cups cold water and bring quickly to a gentle boil; reduce heat and simmer, covered, for 15 minutes. Simmering gently prevents excess loss of fluid volume and volatile oils. Strain while still warm. Allow any solids to settle out, then decant (pour gently, leaving solids in the original container) into a sterile jar and seal while warm. Because the decoction is boiled, it will keep in the refrigerator for a week.

## Syrups

Syrups are water-based solutions of honey, sugar, or sap syrup (e.g., maple, birch). Adding syrup to an infusion or decoction creates a high sugar concentration that preserves the infusion and makes it more palatable (useful when dealing with bitter herbs). Note, though, that simply sweetening an infusion "to taste" can actually speed spoilage by providing food for bacteria. A syrup-based infusion will last longer than the infusion would by itself, while a lightly sweetened infusion might deteriorate more quickly than the infusion alone. Both sweetened infusions and syrups should always be stored in the refrigerator.

### *Syrup-based Infusion*

To make an syrup-based infusion, begin with a "simple syrup." Combine 1 cup water and 2 cups sugar. Bring to a boil and stir until the sugar dissolves. Cool. Store in a sterile jar in the refrigerator for up to a month. To make an herbal syrup, combine equal parts herbal infusion (or decoction) and simple syrup. Stir well and store in a corked or loosely capped bottle in the refrigerator and use within two weeks. Why loosely capped? When sugar or honey is added to a potion, the mixture may ferment. If tightly capped, the bottle may explode!

For a second kind of syrup-based infusion, prepare 1 cup of hot infusion or decoction. After steeping, add 1 cup turbinado sugar, organic honey, or organic maple syrup. Stir constantly over low heat until dissolved and smooth. Cool, then store in a corked or loosely capped bottle in the refrigerator for up to two weeks.

## Using Your Infusions and Decoctions

Once you've mastered these techniques, put them to work! Here are some ideas.

- Craft a therapeutic bath for cleansing, ritual purification, or simple relaxation. Combine 1 cup dried herb and 3 cups water. Bring to a boil and simmer, covered, for 10 minutes. Pour through a strainer into a bathtub of water, then climb in and luxuriate.

- Create a mint- and hyssop-based cough syrup for cold and flu season.

- Lukewarm infusions of eyebright, red raspberry, goldenseal, or bayberry make excellent eyewashes for tired eyes.

- A decoction of thyme, rosemary, or birch makes an excellent foot soak.

A compress, or "fomentation," is a cloth that's soaked in an infusion or decoction, wrung out, and applied to a body part. Compresses can treat infections, relieve aching muscles and joints, and soothe minor sunburn.

### How to Make a Steam Inhalation

For a steam inhalation, place 1 to 2 tablespoons dried herb (rosemary or mint work well) in a large bowl. Pour 2 to 3 cups boiling water over the herbs. Allow to cool for 2 to 3 minutes, then lean over the bowl—with a towel "tented" over your head—and breathe the steam as the potion cools. This is wonderful for colds and allergies, but be careful—it's hot!

# Herbs, Flowers, Plants, and Spices from A to Z

⫷ by Sally Cragin ⫸

O ver the years, I've acquired a variety of books on herbs, ranging from field guides, to cookbooks for cooking everything from weeds to fungi (my husband's special interest), to historical work like *Dr. Chase's Recipes: Information for Everybody*, published in 1902.

Today, it's not easy to know what's a native plant and what's an invasive species. We no longer have to save part of the hay harvest to restuff our mattresses every year; few of us gather rose petals for potpourri to freshen the closet, and I'm the only person in my circle who makes lemonade using a handful of mint from the garden.

My son is growing up with parents who regularly forage weeds and mushrooms, and we share what we know with his classroom. Our hope is that this lore remains a vital practice—not just something you read about in books. What follows is a selective and highly personalized "alphabestiary" of some of my favorite herbs, plants, flowers, weeds, spices, seeds, and other items from the natural world. You'll find crafts (for adults or young artists), kitchen laboratory experiments, and recipes, in alphabetical order.

# A is for Aloe Vera

This spiny succulent is in my top-ten favorites. This plant loves sunlight, survives neglect, and asks only for space to spread its spiky, fleshy green-gray leaves.

### Cosmetic Use

Snap off a leaf and wrap in plastic when you go to the beach. The gel from the leaf is soothing to the skin—especially if you haven't been diligent about reapplying sunblock. I have only used aloe as a topical application, although aloe vera juice is said to have health properties, as well. It also can be used as an ingredient in psoriasis creams.

### Remedy

Apply the juice of aloe vera to cuts and burns to help prevent scars.

# B is for Berries!

Strawberries, raspberries, blueberries, blackberries, huckleberries—how can you choose? Every berry is my favorite, depending on the season. In the past several years, I've found that farming friends are cultivating raspberries that bloom in the spring and in September, which is a blessing.

### *Child Craft*

If you have a variety of berries, you can do a fun painting craft with a small child. Mash a few berries on a plate, being careful to keep the berries separated, so you have an "edible palette" of colors. Use a cotton-tipped stick as a paintbrush and let the children see how subtly different each color is. Raspberries are also fun to feed to a toddler, once you show them how the berry sticks on their thumb.

# C is for Catnip

There is no herb that I know of that is the source of so much mirth and happiness. We have never been able to grow catnip outside, as the cats always find it and roll it into compost, but a bag of the dried herb is reasonable and widely available.

### *Entertainment*

If you sprinkle a bit of catnip onto an old scarf, you can watch your cat roll itself up as it writhes in dazed ecstasy. We always rescue the odd woolen glove after the winter, cut off the fingers, and stuff the little sacks with a pinch of cotton, a half-teaspoon of catnip and more cotton. Use a cloth elastic or yarn to tie off, and you have tiny catnip fish.

Why does catnip make cats so riotous? The process of cat brain activity is not fully understood, but there's a substance called nepetalactone that is presumed to be an influence, although kittens and older cats don't respond so vigorously to the magic herb. Nor us, sadly.

# D is for Dandelion

If dandelions were hard to grow they would be most welcome on any lawn.

### Child Craft

How many dandelions can you pick? The adult can help a child make a chain by slitting the stem an inch from the crown and helping the child put another stem through. This is an entertaining fine-motor activity for all ages, and a great photo opportunity once the chain is completed.

### Recipe

Picking dandelion root in early spring or late fall, once the leaves have passed, is an ancient custom. Wash, dry, and slice the root. You can simmer this for up to 30 minutes on the stovetop. Strain out the root and drink for diuretic purposes.

# E is for Eczema

There are a variety of plants and herbs that are recommended for this annoying skin condition, so here's your chance to experiment.

### Cosmetic Use

Violet leaves or blossoms as a poultice. Red clover blossoms dried and made into a tea (1 cup boiling water poured over 2 teaspoons dried blooms. Steep for 10 minutes, drink three times a day).

Gather the red clover as far from roadways as you can find. Wild strawberry, also known as "Indian Strawberry," which is a groundcover, is also recommended. Make a poultice or an astringent and treat the afflicted area.

# F is for Fern

The most common fern nationwide is the bracken fern. These grow from spring to late summer, and can be harvested for a variety of purposes.

### Recipe

I have cooked fiddleheads, the furled tops of spring ferns, but have yet to have a batch that makes me say, "Oh, you MUST try this!" However, this is a classic "wild diet" ingredient and easy to work with. Gather the fiddlehead (literally, when the new shoot looks like the top of a fiddle) before it gets the brownish fuzz. Boil for up to half an hour and, if the water turns brown, change the water midway. Tannic acid is produced by ferns, which can be constipating.

# G is for Garlic

No kitchen should be without this item.

### Recipe

Bruschetta is a savory topping for crackers or melba toast and an excellent appetizer for parties. Chop 2 to 6 plum tomatoes into small cubes. Add salt, pepper, and at least one clove of mashed garlic per 2 tomatoes. Drizzle with olive oil and let marinate until ready to serve.

### Remedy

Throat soother: Mix a mashed clove of garlic with a generous teaspoon of honey in a cup filled with hot water. Drink to clear and soothe a sore throat.

# H is for Heal-all

Trust me, you have this growing in your yard. It's the very low groundcover with delicate purple flowers that are a cross between a violet bloom and a snapdragon.

### *Recipe*

Leaves and flowers can go into a salad.

### *Remedy*

This is a universally favorite all-purpose herb (hence the name). The Chinese made tea from the leaves, which have been used for circulation and liver problems as well as conjunctivitis and other skin troubles.

# I is for Insect Bites

Many herbs and plants are useful for insect bites. Sweet Melissa, also known as lemon balm, can be rubbed on bruises. Leaves of plantain, which you have in your yard (it's the green groundcover with the long cattail-like flower stalk) also works well. Native American Indians used the leaves of the giant ragweed (the most dastardly allergen in my circle) to soothe bites, which says a lot about the strength of their immune systems. See jewelweed, below.

# J is for Jewelweed

This is a common plant in meadows, streams, and wet places. It has one specific traditional use, and it's a good one

### *Remedy*

To make a balm for poison ivy, crush the plant and rub on the skin as soon as you realize you've brushed against poison ivy.

The flowers are gorgeous—orange and yellow—and it's called jewelweed because the leaves repel water (which form "jewels" on the surface). You'll be a hero on the woodland walk by pointing this out.

# K is for Kelp

This long, ruffled frond is the equivalent of Japanese knotweed in the oceans. The fronds can be 18 feet in length when mature, but it's usually the juveniles that wash up on the beach. It's a little bit of trouble to use kelp, but it makes you feel like a very adventurous cook.

## Recipe

Wash and dry the frond, and slice into toothpick-size slivers. Dry in the sun and soak in water again before adding to stew.

# L is for Leaves

All leaves are good for collages.

## Child Craft

Gather as many different leaves as you can, and spread them out. Ask your child to describe them using adjectives such as smooth, pointy, narrow, thick, dark green, light green, etc. (Older children can use a more biologically complex vocabulary, such as three-lobed for a maple leaf.) Move the leaves around and see what animals you can make. Two beech leaves on a thick scrub oak leaf can be a rabbit. One large oval leaf with smaller ovals can turn into a fish. Press your leaves first if you want these collages to last.

# M is for Mint

Common and precious, mint is happy to grow anywhere. We have mint growing on—no joke—a granite outcrop near our porch. The mint must have found enough dirt and is now thriving.

### Recipe

To make mint lemonade, take at least a dozen 6- to 8-inch snips of mint tops. Crush in your hands and add to a container with 6 cups of water. Let sit in the sun for the afternoon. Drain and filter the mint and add 1 cup lemon or lime juice plus ½ cup honey, warmed and stirred into ½ cup of water. Shake thoroughly in a two-quart pitcher and serve over ice. I've brought this to committee meetings at our school, and it always seems to help pep up the discussion.

# N is for Nuts

Yes, not an herb, not a spice, but the product of a plant, and another all-purpose kitchen item.

### Children's Craft

My five-year-old son doesn't like the meat, but loves walnut shells. You can use the shells for making a tiny boat. Put a daub of clay in the bottom, tape a triangle of paper to a toothpick, and sail away! Paint walnut shells with red and black acrylic paint to make a ladybug. A bit of yarn, two oval shapes of paper and two "googly" eyes make a mouse. Clap two shells together to hear the sound of tiny horsehoofs.

### Recipe

The saddest salad of iceberg lettuce and late-winter tomatoes can be perked up with the addition of toasted almonds. Put sliced almonds on a cookie sheet in a 200°F oven or toaster oven, and check after a few minutes. Or, make the quickest, easiest peanut butter cookies ever with:

> 1 cup peanut butter
>
> 1 cup sugar
>
> 1 egg

Mix ingredients together, roll into balls, press down with a fork, and bake in 350°F oven for 10 to 12 minutes.

# O is for Observation and Opportunity

Sometimes the best way to experiment with herbs, plants, nuts, seeds, and recipes is to buy something you've never seen before at your local natural-food store, and learn from there. I was prompted to start adding watercress to sandwiches after reading Beatrix Potter books aloud. We have a small library of useful books devoted to weeds and wild plants. I recommend *A Field Guide to Medicinal Plants and Herbs* in the Peterson Field Guide series. There is an Eastern and Central North America edition along with a Western edition. The color plates are very helpful and this is a great educational tool to use with children as they can gather and identify plants using the book and the leaf templates included.

# P is for Parsley

Parsley is one of the aromatic herbs that are essential for Italian cookery. You'll want to use the flat-leaf parsley for soup, or chopped in a salad. (See R, S, T, Plus P.)

# Q is for Quick Crafts

A long stick can be a fishing pole, a magic wand, or a conductor's baton. Ginkgo leaves gathered and bundled can make a rose. Dandelions can be a pirate's treasure (all the golden flowers are coins) or made into a crown or necklace. Milkweed puffs can be anything from doll hair, to pillow-stuffing. The seedpods dried out and sliced in half can become boats that you and your child race across a bowl of water.

# R, S, T, Plus P are for Rosemary, Sage, Thyme & Parsley

These aromatic herbs are essentials for Italian cookery. Rosemary is key for roasted potatoes, lamb, vegetables and focaccia. My husband has two green thumbs so he can usually get a rosemary plant to winter-over in our living room, but this is one plant that will not forgive you if it's dry. Rosemary is also great for a potpourri. Sage goes with meat dishes and salad, and it's the dominant flavor in saltimbocca (means "hop in the mouth"), a recipe made with veal that is popular in Italy, Spain, and Greece. Like rosemary, sage is happiest when added to other herbs and spices so it's not the dominant motif. Harvest sage before the flowers bloom and you can use the leaves fresh, or hang to dry.

### Remedy

Rosemary tea is good for the circulation, and the cold tea can be used as a mouthwash. Thyme tea has a folk tradition of being good for relieving cramps and as a "blood purifier."

### Remedy

Clary sage (Salvia sclarea) is good for nausea and treating colic.

# U is for Urinary Tract Infections

I am going to pass along information I have been told is helpful, and wish you all good health.

### *Remedy*

To make wintergreen tea, cover 1 tablespoon of leaves with boiling water and steep for 15 to 30 minutes. Pipssewa is a slow-growing relative of wintergreen that is native to dry woods, but check with local state agencies before harvesting. You can make a tea by putting 1 tablespoon of chopped dried leaves in 1½ cups of water. Simmer for at least 15 minutes and strain.

# V is for Violets

As you probably know, violets aren't always violet. One of my earliest activities as a child was my quest for candied violet candy. Here's one recipe for those with excellent fine-motor skills.

### *Recipe: Violet Candy*

Gather a few dozen purple violets in the spring. Wash and dry. Gently brush the blooms with egg white (that is at room temperature) and sprinkle with confectioners' sugar. Let the coated blossoms dry, then snip the stems.

### *Recipe: Violet Tea*

Make some violet candy and then invite friends for tea. Dried flowers will be more aromatic than fresh blooms, but the ratio is 1 tablespoon blossoms (washed and dried, and preferably collected in early morning), to 1 cup of water. Steep 5 minutes.

# W is for Wintergreen

Wintergreen is also known as teaberry. This low-growing plant is easily identified in the fall when bright red berries appear.

Crack the leaf and inhale the aroma. You can also chew on the berries. The magic ingredient is methyl salicylate, the basic building block for aspirin. If you are gathering the leaves and drying them, be patient—the leaves are thick and are dry when they easily crack, rather than bend, between your fingers.

### Remedy

Gather wintergreen leaves, slice and put in a glass jar. Cover with isopropyl alcohol and let sit for several weeks. This ointment is useful for bug bites, or can be used as a liniment.

### Recipe

One tablespoon of dried wintergreen leaves added to water that has been brought to a boil. Let steep for up to a half-hour. This is said to be useful for bladder infections, but it should be avoided by those with aspirin allergies.

# X is for eXtra Ideas

I knew when I pitched the idea of an "alphabestiary" of herbs, plants, and spices that there would be special favorites that fell through the cracks. So here are eXtra ideas for you! For the most part, I am including recipes that use common, household items.

### Recipe

Cosmetic lemon toner can be made using tea bags, but I like using mint from the garden. Pour a ½ cup of boiling water over a handful of crushed mint leaves (peppermint or spearmint is fine) and add 2 tablespoons of lemon juice. You can also add 1 or 2 tablespoons of witch hazel, but if you just use the two ingredients, you'll need to use this up quickly. Daub on face with a cotton ball—it's very refreshing and leaves no residue.

### Recipe

Cucumber lotion for sunburn is made by chopping a cucumber and straining out the juice. Add glycerine and rosewater in equal parts to the juice for a lotion (refrigerate unused portion).

### Remedy

This sore throat remedy from Dr. Chase dates from 1902. Steep 1 tablespoon sage leaves in 1 cup of boiling water. Add 2 tablespoons each of honey, vinegar, and salt; and 1 teaspoon of cayenne pepper. Strain, mix, and bottle. Gargle four times a day with the remedy.

## Y is for Yarrow

Very common in fields and roadsides, this plant has clusters of small white, gold, or rose-colored five-petal flowers and a sturdy green stalk. Its Latin name, *Achillea millefolium*, references its folkloric properties, as it was said to have been used by Achilles, the Greek warrior, to staunch his soldiers' wounds. The dried flowers have been used for a tea that provides relief from colds.

### Recipe

Add peppermint leaves and dried yarrow to water that has been brought to a boil. Let the mixture steep for 15 minutes. This tea is said to help with fevers.

## Z is for Zingiber officinale

Also known as ginger, this root originated in Asia, where it has many medicinal and culinary uses. It was brought to the West thanks to Silk Route trading practices. It has been cultivated in the West Indies since Spanish colonial days. You need a root in your kitchen at all times for a variety of purposes. Cover the cut end of ginger with a daub of oil or wrap the root in plastic wrap to keep it from drying out.

### *Remedy*

Sore throats will be soothed with this simple recipe for ginger tea. Grate at least 2 tablespoons of fresh root into a glass measuring cup and cover with a pint of boiling water. Let this steep for 10 to 15 minutes. Strain the brew into a cup and add honey and lemon, if desired. You can also add ginger root along with maple syrup to dress up acorn squash.

# Crafting Wreaths from Herbs

## ≈ by Ellen Dugan ≈

*She wore a wreath of roses*
*The first night that we met.*
~Thomas Haynes Bayly

Creating arts and crafts with herbs is one of the many benefits of growing your own herbs in the garden. In this article we will explore making wreaths that you can make as gifts and to decorate your own abode.

Crafting something with your own two hands is relaxing and invigorating at the same time. When you put your heart into the project, you imbue the object with positive emotions and energy, which then radiate out into the home. There is a natural and enchanting beauty in herbs. The foliage and flowers are fragrant; their shapes, colors, and forms are beautiful. So why not take some of that beauty that nature provided us with, and combine it with a bit of your own imagination and see what you can create?

## Crafting an Herbal Wreath

A wreath may be used year-round, not only at the winter holidays. There is something so cheerful about a wreath in the spring and the summer, and the rich, robust colors of an autumn wreath are glorious. Wreath making is an ancient practice that is bound up in humanity's desire to create circles. Why circles? Well, all over the world the circle is a sacred shape, whether it is an eternal ring, the wheel of the year, a medicine wheel, or the outline of the sun and the full moon. The circle can symbolize spiritual protection; it is utilized in meditation and prayer; and to many, it symbolizes both hope and continuity.

The wreath was originally used as a symbol of sovereignty and of victory. Think of the laurel wreaths that were once used to adorn Olympians in ancient times. All over the planet people create wreaths and festive garlands out of natural supplies— fresh and dried herbs, flowers, feathers, shells, pinecones, greenery, berries, grasses, dried leaves, and fruits. These decorated wreaths are used to celebrate seasonal festivals, and special events in the family. Wreath making has a proud and enchanting history, and you can become a part of that history.

Keep in mind that much more can be done with a wreath than just hanging it on your front door. What about hanging it on the garden gate? Or inside your home in a place of prominence? As long as we are thinking outside of the box, consider laying a decorated wreath flat on your dinner table. Tuck a few tall candles around it, or a large pillar candle in the center, and use this as a natural centerpiece. If you want some height, lay the finished wreath on a footed clear glass cake stand. Tuck a few candles in glass globes around the outside of that—you'll amaze your guests at your next gathering.

For scented herbal napkin rings at a dinner party, you can make diminutive wreaths out of finer materials such as ivy, boxwood, thyme, fresh lavender, or rosemary stems. Now doesn't that nifty idea just tickle the imagination?

## Gathering Supplies

Before you head off to your local arts and craft store, take a moment and look carefully around your own garden. This will help jump-start your creativity and help you to save some of your hard-earned money. Craft making isn't about spending lots of cash. Instead it is about taking the time and creating something with love for you, your family and friends to enjoy.

You should definitely check out the herbs and flowers growing in your garden bed. But look a little further. As a matter of fact, look up. Check out the trees and shrubs growing in the yard as a possible source of botanical materials, as well. Many common trees and shrubs, such as lilac, holly, and viburnum are, in fact, classified as herbs. Take a look at the maple, magnolia, pine, birch, willow, rowan, elder, elm, and oak trees. Oh, and those are just a few. Any trees or shrubs that produce fruits will fall into the herb category.

Break out your favorite herbal reference guide and start identifying all of the enchanting varieties of herbal trees and shrubs that are around you. Go outside and take another look. What do you see now?

While you are perusing the landscape, I suggest that you also look down on the ground. There are fallen leaves, pretty twigs, acorns, possibly a fallen feather or two. What about working with the roses from your rose bushes in the garden?

Are there any pretty dried rose hips or seedpods to be found? How about some lovely, faded and dried hydrangea blossoms? What about the ivy growing in the shade?

Ah, now you're thinking about it. But don't stop there. If you live close to the beach, perhaps you'd like to incorporate small pieces of driftwood or a few sea shells or starfish into the design. If you live in a more arid region, how about working with small interesting stones, native plants, and dried sagebrush? Put on your thinking cap and see what you can conjure up! These other items from nature can add interest and texture to your herbal wreaths, so take a careful and thoughtful look around you at nature and see what nature can offer you.

## The Language of Herbs and Flowers

While you are pondering which herbs and plants you would like to work into your crafting, here's something else to consider—the language of flowers, or "florigraphy." Florigraphy became in vogue during the Victorian era. Every flower, herb, and leaf had a message and a specific significance to a bouquet. Florigraphy was a "secret" way to send along a message to a lover, or to declare your intentions. Today, it is a charming way to add a little something extra to your herb crafting.

If the plant you wish for is out of season or not in your gardens, then take a look for it in the dried floral section of an arts and craft store. Peruse this fascinating list of shrubs, vines, trees, flowers, and herbs and then choose your botanical materials with intention to add another whole dimension to the herb-crafting process.

### The Messages of Flowers

Alyssum—worth beyond beauty

Angelica—inspiration

Aster—beauty in retirement

Basil—good wishes

Bay—glory

Boxwood—boundaries

Carnation—encouragement and energy

Chamomile—patience and comfort

Cinquefoil—beloved daughter

Clematis—ingenuity

Coneflower (Echinacea)—health and strength

Daisy—innocence

Dianthus—forever lovely

Dusty miller—respected grandmother

Elm—enchantment

Fennel—strength

Fern—passion and fascination

Feverfew—good health

Forsythia—good nature

Foxglove—faery magic

Grapevine—prosperity and plenty

Holly—foresight and domestic bliss

Honesty (moonwort)—"I have nothing to hide"

Hosta—devotion

Hydrangea—protection and a devoted heart

Hyssop—cleanliness

Ivy—fidelity, everlasting love

Jasmine—enchantment of the night

Juniper—protection of a new home

Kalanchoe—popularity

Lady's mantle (Alchemilla)—protection and women's health

Lamb's ears (Betony)—surprise

Lavender—good luck and happiness

Lemon balm—sympathy and healing

Lilac—first blush of love

Magnolia—love of nature

Marigold—beloved ancestors

Marjoram—blushes

Meadowsweet—lovely bride

Mint—refreshment and warmth

Moss—maternal love

Nigella (Love-in-a-mist)—"kiss me quick!"

Oak leaves—wisdom and strength

Oregano—substance

Pansy—cures a broken heart

Parsley—health

Peony—bashfulness

Pine—endurance and life eternal

Pussy willow—friendship and warm fuzzy thoughts

Queen Anne's lace—protection, and returning home

Quince—temptation

Rose—love

Rosemary—remembrance

Rue—grace and clear vision

Sage—wisdom and immortality

Sedum—peace

Sorrel—affection

Sunflower—fame and riches

Sweet woodruff—eternal life

Tansy—safe pregnancy

Tarragon—lasting interest

Thyme—courage and strength

Tiger lilies—tempestuous passion

Valerian—easy going nature

Verbena—enchantment

Viburnum—protection and charm

Wheat—harvest and abundance

Wild strawberries—perfection

Willow—love and protection

Yarrow—witches' herb, enchantment

Zinnia—thinking of absent friends

## The Mechanics of Wreath Making

There are no hard and fast rules to crafting your own herbal wreaths. You may choose to work with a store-bought grapevine wreath as a base, or even a straw or moss wreath. You may even decide to shape your own wreath by hand with vines gathered from nature. For the more adventurous crafter, try working with a wire frame and then bind bundles of fresh herbs onto the frame with floral wire. Go with whatever procedure of wreath building that speaks to you.

### Basic Supplies

Basic supplies include: garden scissors or snips to gather your herbal materials with, sixteen-gauge green floral wire, a low temperature hot glue gun, green florist's tape, wire cutters, the base on which to build the wreath, your herbal supplies, whatever other natural items you choose to add, and 3 to 4 yards of ribbon to create a bow.

### Crafting Techniques

The simplest way to create an herbal wreath is to use grapevine wreath as your base and then to hot glue sections and stems of your fresh or dried herbs on the wreath. Tuck the stems into the grapevine and add a dollop of hot glue to hold them in place.

You may also wire up bundles of the herbal material. Create tiny bundles or bouquets of the herbs you choose to work with and then wire them together. Start at the base of the stems of the bundle and then wrap the wire up, spiraling it around and up toward the leaves and/or blossoms of the herbs. Snip the end off the wire with the wire cutter and bend the end down toward the stems, so it stays smooth and there are no sharp edges of wire poking out. Then tuck the stems of the little bouquet or bundle of herbs deep into the grapevine wreath.

As you place the botanicals on the wreath, remember to make them full and lush. Don't skimp on the botanicals. There is nothing sadder than a skimpy, skinny wreath. If you choose to go with larger flowers or a few arranged bundles of herbs, then consider this tip from floral designers. To make your wreath look balanced, always use odd numbers of larger flowers—or in this case, the larger bundles of herbs. Think of creating triangles throughout the design of your wreath. If there are three or five points of interest, the wreath will look less like a clock face.

Interestingly enough, if we keep this "clock face" theme in mind, here is another floral designer's trick for wreath making and decorating that I can pass along to you. If you imagined a clock face on the base of your wreath, a pretty triangular arrangement of larger flowers or bundles of herbs would be at two o'clock, seven o'clock, and ten o'clock. This way your "triangle" is offset, and it pulls the eye around the design of your wreath instead of resting in one place. Remember to soften up those bundles or larger flowers with foliage and twigs that radiate out beneath the main herbs or flowers and you have something really eye-catching and interesting.

### Finishing Touches

Here is a general rule of thumb for adding a bow to your finished herbal wreath: keep it in scale with the botanical materials on the arrangement. Sticking a massive, wide-ribbon bow on an arrangement made of fine and dainty herbs will cause the eye to go straight to the bow—and nothing else. The most interesting arrangements typically are asymmetrical, so offset the bow a little bit—experiment. The wreath-making police are not going to break in and write you up for an infraction because you didn't slap your bow on the top center section of your wreath.

Finally, there is no rule that says all bows must be made from wide wire-edge ribbon. Go with thinner ribbons if your materials are dainty in scale. Try a pretty one-quarter inch wide ivory satin picot ribbon, and let those loops of the bow dangle as they will. Or work with sheer half-inch-wide ribbon in various shades and colors to add romantic, soft addition to your herbal wreath. Bottom line, go with the color and style of ribbon that you find most pleasing.

For more information on the mythology and folklore of plants please refer to my books: *Herb Magic for Beginners*, *Cottage Witchery*, *Garden Witchery*, and *Garden Witch's Herbal*, are published by Llewellyn. You'll find these books are stuffed full of fascinating herbal information and lots of entertaining ideas for your home and garden.

Now, go break out your glue gun and the ribbon, and take a good long look at the botanical material you have on hand in your own garden. Dare to have some fun with flowers and herbs. Embrace your creativity, and use your imagination! I am sure the results will be absolutely charming.

# Strew, Dye, and Festoon with Herbs

### ⚘ by Nancy Arrowsmith ⚘

Although housework is often considered drudgery, the knowledge of small skills, the discipline of routine, the familiarity of a light knowing touch, and the pleasures of sweet odors, rich viands, and cleansing herbs can make it into a lighter task. Sachets, potpourri, and bowls of scented herbs can help to sweeten and brighten a room, and moth-repelling mixtures will discourage moths and scent linens. Bunches of herbs hung on a string can even transform a sterile modern kitchen into a comforting place. Herbs can be used directly as cleansing solutions or added to other household mixtures. Dyes can be processed from them, soaps made from them, or beer brewed from them. They are extremely versatile household helpers, and it is a pleasant art to gradually appreciate their many household properties and to master their manifold applications.

*Some respite to husbands the weather may send,*
*But housewives' affairs have never an end.*
~Thomas Tusser, BOOK OF HOUSEWIFERY

# Herbal Dyeing

Although dyeing is usually done with chemical products, many flowers, herbs, and shrubs are also well suited for this purpose. Plant dyes were once widespread, but are now becoming so rare that their value has risen proportionately. They produce warm, comforting tones in an astounding array of colors and nuances. The principal goal when dyeing with natural materials is to achieve a relatively fast color with the help of a mordant (from the Latin *mordere*, meaning "to bite"), which prepares the fibers to absorb color. Wool will take on color more readily and reliably than cloth. When using natural materials, keep in mind that the resulting color may be totally different from the color of the dyeing bath. Results vary widely according to the mordant and the strength of the dye, the hardness or alkalinity of the water, and the potency of the herb used. The intensity of the desired shade can be regulated by increasing the amount of the dye material used, by letting the wool draw longer in the dye bath, or by dyeing a second or third time. Easily available natural mordants are wood-ash solutions, stale wine, sorrel roots, willow or oak bark, washing soda, salt, vinegar, and powdered oak galls. The chemical substances alum, oxalic acid, bichromate of potash, copper or ferrous sulphate, and stannous chloride or tannic acid—although more drastic—are usually preferred as mordants because of the relative precision possible through exact measurement.

Here is a short list of the steps to be followed when dyeing wool for the first time:

Wet 1 pound of wool, squeeze, but do not wring dry, and set aside. Dissolve 3 to 4 ounces of alum and 1 ounce of cream of tartar in a little boiling water, and combine with 4 gallons of softened water in a large, covered, enameled or stainless steel pot. This container should be used solely for dyeing. Immerse the wool until completely covered with the warm liquid. Cover the pot, and heat the contents slowly. Simmer for 1 hour. Cool until lukewarm, then take out the wool. Gently squeeze dry, and roll in a towel. Some people prefer to let the wool cool in the mixture overnight and only remove it in the morning.

Place at least 1 pound of dyeing material (the rule of thumb is 1 pound of dyeing material for each 2 pounds of wool, although this will vary with more or less concentrated dyeing material) in at least 4 gallons of softened, cold water, without the wool. Cover and let soak. Flowers usually only have to be soaked for 1 hour, but leaves should be left overnight. Woody stems may have to be heated and soaked for a week, reheating every day (if you do not heat the dye material every day or two, mold begins to form). Some dyestuffs must be fermented with either washing soda or ammonia to produce fast colors. Strain out the leaves and other residue carefully.

Heat the dye bath to 140°F for heat-sensitive colors such as red or blue (madder, cleavers, indigo) or to the boiling point for strong browns and oranges. Cool until warm, and then add the wool, immersing it completely. Stir carefully a few times. Cover the pot, and simmer slowly until the desired tone is obtained.

Take the pot from the stove, and either remove the wool or let it cool in the dye bath overnight. Intense colors can be obtained by insulating the tightly closed container in a hay box (a wooden box insulated with hay to keep the temperature constant) or under a comforter until cool. Rinse the wool in softened water until it stops "bleeding" and then hang it up to dry. Some dyers add ammonia, vinegar, or salt to the first rinse water to help "set" the colors. Some plants, such as yarrow, are very sensitive to ammonia, and the entire dyeing solution will change color dramatically the minute ammonia is added.

After a few attempts with alum, experimentation with other mordants can begin. Samples of the different dye experiments should be saved, with a few notes on the methods and amounts used and their effectiveness. Since it is very difficult, if not impossible, to match colors precisely while working with natural ingredients, all the wool needed for one project must be dyed at one time. The great variety of shades and tones that can be produced and the unpredictability of results is one of the great challenges of dyeing with natural materials. What greater joy than suddenly, unexpectedly discovering a totally new color that can be produced from a familiar plant found growing in masses around the house?

Yellows, browns, golds, and greens are relatively easy to obtain with a wide variety of dye materials. The colors red and blue, as well as black, are much more difficult to produce. That is why plants such as madder, woad, and indigo have assumed such importance over the centuries. Madder roots produce deep red and purplish-red colors as well as shades of pink and orange. Woad and indigo are used to prepare blue, green, and even black dyes. Another very useful dye plant is weld, which produces fast and clear yellow shades.

There are many other plants of interest to the dyer. Walnut hulls, oak leaves, horse chestnuts, tea leaves, and lichens will all produce browns without a mordant. The composite flowers (marigolds, tansy, daisies, yellow chamomile, etc.) all dye yellow, as do the flowering tops of lady's bedstraw. The roots of lady's bedstraw and cleavers dye, according to the mordant used, pink, orange, or red. Hollyhock flowers are reported to produce a pale blue color that, unfortunately, is not too fast. Yarrow dyes wool yellow and green. Nettles and marjoram impart a lighter green shade.

> *She is not afraid of snow for her household:*
> *for all her household are clothed with scarlet.*
> *She maketh herself coverings of tapestry;*
> *her clothing is silk and purple.*
> ~Proverbs 31:21–22

## Strewing, Garlanding, and Festooning

One of the most pleasant and delightful ways of using herbs has, to our great loss, been almost forgotten during the last few centuries. One often reads of herbs strewn in banquet halls and kings and queens walking on carpets of rose blossoms, but who today has had the overwhelming joy of walking barefoot across a room cushioned with sweet-scented herbs?

This old custom had a very mundane origin. When floors were made of stamped earth, cold stone, or rough-planked wood, they were often strewn with absorbent materials such as sawdust to simplify the cleaning process. Rushes were thrown down on more festive holidays, adding a sweet note, clean and fresh, to the room. On very high occasions such as weddings and banquets, the most fragrant flowers and herbs were picked to throw at the feet of those celebrating there. Sir Isaac Newton observed that:

> . . . at bride-ales the house and chambers were wont to be
> strowed with these odoriferous and sweet herbes to signifie
> that in wedlocke all pensive saleness and tow'ring cheer, all

wrangling, strife, jarring, variance and discorde ought to be utterly excluded and abandoned.

The ancient Romans were so lavish in strewing herbs at banquets that they used to steep their wine with them, and gave their guests floral washing waters and herbal garlands to drive away the noxious effects of wine fumes:

> The use of flowry Crowns and Garlands is of no slender Antiquity, and higher than I conceive you apprehend it. For, beside the old Greeks and Romans, the Aegyptians made use hereof; who, beside the bravery of their Garlands, had little Birds upon them to peck at their Heads and Brows, and so to keep them from sleeping at their Festival compotations.

> ~Sir Thomas Brown

Not only were guests wreathed in garlands, but lovers, poets, and victors were also honored with them. In later centuries, people preferred to perfume their food with strong floral and herbal essences rather than strewing the dining room with fragrant herbs. Our times have grown particularly stingy. Even the parsimonious practice of hanging a bunch of sweet-smelling herbs from the ceiling has fallen away. But, despite our present frugality, I am convinced that herbs will be strewn, and flowers worn in buttonholes again.

For example, we can bring the invigorating air of mountainous regions into our houses in the fragrances of organy, wild thyme, horse and water mint, sage, juniper, fir, pine, and larch needles. With a few herbal pillows here, some potpourri there, a lighted aroma lamp in the hallway, we can trigger memories of mountain holidays.

# Beyond Pine-scented Cones

～ by Laurel Reufner ～

I love pine cones; they're like little wooden flowers and each one is unique. A few placed in a pretty bowl or basket make a lovely display. Some scent and maybe some glitter will jazz up the display a bit, or some potpourri can be added for a different kind of interest. Pine cones can be coated in wax to make firestarters, or spread with nut butter and rolled in bird seed for a wintery wildlife treat. There are just so many things you can do with these lovely beauties. Let's explore some of them together.

Probably the easiest way to acquire pine cones is just to buy them from a craft store. Odds are that you'll have a variety to choose from and you won't need to do anything special to prepare them for use once you get home. If you're in a big hurry, or it's really wet and rainy outside, this is the best way to go. However, it'll be a lot more fun to go gather your own. While you can gather pine cones any time of the year, autumn is definitely the best since the cones are at their freshest and have been the least warped by the weather, animals, and life in general. Grab a partner in crime, some kids or the dog, and a bucket or bag, and then head out to an area where pine trees grow. Remember that pine cones have sap, so don't use a container that you want to keep sap-free.

Once you get home with your cones, there are a couple of ways to clean them up and get them ready for use. Both are pretty thorough in getting rid of bugs, although I think the latter method is best at dealing with any sticky sap.

For the first method, put the cones in a bucket and fill full of cold water. Leave it sitting outside overnight, although be careful not to let it freeze. The next day, set the cones inside near a nice sunny window to dry and open back up.

For the second method, spread the pine cones out on a foil-lined baking sheet and place in a 200°F oven for about an hour. This will not only dry out the cones, getting them to open up fully, but any little bugs that might be in them will be killed, and the heat will melt off any remaining sap.

Now that you've got your cones, and they've been cleaned, it's time to have some fun.

## Crafting with Cones

This first craft—making dragon scales—is great to do with kids of any age. You'll need some floral cutters or a really good pair of kitchen shears to snip the "scales" from the pine cone. Start at the base of the cone, where it's easier to get to them, and remove a small pile of the pine scales. Decide what color you want your dragon to be and begin painting "the scales." The nice part about this particular craft is that even young kids can enjoy the painting part. Allow each side to dry completely before flipping them over and painting the other side. Add a little iridescent glitter to make them sparkle like the real thing. Once dry, store them in a special bag or a little box.

This craft can also be used to instill a bit of confidence in a child. Red scales could be used for courage, yellow to do better in school, and blue for a child needing more calmness. Maybe you could let your child pick the color for the attribute they want to work on. And when in doubt, gold is always a great color for a magnificent dragon. It also helps instill confidence, in general.

## Decorating with Cones

As mentioned earlier, pine cones make decorative and fragrant centerpieces for your home. They can be arranged on a plate or tray, or tucked into a pretty bowl or basket. Tuck in snips of rosemary, lavender, sage, or even whole spices such as cinnamon sticks, star anise, or whole nutmegs for a bit of nature's bounty brought inside. This makes a lovely potpourri to freshen up a room. (I included some recipes for you to try.)

A pine cone wreath also makes a wonderful home decoration. A grapevine wreath and either some craft wire or a glue gun, plus a good quantity of cones, are all you need to create a beautiful wreath. Depending on your cones and the size of your wreath, attach the cones two to three across on the grapevine. Use a variety of sizes to create texture and make it more interesting. Smaller pine cones can be used to fill in small gaps between the larger cones. Add a jaunty wire-edged ribbon bow to finish it off. Tuck in some colorful berry sprays for even more color.

### Winter Citrus Pine Potpourri

1   cup pine cones, small to medium-sized

1   cup hibiscus flowers, whole

½   cup cinnamon pieces, 1- to 3-inch lengths

½   cup orange peel, dried

½ to 1 cup bay leaves

½   cup orris root chunks

½   dram citrus spice oil mix*

1. Add citrus spice oil mix to the orris root and allow mixture to sit overnight so the orris root fully absorbs the oil's fragrance.

2. Combine all of the ingredients and allow the potpourri to sit for three weeks. Shake it often.

*To make citrus spice oil mix, combine 15 drops each of cinnamon and sweet orange (or sweet bergamot) essential oils, 15 drops clove essential oil, and 12 drops nutmeg oil.

### Pine-scented Potpourri

½   cup bay leaves

½   cup balsam needles

½   cup miniature pine cones

½   cup rose hips

1   tablespoons orris root or cellulose fiber

20 drops pine-scented oil

To mix the potpourri, follow the same instructions as for the Winter Citrus Pine Potpourri.

# Scented Pine Cones

Another wonderful way to use pine cones is to scent them. All you'll need are some pretty cones and a good essential or fragrance oil, such as those used to make potpourri. Think warm, earthy scents—patchouli or even bay are good choices. Spicy scents work wonderfully, as well.

Place your pine cones into a resealable plastic bag and add 10 to 15 drops good essential or fragrance oil. Shake well to distribute the oils on the pine cones and leave the bags closed for at least 24 hours. Decorate them by brushing on a mixture of 1 part glue and 1 part water. Shake glitter over the cones, giving them a light tap to remove the excess. Let dry and then display.

Another method to easily scent pine cones uses dry, powdered spices. Mix up a combination of spices that you like. Some good ones to use include cinnamon, cloves, nutmeg, anise, and ginger. Use a brush to paint the cone with a mixture of equal parts water and glue. Shake the spice mix onto the pinecone, taking care to get an even coating. Gently tap any loose spices out onto a piece of paper so you can reuse them. After the cones have dried, display however you wish. You could also add some glitter to the spice mix for a slight twinkle on the cones.

My last method for scenting pine cones utilizes melted wax. While there are now waxes you can be melted in the microwave, the double-boiler stovetop method is really easy. Look for boxes of paraffin in the canning supplies section at your grocery store. You'll also need a clean tin can that is 2 to 3 inches taller than your tallest cone.

Use a marker or something with which you can scratch the can. Make a mark on the inside of the can that is even with the height of your tallest cone. You don't want your wax to be any deeper than this, otherwise it might overflow. To melt your wax, simply chop it up into chunks and place them in the can. Set the can into a pan that's about half full of water and set the pan over medium heat. After the wax has completely melted, add your essential or perfume oil and stir to blend. (A wooden chopstick makes a great stir stick.)

You can either tie a piece of string around the end of the pinecone or use a pair of inexpensive tongs to dip the cone into the wax. You'll also want a large piece of wax paper nearby to rest the cones on after dipping. You want to give these scented cones at least three coats of wax, letting them dry between dippings. If you want them extra fancy, sprinkle the cones with glitter after the last dipping. You could also coat the cones with some powdered spices for additional yummy smells. Display, taking care to keep them away from heat sources or sunlight.

All of the scented cones make great firestarters, especially the wax-dipped ones. If you're planning to use them to start a blaze, just light the scales along one side of the cone. Or tie a bit of candle wicking or string around the base of the cone and light that to get them burning.

## Colored-flame Pine Cones

Our final craft project is to make colored-flame-producing pine cones that are pretty when burning, and a lot of fun to make. You just soak the cones in a bucket of water that contains the color-producing chemical or your choice.

To get started, add the chemical of choice to a half gallon of water and stir to dissolve. Keep stirring the dry chemical until it is completely dissolved in the water. (Using warm water will make the job easier.) If you're using a liquid chemical, you won't need to worry about mixing it with water.

Next, find a tall narrow container to pour your chemical into. The displacement caused by the added pine cones will help make sure they're completely submerged. (Use only one chemical per bucket of water.) Allow the pine cones to soak for at least eight hours. Allow them to dry for at least three days before using. Finally, don't soak the cones in more than one chemical; otherwise, you'll undo your hard work and wind up with only regular colored flames.

- Bright red flames are produced by using strontium chloride, which can be found with aquarium supplies. It is commonly used in the care and keeping of certain corals.

- Deep red flames are produced by boric acid. It is also found with aquarium supplies, and commonly used to keep the pH balanced in saltwater aquariums. You also might be able to find boric acid at your local pharmacy or craft supply store. Check the soap making supplies.

- Orange flames are produced by using calcium chloride, which is used in ice melting compounds and as an ingredient in brewing. You might be able to find it at stores catering to the home brewer.

- Yellow flames are created with regular old table salt.

- Yellow-green flames are produced by using borax. This chemical can easily be found in the laundry aisle, in a box labeled 20 Mule Team Laundry Soap.

- Bright-green flames are produced by using alum. Look for it in either the canning section or with the herbs in your local grocery store.

- Green flames are produced by using copper sulfate, which can be found in with aquarium supplies. It's used to treat ich in both fresh and saltwater aquariums.

- Blue flames are produced by using copper chloride. The chemical can, hopefully, be found with aquarium supplies.

- Purple flames are produced by using potassium chloride. This compound is a common salt substitute. Look for it in with the dried herbs in your grocery store.

- Violet flames are produced using a combination of chemicals. Mix 3 parts potassium sulfate with 1 part potassium nitrate, otherwise known as saltpeter. Both chemicals can be found at the aquarium store.

- Pink flames are produced by using plaster of Paris. Find it in either the craft aisle or a hardware store; it might be cheaper in the hardware store.

- White flames are produced by using magnesium sulfate, better known as Epsom salts. Find it at the pharmacy.

To use your colored flame pine cones, simple add them to an already burning fire. If you'd like to add scent to go with your color, use one of the above methods for scenting the pine cones. DO NOT dip these cones in wax to make them fire starters. They're meant to be added to an already burning fire. Also, certain chemicals in the wax could negate your lovely colored flames.

Some of these chemicals can be nasty but, with simple precautions, you should be fine. Work in a well-ventilated area with little to no wind, and cover your nose and mouth with a dust mask to avoid irritating your air passages. Also, wear gloves when working with either the chemicals or the wet pine cones. Finally, make sure not to leave the pine cones where small children or dogs can get into them. They wouldn't be very healthy chew toys.

# Herb
# History,
# Myth, and
# Lore

# Hidden and
# Forbidden Herbs

## ❧ by Nancy Bennett ❧

What is it about some herbs that make us feel so passionate? Does basil make you feel warm and comforted, and does garlic really arouse your senses and make you feel fresh and free? Various herbs have had hidden uses since ancient times. For example, anise was used in many Middle Eastern countries to excite the lovemaking of newlyweds and to cure impotence. Basil was known for evoking passion, and it is still in used in Haitian voodoo rituals.

## Myth or Not?

Anise on a wedding day will not keep the dogs at bay. Fragrant, spicy anise has had a following among the romantically engaged since ancient times. It was the Romans who first used it in a spicy cake that was served at the end of large meals to ease digestion. This cake, known as Mustacae, was the forerunner of our spiced wedding cake. Nowadays this cake is given to guests either to eat, or to sleep on and dream of their future love. Anise is one of the most ancient herbs, possibly originating in Egypt over 1,500 years ago. In the Middle East, anise was often served to the bride and groom to add spice to the honeymoon. For the male, it was supposed to cure impotence, and for females, to promote estrogen; then, later it helped with breast milk production. Not only humans were lured by the charms of anise: It is also useful for attracting dogs, luring fish, and for baiting mice! Anise seed can also be combined with other herbs to make a tea to ease hot flashes in women.

As a spice, anise has many uses. Try it in Scandinavian Christmas cookies, or as a main course addition, used to add flavor to pork or beef roasts. Anise also works well with fish, and it is found in many ethnic foods.

## Garlic to Ward Off Vampires and Jealousy

Garlic has had many uses. The Greeks used it as a blood tonic to help troops build up courage, and as a medical antiseptic on the battlefield. Garlic was used to ward off vampires and jealous nymphs that bothered pregnant women. But its boldest claim to fame is that of a pungent aphrodisiac. A groom in Palestine might wear a garlic flower in his lapel, an old custom to ensure a successful night of romance with his new bride. It was once believed that garlic actually raised a man's sperm count. The name garlic comes from the word "spear," and the shape of a garlic plant has a phallic connection. Women have found garlic helpful for the heart and in keeping with a healthy love life. You might do as I did on my honeymoon, and share a meal of roasted garlic on toasted bread with your love.

### To Make Roasted Garlic

Preheat your oven to 400°F. Take a whole clove of garlic and remove most of the paper layer, leaving one to hold the cloves together. Cut off the top so all cloves are exposed. Drizzle with about 2 tablespoons of good olive oil. Roast in the oven 25 to 30 minutes, or till tops are brown and cloves are soft. You will know by the wonderful smell when they are done.

Cut up some thick bread and toast it, then cut it into triangles. Call someone you love. Squeeze the garlic onto the bread (it's remarkably sweet this way) and pass the wine.

## Basil to Warm Your Ancient Fires

Basil is a beautiful fragrant herb and is most often found in homemade pesto, but it has been associated with the Haiti goddess of love, Irzulie, and was often employed as an aphrodisiac. In Romania, if a woman (or man) offers a leaf of basil to a potential partner and they accept it, the couple is betrothed; and in Italy, if a woman puts a pot of basil on her windowsill, she is advertising her desire for a gentleman caller. Basil is also associated with love and eternal life in accordance with Hindu tradition, and is sacred to the goddess Tulasi. Poor Tulasi was tricked into making love to a man not her husband by the god Vishnu. In her anguish over her unfaithful behavior, she killed herself. The god Vishnu was touched by Tulasi's actions and caused holy basil to grow from her ashes as a symbol of the faithfulness of women.

If your passion meets a dead end, don't despair. The custom of putting a leaf of basil on top of the funeral pyre was also used in India, to ensure a way into heaven.

# Message Amidst the Clover

Wearing herbs can have sensual and secret meanings, too. Catnip worn or sent to another means, "I am intoxicated with love." Want to reject a lover? Send him or her a dandelion, which means, "I find your presumptions laughable."

# Wandering and Wanton Herbs

Oh poor mint! It's named after a nymph named Mythne who caught the eye of Hades and instigated the wrath of his beloved, Persephone. Mythne was caught in a comprising position, and she was killed and trod upon by Persephone's heel as a warning to others. Roadsides were once lined with this fast-growing, fragrant, and delicious herb. Many gardeners consider mint a weed, but under control—in a pot or a secluded area—it will not get underfoot, and if it does, what a scent!

# Forever Herbally After

There are many other "romantic" herbs. Greek couples wore hawthorn blossoms on their wedding day. Rosemary had the power to persuade a maid or man to fall in love. Prick your intended with a rosemary twig, and they will hold you in their heart forever—or so it is believed. In North America, wild herbs also made it into romantic favor. Among the Menominee tribe, bleeding heart was used as a love charm. Young braves picked the flowers and threw them at an intended love. If the flower hit the maid, then she was sure to fall in love with him. Any way you look at it, herbs are always at the heart of the matter. Add them into your garden and your cooking, and love may soon be growing.

# Sacred San Pedro Cactus

### ❦ by James Kambos ❦

When humans migrated into the Western Hemisphere from Asia more than 40,000 years ago, they encountered plants and animals different from any previously known to them. The southward and eastward movement of these people over many millennia eventually led them to the more arid regions where they encountered a variety of cacti (the plural of cactus). Cacti, members of the Cactaceae family, are native to North, Central and South America. Over thousands of years, some of these cacti took on more significance than others, becoming dependable sources of food or having divine attributes. Approximately 23,000 years ago, humans migrated into South America by way of the Isthmus of Panama, and again found strange new fauna and flora. Survival for these potential desert and semi-desert dwellers depended on their successful use of the natural resources, whether as sources of food or fiber, or as a means of dealing with their spirit world.

As a method of communing with the spirit realm—to interact or intercede with the supernatural sphere—and as a course to heal the sick, two phytochemically rich cacti took on significant roles in the lives of Native Americans. They were the better-known peyote cactus (*Lophophora williamsii*) that is found in southwestern North America, and the far lesser-known San Pedro cactus (*Echinopsis pachanoi*, changed from *Trichocereus pachanoi* in the early 1980s). San Pedro cactus is prevalent in a "chili pepper-shaped" mountainous region of north central South America, and it is this more obscure San Pedro cactus that we shall explore.

The San Pedro cactus is native to a long narrow swath of the central Andes Mountains (from Ecuador through Peru and into Bolivia) at an altitude between 6,000 and 9,000 feet. (Other species within the genus may occur as far south as Argentina.) Its physical appearance gives no inkling of its ancient history and continuing modern-day importance. Its overall structure is rather unassuming, actually. It is a sturdy, columnar, often branched, frequently (but not always) spineless 9 to 20 foot tall cactus. It looks like the unassuming organ-pipe-like cactus used as the "living fence" surrounding part of the grounds of the Museo Frida Kahlo (Frida Kahlo Museum) in Coyoacán, México; or as the living barriers, which constrain livestock, avert banditos, or demarcate property lines, one can see when visiting parts of rural Peru or Chile. The columns have six to eight longitudinal ribs, which facilitate a body-wide accordion-style expansion or contraction of the cactus, depending on its water content. It is common knowledge, of course, that one unique characteristic of cacti, in general, is their ability to store water for times of severe drought, which for many species may mean most of the year.

Given natural genetic variation, the number of ribs may vary from plant to plant. Those rare specimens with four ribs are considered most valuable, as they are thought to have healing and magical qualities. These particular examples are known as "cactus of the four winds or "cactus of the four roads." Additionally, plants from the highlands are said to be the most potent of all, possibly as a result of climatic or soil factors.

The stems of the San Pedro are glaucous (covered in a bluish waxy substance that rubs off easily with the fingers) when young, becoming dark green with age. The most spectacular physical feature of this cactus is its funnel-shaped, luminously white flowers that are nocturnal, opening only at night. These beautiful flowers can be between 7½ and 9¼ inches wide. The flowers are wildly fragrant to attract night-flying moths and fruit bat pollinators, and they are well worth a late-night standing ovation at a midnight flower-watching party! Upon pollination, the plant produces oblong, dark-green, 2 to 2½ inch long fruit that is covered with long dark hairs and is readily eaten by wildlife.

For our purposes, the most important feature of this cactus to ancient and modern shamans and *curanderos* ("men who cure") alike is its psychotomimetic (describing factors that produce a condition resembling psychosis) properties, due to a wide range of alkaloids. The term alkaloid is used by chemists to describe the nitrogenous metabolic products of plants that have alkaline properties and are, therefore, "like or as an alkali"—alkaloid.

It should come as no surprise, therefore, that earlier humans, discovering how San Pedro cactus greatly altered their senses upon consumption (and imagine the undisciplined trial and error testing that occurred), believed that it was a divine gift and a means by which they could influence the sphere of sorcery and communicate with their spirit world. And believing, as they did, that spirits controlled health, sickness, and death, the San Pedro cactus became a powerful weapon for them in the arsenal used to communicate with, and hopefully manipulate, these spirits.

Spanish missionaries and conquistadores went to considerable efforts to try to eradicate the use of the San Pedro cactus because it was believed to be a form of pagan devil worship. The following undated account is from a sixteenth- or seventeenth-century unidentified Spanish officer in Cuzco, Peru:

> Among the Indians, there was another class of wizards, permitted by the Incas to a certain degree, who are like sorcerers. They take the form they want and go a long distance through the air in a short time; and they see what is happening, they speak with the devil, who answers them in certain stones or in other things they venerate.

An additional account states the shamans:

> [They] drink a beverage they call achuma which is a water they make from the sap of some thick and smooth cacti . . . as it is very strong, after they drink it they remain without judgment and deprived of their senses, and they see visions that the devil represents to them . . .

And further early testimony from an anonymous, undated ecclesiastical report from Peru states:

> This is the plant with which the devil deceived the Indians . . . in their paganism, using it for their lies and superstitions . . . those who drink lose consciousness and remain as if dead; and it has even been seen that some have died

because of the great frigidity to the brain . . . Transported by the drink, the Indians dreamed a thousand absurdities and believed them as if they were true . . .

But the practice continued among the Mestizo culture of Peru despite the Church's prohibitions. The cult slowly became a syncretic blend of Roman Catholic and pre-Hispanic elements, which helps explain the name San Pedro (Saint Peter, in English) cactus. Many Christians believe that Saint Peter holds the keys to heaven, thus the effects of the cactus suggested to the Mestizo people that it was the key for them to reach heaven while still earthbound.

Additionally, the rituals are conclusively moon-oriented, which further corroborates the amalgam of pagan and Christian elements. Anthropologist and author Douglas Stone wrote in 1972:

[The] San Pedro is always in tune with the saints, with the powers of animals, of strong personages or being, of serious beings, of beings that have natural power . . .

In the northern Andean area, the cactus is known as huchuma, and in Bolivia as achuma. In fact, the Bolivian expression *chumarse* (meaning to "get drunk") is derived from the word achuma. In Ecuador it is called either aguacolla or gigantón.

San Padro cacti are rich in mescaline, which has psychotomimetic effects similar to those of LSD and psilocybin (mushrooms with psychoactive ingredients). The dried cactus contains 2 percent of the chemical and the fresh product contains 0.12 percent, in the same way that dried culinary herbs are more potent than their freshly picked counterparts. Mescaline is a compound closely related to the brain hormone norepinephrine (noradrenaline). Norepinephrine belongs to the group of physiological agents known as neurotransmitters because they function in the chemical transmission of impulses between neurons (nerve cells). Mescaline and norepinephrine have the same basic chemical structure; both are derivatives of a substance known to chemists as phenylethylamine. Mescaline causes one to experience vivid colors and other enhancements of the senses. One does not actually lose consciousness, nor does one actually hallucinate, but the effects on the mind are impressive, to say the least. Other alkaloids have been reported from the plants as well; namely 3.4-dimethoxyphenylethylamine, 3-methoxy-tyramine, as well as traces of other bases. A similar alkaloid, N,N-dimethy-tryptamine has been isolated from a related species, *E. terschekii*, indigenous to northern Argentina.

In general, we experience life from a rather one-sided point of view. This is our so-called "normal state." However, through hallucinogens, the overall perception of reality is profoundly challenged or even expanded. These different aspects or levels of one-and-the-same reality are not mutually exclusive. They form an all-encompassing, timeless, transcendental reality. The possibility of changing the "wavelength" of the ego's acuity and, subsequently, to produce alterations in the awareness of veracity, constitutes the real significance of hallucinogens. This ability to create new and different takes on the world is why hallucinogenic floras were, and still are, regarded as sacred.

As far as the ancient use of the San Pedro cactus in everyday mystical life, the archaeological evidence in many of these arid regions is scarce, yet some interesting information has been obtained from plant samples, stone carvings, ceramic ware, paintings, and textiles. For example, ceramic pipes and, for lack of a better description, "cigarettes," probably depicting the San Pedro cactus, have been found at a coastal site north of Lima near Casma, with an age of about 3,000 years. Researchers suggest that these may represent a method by which early native South Americans obtained the psychotomimetic effects of mescaline—it was often combined with tobacco. An engraved, low bas-relief depicting the principal Chavin deity was excavated from a circular, sunken plaza in the court of the Old Temple of Chavin de Huantar (their culture is dated about 1200 to 800 BC) in the northern highlands of Peru. It is an anthropomorphized creature with serpentine hair, jaguar fangs, and a two-headed snake as a belt. In its eagle-like claws, the character clutches a four-ribbed piece of San Pedro cactus. This is the earliest depiction of the San Pedro cactus, dating to 1300 BC. A ceramic pouring vessel from the same culture depicts a jaguar sitting amongst stems of the San Pedro. The jaguar, which is always associated with shamanism and hallucinogens in South America, unquestionably—according to anthropologists—indicates that this cactus was used in sacred rituals at least three thousand years ago. A fascinating piece from the Chimú culture (dated to AD 1200) portrays an owl-faced woman (she may be wearing a jaguar's head as a headdress), who is probably a herbalist and shaman. She is holding a piece of San Pedro cactus so large she uses both of her stylized hands. Even today, the women who sell pieces of this cactus are usually both herbalists and shamans, and according to beliefs, the owl is associated with these women. Fascinating, isn't it?

The stems of the cactus, normally purchased at the market in stalls tended by these aforementioned women, are sliced crosswise like a loaf of bread or a cucumber and boiled in water for up to seven hours. The cactus slices may be boiled by themselves, or may be combined with additional sanctified herbs, which are boiled separately and added later, in a sacred brew called *cimora*. Ethnobotanist and author Wade Davis, wrote in 1983:

> . . . the matter of cimora still needs clarification. Clearly, however, cimora is not simply a mixture of the San Pedro Cactus and a few other plants.

A strict diet is adhered to prior to partaking of the brew. Animal fat, grease, salt, chili peppers, and pieces of vines that entangle (such as beans and other legumes) are to be avoided. I understand the avoidance of fats, which may coat the stomach and impede absorption of the chemicals, as well as the vines, whose twining nature may metaphorically "ensnare" or "truss up" the spirit forces, but the exclusion of salt and hot peppers escapes me. Unless of course, it pertains to the age-old belief that salt drives away the spirits and that, even more simply, hot peppers make one sweat, therefore "expelling" or "eliminating" the conjuring powers of the cactus. My hypotheses are all possible, perhaps, but I cannot say for certain. An anonymous Shaman in Peru stated:

> . . . the drug first produces . . . drowsiness or a dreamy state and a feeling of lethargy . . . a slight dizziness . . . then a great "vision," a clearing of the faculties . . . It produces a light numbness in the body and afterward a tranquility. And then comes detachment, a type of vital visual force. . . inclusive of all the senses . . . including the sixth sense, the telepathic sense of transmitting oneself across time and matter . . . like a kind of removal of one's thought to a distant dimension.

Although cimora may be drunk, it appears that the preferred method for ingesting the San Pedro is through the nose. Perhaps contact with the mucous membranes improves the absorption of the chemicals. As stated earlier, tobacco is often used in combination with the San Pedro cactus. Tobacco users believe that it enhances the effects of the plant by clearing the mind and augmenting other effects such as visions, imagination, and sight.

After first ingesting the San Pedro cactus, it has been observed that the person undergoes a bout of nausea and vomiting. These symptoms are considered to be beneficial as it "purges" the potential patient of impurities. The healing ritual consists of an all-night session composed of two parts. The first, led by the *curandero* (meaning "folk healer" or shaman) who is under the influence of the San Pedro cactus, lasts about two hours and involves singing, praying, and whistling.

It is during this first phase that the healer divines the cause of the patient's illness and how best to cure it. Both the patient and the curandero's assistants also take the San Pedro cactus with tobacco through the nose. All involved drink a cup of San Pedro tea, or an infusion of it, at the end of the first session.

The second phase consists of the curandero's treating the patient through the use of various plant-based folk medicines. The cactus permits the emergence of the visionary power of the healer, who visualizes the aspects of the patient's life, which represent the causes of the problems. Although any San Pedro cactus may be used, as stated previously, it is the rarely encountered four-ribbed specimens that are believed to have exceptional healing properties, as noted by anthropologist and author Douglas Stone:

> Four-ribbed cactus . . . are considered to be very rare and lucky . . . to have special properties because they correspond to the "four winds" and the "four roads," supernatural powers associated with the cardinal points . . .

## A Personal Experience

About thirty years ago, I tried the San Pedro cactus myself. I had a small potted one as a houseplant, when I read an obscure treatise about it and its psychochemical attributes. Of course, this was light years before home computers were the norm and Google searches could give a person extensive information about any desired subject, and previous to ethnobotany becoming a cutting-edge and highly recognized discipline with all of the literature it generated. I simply sliced the stem like a cucumber, pared off any spines with a small kitchen knife and ate it. It wasn't as unpalatable as peyote or psilocybin mushrooms, let's say, but it wasn't a taste sensation, either. I did experience some minor effects, however. I felt an increased awareness of my surroundings and a definite amphetamine-like feeling—as if I had consumed way too many triple espressos. I did not experience any nausea—thankfully—probably because of the small amounts I ate. Nor did I even remotely hallucinate. Naturally, I persevered conducting my little tests and, sadly, nibbled the unassuming cactus into oblivion. Nowadays, of course, with information so readily at hand, I would never be so foolish as to try home experimentation.

The San Pedro is still used in traditional medicine. It is still perceived to have great power for divination, in undoing love witchcraft, for fighting various forms of sorcery, and to assure success in personal ventures. Some even partake of it orally to heal disorders of the stomach, kidneys, liver, and blood. A decoction of the stem is used externally to treat baldness, and it is used primarily for therapeutic purposes to treat alcoholism and mental illness.

## Edible Cacti

The fruit of many cacti, like those of the genus *Opuntia*—the prickly pear cacti, the saguaro cactus, and the dragon fruit, for example—is deemed eminently edible and forms an integral part of the cultures of native peoples of the Americas. The fruit of some other *Echinopsis* species—such as those of *E. chiloensis*, known as cardón de candelabro or quisco, and *E. spachiana*, called the torch cactus—is eaten quite safely and regularly. But amazingly, I have read reports that the fruit of the San Pedro is eaten as food in parts of South America, but given the plant's natural battery of chemical compounds, I think it would be quite unwise to experiment with it—if your plants ever produce fruit, that is. Imagine the possible unexpected and unwanted repercussions.

## Cultivating San Padro Cacti at Home

The San Pedro cactus is easy to cultivate at home and readily available, as well. It requires a rich, but flawlessly drained soil. Add plenty of compost or well-rotted manure for nutrition, and plenty of sharp sand or turkey grit for drainage, if your soil isn't up to snuff.

They can be grown outdoors in the full sun in areas (thanks to their high altitude habitat) where there are only brief or rare periods of 20°F. That is in USDA Zones 10 and 11, which includes Hawaii, of course, as well as the southernmost portions of California, Texas, Louisiana, Mississippi, Alabama, Florida, as well as points south. The use of pea gravel or small stones as mulch around the plant lends an attractive, natural appearance and helps keep weeds down. In northern climes, it makes an admirable, if slow-growing houseplant and a great addition to the cactus collection.

Cultivate it in a fully exposed south- or southwest-facing window, or in an unshaded greenhouse or unobstructed sunroom or bay window. Utilizing unglazed terra cotta containers helps avoid waterlogged soils—a death knell for any cactus. Fertilize using your favorite water-soluble plant food twice monthly during active growth. Give indoor specimens an outdoor summer vacation in full sun if possible—it will work wonders for lackluster examples. As for insect pests, watch for mealy bugs and scale insects on houseplants and use your favorite horticultural oil or organic insecticide for eradication.

# References

Anderson, Edward F. "The Cactus Family: Chapter Two." *Ethnobotany of Cacti*. Portland, OR: Timber Press, 2001.

Calderon, Eduardo, Richard Cowan, Douglas Sharon and F. Kaye Sharon. *Eduardo el Curandero: The Words of A Peruvian Healer*. New York: Random House, 2000.

Davis, Wade E. "Sacred Plants of the San Pedro Cult." Botanical Museum Leaflets. Cambridge, MA: Harvard University, 1983.

Rätsch, Christian. *Le Piante dell'Amore: Gli afrodisiaci nel mito, nella storia e nella practica quotidiana*. Gremese, editore. Luzern, 1990.

Schultes, Richard E. and Albert Hoffman. *Plants of the Gods: Their Sacred Healing and Hallucinogenic Powers*. Rochester, VT: Healing Arts Press, 1992.

# Holy Smoke: Beyond the Smudge Stick

### ❧ by Amy Martin ❧

The smudge stick—dried leafy herbs on stems, bound or woven together—can be bought in so many shops, you might think that burning these little bundles is the only way to smudge.

Oh, the fun that you are missing! Try smudging Mesoamerican-style and you'll never go back to smudge sticks. Toss loose herbs on hot charcoal to create billows of smoke that immerse you in aroma. It's like a sweat lodge, but with smoke instead of steam—an astoundingly thorough purification.

Why smudge? Because it works! Modern life brings us into contact with the stress of cranky coworkers and roommates, bosses that bully, and just plain jerks. Cops and crazy drivers plague the twice-daily commute. The

daily news makes it seem like the world is hopelessly mad. All of that negativity tends to hang around us like the permanent dust cloud of Pigpen in the comic strip "Peanuts." Metaphysics and mystics call it our aura, the etheric body that extends out from our physical one. We bathe our corporeal bodies regularly. Why not our vibe?

## Hibachi 101

First, get over the idea that fire making is messy and requires a Boy Scout badge. Look for and buy those one-use bags of charcoal. You just light the bag and it ignites the charcoal for you, leaving behind a pile of hot embers. Or you can take a little more effort and use hardwood charcoal made of recycled lumber, or briquettes made from coconut shells, and ignite them with a plant-derived ethanol lighter fluid. Using a charcoal chimney can help the lighting process immensely.

It's hard to beat a Weber hibachi. They're lightweight, very portable, easy to use, and priced around $30. A bottom vent allows the ashes to drop out, and a tight lid with a smoke vent makes for good safety. For a more substantial hibachi, try the cast iron ones. You'll also need a few fire tools: a bellows to encourage recalcitrant fires, a metal rod for stirring the ashes, and a long-handled lighter. Keep on hand a jug of water or a fire extinguisher for safety, and some wet wipes for cleanup.

## Herbal Adventures

Smudge sticks are limited to relatively large leaves on a stem such as sage, or long thin leaves such as sweetgrass that can be bound or braided. A hibachi-based smudge can incorporate any size or shape of leaf, plus resins, woods, roots, seeds, berries and flowers, even essential oils. It's limitless! White sage is a traditional purifier from the Native American tradition. Also tap into Western herbs like blue vervain, which coaxes negativity out of its hiding places; and hyssop, which flat-out frightens the bad stuff away. Mugwort lifts out negativity with a strong tidal pull.

## Beyond the Leafy Herbs

Benzoin, a tree resin, and ground calamus root brighten away negativity. Frankincense, copal, and sandalwood, all from trees, combine into a lush, sweet smudge that invigorates the mind.

Include protective herbs so that the vigorous smoke cleansing doesn't leave the smudgee vulnerable. Wood betony and yerba santa are best, but smell musty. Almost as effective and far more aromatic are bay laurel leaves.

A smudge can be fashioned for any occasion. A male-honoring smudge might be musky with highly spiced overtones. One for women could reflect their complexity, with sweet and warm aromas brightened with elements of green herbs and grounded with earthiness. Here's an example of a smudge for celebrating the moon:

### Lunar Purification

½  cup buchu (1 part)

½  cup calamus root (1 part)

1   cup mugwort (2 parts)

1   cup myrrh resin (2 parts)

1   cup sandalwood (2 parts)

Crush the calamus, myrrh, and sandalwood, if necessary, then grind with the buchu into a rough powder. Add mugwort and blend. This recipe produces a beautiful fluid smoke with a sweet, relaxing aroma. Mugwort, an herb of the moon, is the core lunar connection and it aids in dream divination. It's paired with buchu, a little-known moon herb that is very psychedelic. Myrrh resin and sandalwood provide the base aroma and add purifying strength. Calamus root brightens the energy and adds a spicy note.

## It's Better Together

Hibachi-based smudges put the herbs and their power at center stage. When being blessed with a smudge stick, it's easy to be aware of the person who's doing the smudging. But with loose herbs on a hibachi of hot charcoal, it's just the smoke and the smudgee. Everyone's been through the interminable wait while individuals within a group are smudged with a stick. But to smudge a group of people using hibachi smudges, all they have to do is stand downwind, or use large hand fans to direct the smoke.

## Just Do It

To become immersed in smoke is a baptism, a complete submission to another world. The animated smoke feels alive with strong aromas that can transport the mind and liberate the spirit. If you have herbs, a fire container, and charcoal, it's easy to do.

# *Flying Ointments*

### ≫ by Susun Weed ≪

Have you ever wanted to fly? On your own? To leap from the edge of a cliff and fall up? To soar until your perspective changes and your problems seem small? To float in bliss on a pink cloud? Many people have wanted to fly; and some have attempted it. With the proper mindset and setting, and the judicious application of some psychoactive herbs to the skin, anyone can fly. I've done it, as have many others, including some Harvard professors.

Of course, we can fly in our dreams. We can fly in our imagination. We can fly in a shamanic trance. We can pretend to lift out of our body and fly through the air. We can envision what it would be like to be a superhero who

can fly. We can learn how to shapeshift into the body of a bird. We can read stories that carry us up in the air with Harry Potter, or the witches of yore, on magical brooms. Dreams, imagination, stories, and trances can help us spread our wings and fly, and they are quite safe. But some people have wanted more. Some have been willing to risk their safety in pursuit of a more real experience of flying. They created flying ointments.

The classic image of a witch is someone flying through the air, sometimes on a broom, sometimes in a cauldron, with her hair streaming out behind her and a black cat for a companion. The flying oil was made in her cauldron, and it was probably applied with the aid of a broomstick. The cat guarded her garden, where she grew the special plants needed for her flying ointment. Flying ointments have a long and colorful history. Lucian describes a sorceress in Onos in this way:

> Hereupon she opened a fairly large chest containing a large quantity of boxes, and took one of them out; what was actually inside it I cannot say, except that it looked to me like oil. She then rubbed it in all over her body, from her toenails to her hair, and suddenly feathers burst out all over her, her nose became a crooked beak, she took on all the characteristics of a bird which distinguish it from other animals, and in short, stopped being what she was and turned into a raven . . .

My own interest in flying oils began when I visited my friend Dolores one fine autumn day. I commented on the delicious aroma coming from her kitchen, hoping to be invited to eat with her. Instead, she asked me if I would like to try her flying ointment—when she was done cooking the toad.

The toad! I was astonished; it smelled wonderful. I believed she was serious, as we had recently experimented with a marvelously successful third eye-opening tincture. (The recipe is included at the end of this article if you wish to try it.) We did eat together that evening, as I recall. It was a feast of sweet corn and winter squash, cheese from my goats, and cooked greens gathered from the garden. Then we went outside, built a fire in a secluded spot, took off our clothes, rubbed our bodies well with the now-cool ointment, and flew together. Dolores has gone on to restore traditional herbal medicine in Puerto Rica, while I have continued to explore flying with the aid of herbs.

Traditionally, poisonous psychoactive plants in the night-shade family have been combined with cooked toad to produce a classic flying oil capable of altering brain chemistry, increasing skin sensitivity, and thus producing the illusion of flying. The use of these ointments can be risky. Great care is advised when working with the plants.

In 1954 researcher Siegbert Ferckel rubbed an ointment containing belladonna, henbane, and thornapple into his chest, particularly around the heart. He describes his experience:

> Less than five minutes had elapsed before my heart began to beat wildly and I was overcome by a powerful sensation of dizziness . . . my face was totally distorted; my pupils were almost as large as the eyeballs themselves, my lips were bluish and very swollen, and my whole face was chalky-white . . . Suddenly the walls and ceiling began to undulate and to crash together with a loud bang . . . Faces came towards me out of the darkness . . . It slowly grew completely dark around me, and I soared upwards at a great speed. It grew light again, and I saw hazily, through a pink veil, that I was floating above the town. The figures which had oppressed me before in my room accompanied me on this flight through the clouds . . .

I prefer to use safer, nonpoisonous, not so psychoactive, North American plants for my flying oils. But it helps to know about the plants that were traditionally used, too.

Nightshades, or plants in the Solanaceae family, are the most important ingredients in flying oils and flying ointments. The Old World knew only two genera of nightshades: henbane (*Hyoscyamus*) and belladonna (*Atropa*). Both are deadly poisonous, highly medicinal, and strongly associated with magic. The nightshades of the New World are mostly edible: tomatoes, potatoes, peppers, and eggplants. Interestingly, the aura of unpleasant magic extends to the edible nightshades. Despite extensive scientific evidence to the contrary, people blame nightshades for a variety of health problems, most especially joint pain. New World nightshades do include two genera used magically and shamanically: tobacco (*Nicotiana*) and tree datura (*Brugmansia*).

For a flying oil to be effective, it must contain one or more of the many nightshades. If you can't get—or feel uncomfortable using—the dangerous, powerful nightshades (henbane, belladonna, mandrake, or datura), substitute fresh tobacco leaves or the green berries of your local nightshade (i.e., black nightshade or bittersweet nightshade). In a pinch, you could even use the fresh green leaves from tomato or potato plants.

Henbane, if you can get it, is one of the most effective nightshades in creating the sensations of flying. Of the three most widely used henbanes—Egyptian henbane (*Hyoscyamus muticus)*, white henbane (*Hyoscyamus alba*), and black henbane (*Hyoscyamus niger*)—the first is the strongest and the last is the most widely grown and used. Annual or perennial varieties of henbane can be grown in most gardens. In Montana and a few other northern states, henbane has escaped cultivation to become a well-established weed.

Gardeners beware! Henbane smells rank and is no beauty. Various authors have outdone themselves in describing its look and odor: "clammy pubescent fetid narcotic herb," "darke and evill grayish slimy leaves," and "stinking trouble" are but some of them. And Pliny tells us that:

> Hyoscyamus . . . troubles the braine, and puts men besides their right wits; beside that, it breeds dizziness of the head . . . it is offensive to the understanding . . . if one take in drinke more than four leaves, thereof, it will put him beside himself.

Just smelling the leaves can produce dizziness, stupor, and the impression that you are flying. Both the dried seeds and fresh leaves of henbane can be used in flying oils and ointments. Herbalists and doctors still use the flowering tops as an antidote to mercury poisoning, as a treatment against morphine addiction, to ease pain, and to produce sleep. Henbane contains the psychoactive alkaloid hyoscyamine, as well as generous amounts of the cerebral sedative scopolamine. Overdoses redden the facial skin, dry the mouth, burn the throat, dilate the pupils, cause nausea and delirium, and may produce convulsions, coma, and death.

Belladonna (*Atropa belladonna*) is another nightshade that is famous for creating the illusion of flight. It is also known as deadly nightshade, sleeping nightshade, devil's herb, sorcerer's herb, naughty man's cherries, and death cherry. Its botanical name, *Atropa*, means "inflexible or unalterable," and is derived from the name of one of the Fates, the one who severs the thread of life. Witches's trances and hallucinations are thought to have been produced by an ointment [of belladonna leaves and berries] rubbed on the body. As belladonna does not grow wild in North America, the name "deadly nightshade" is often applied to our weedy nightshades: *Solanum nigrum*, with its shiny black berries, and *Solanum dulcamara*, with its lurid purple flowers. Neither is really poisonous; both work well in flying oils. Belladonna is still one of the chief sources of scopolamine, the infamous "truth serum," and of atropine, used by ophthalmologists to dilate the pupils of the eyes. Atropine is used in dozens of ways in modern medicine. It is one of the few antidotes for poisoning from the insecticide parathion or from nerve gas.

The genus *Datura* in the Solanaceae family has species native to every continent in the world, and their magic has been recognized and used by virtually every culture. In fact, the daturas have been cultivated for 40,000 years and, therefore, there are no wild species anymore. Prehistorical stories from India tell of the uses of datura. The eleventh-century physician, Avicenna, valued datura. The seeds, roots, and leaves of daturas are all sources of scopolamine, with the root being the safest part to use and the seeds the most dangerous. Thornapple or jimsonweed (*Datura stramonium*), is most often cited as being used in flying oils. It can take one back in time, as well, to visit with the ancestors and the ancient ones. South American shamans fly with the tree daturas (*Brugmansia*), which are easily cultivated, though not frost hardy.

Mandrake (*Mandragora officinarum*) is another nightshade rich in hyoscyamine and scopolamine, making it a favorite ingredient in flying oils. Harvard professor Richard Evans Schultes says:

> Mandrake . . . was an active hallucinogenic ingredient of many of the witches brews . . . It was undoubtedly one of the most potent ingredients in those complex preparations.

Monkshood (*Aconitum napellus*) is also known as wolfbane or aconite. It is not a nightshade, but it is found in many flying oil recipes. Applied to the skin, aconite ointment causes heightened sensitivity. It produces tingling sensations, then numbness valued by herbalists treating those with intractable pain. Used with the intention of flying, however, aconite ointment makes it easy to hallucinate that the skin is covered with feathers or fur and that one is lifted off the ground.

Toad is another must-have for a powerful flying oil. The few modern investigations into flying oils and flying ointments have concentrated on the toad. A group of Harvard scientists all reported visions of flying after ingesting toad skin. Fortunately, their trip lasted only a few minutes. Shamans report the use of toad skin unleashes an "overwhelming cyclone of energy" that brings about a complete loss of ego, a reunion of self with Self, and a reconnection with all other life. The vast majority of those who use toad skin as a psychoactive today smoke it. Extracting into oil, as the old recipes instruct us, may be a safer way to use it, though.

I use ordinary garden toads in my flying oil, preferring those that have died naturally. But those who want to craft an especially strong flying oil may wish to search out special toads. Down Under, you can find the cane toad (*Bufo marinus*), which secretes a psychedelic venom loaded with bufotenine from glands on its back. Closer to home, you have only to find the Colorado River toad (*Bufo alvarius*), which also produces a neurotoxin in its skin. These secretions can be extracted from the live animal, dried, and smoked. They can be formulated (from toads) to be transmitted directly from the oral mucosa to the blood, so both smoking and application to mucosal surfaces such as the genitals produces effects. The active chemical in toad skin is 5-methoxy-N,N-dimethyltryptamine (5-MeO-DMT). This is a close analog of the neurotransmitter serotonin and the hormone melatonin, so toad skin clearly can trigger intense mental states. Andrew Youil says toad smoke "possibly has special actions in particular deep-brain centers that may be related to emotion and the seat of consciousness." *Caution: Eating toad skin or toad eggs has caused death.*

If you prefer to leave the toad out of your flying oil, the flowers of cannabis or the flowers of hops may be used instead, but with far less effect. Psychoactive plants that are legal and easily available, and that can be absorbed dermally, include Indian tobacco or pukeweed, garden rue, wormwood, and mugwort/cronewort (*Artemisias*), poke berries, fresh catnip in flower, and mullein flowers.

Use your imagination when crafting your flying oil. Ask the plants in your garden if any of them would like to be included. And do be sure to use your flying ointment in a ritual setting. You are far more likely to enjoy the effects if you fly with others of a likemind on a night lit by the full moon, with soft turf, dry sand or velvety cushions to fall back into.

## Classic Flying Ointment
*For External Use Only (Poison)*

Boil together the leaves of belladonna (*Atropa belladonna*), thornapple/jimsonweed (*Datura stramonium*), and monkshood (*Aconitum napellus*), with a handful of celery seeds and a toad in a heavy pot of oil. When the toad falls from the bones, stop boiling. Strain the oil. Thicken it with beeswax to your desired consistency. When cool, rub on forehead, chest, armpits, and genitals.

## Olde Recipe for A Flying Oil
*For External Use Only (Poison)*

Boil one toad in oil for some time. Then pour the oil over a quantity of poison hemlock (*Conium maculatum*), European mandrake (*Mandragora officinarum*), belladonna (*Atropa belladonna*), and henbane (*Hyoscyamus*). The fresh leaves, seeds, and roots may all be used to great effect. Set in the sun and steep for a fortnight or more. Strain the foul-smelling oil from the plants. The oil is to be smeared liberally onto the chest and into the armpits, then rubbed generously onto a broom handle and applied to the vaginal lips as well.

# A Modern Flying Ointment
*For External Use Only*

Mix together as many of the following plants as you can find. Your flying ointment will be stronger if you use fresh, rather than dried, plants. ***These plants are considered highly poisonous. Some people have skin reactions to touching the fresh plants. Handle with care***.

> Roots of jimsonweed (*Datura stramonium*)*
>
> Roots of monkshood (*Aconite napellus*)*
>
> Leaves or seeds from second-year plants of henbane (*Hyoscyamus niger*)*
>
> Green berries of black nightshade/garden huckleberry (*Solanum nigrum*)
>
> Green berries of bittersweet nightshade (*Solanum dulcamare*)
>
> Flowers (if available, but leaves will work) of marijuana (*Cannabis sativa*)
>
> Seeds and leaves of Indian tobacco (*Lobelia inflata*)
>
> Flowers of mugwort/cronewort (*Artemisia vulgaris*)
>
> Leaves and flowers of wormwood (*Artemisia absintheium*)
>
> Berries of poke (*Phytolacca americana*)*
>
> Leaves or seeds of garden rue (*Ruta graveolens*)*
>
> Flowers of mullein (*Verbascum thapsus*)
>
> Fresh catnip in flower (*Nepeta cataria*)

Pour pure olive oil, warm lard, or coconut oil over the plants until they are completely covered. Make sure nothing protrudes. An extra head of fat/oil protects against mold. If using lard or coconut oil, set your brew in the sun or keep it in a barely warm oven. If using olive oil, keep your brew inside, away from the sun. Strain out the herbs after six weeks. To thicken: add some melted beeswax to the oil; chill the lard or coconut oil. If you wish, stir in a half cup of oil made from boiling a toad in oil for several hours.

## Third Eye-opening Tincture

2   parts tincture of fresh flowers of mugwort/ cronewort (*Artemisia vulgaris*)

1   part tincture of fresh flowers of chicory (*Cichorium intybus*)

1   part tincture of fresh flowers of purple loosestrife (*Lythrum salicaria*) or fireweed (*Erechtites hieracifolia*)

Pick flowers early in the morning and tincture in 100 proof vodka. (No, 80 proof will not work.) You will want at least 2 ounces of cronewort tincture and 1 ounce of each of the other tinctures. This will involve picking a lot of flowers! Allow the tinctures to mature for at least six weeks. When each tincture is ready, and not before, combine them in the required proportions. Take a full teaspoon dose of the combined tincture on an empty stomach. Fasting from all food for at least twelve hours prior to your experience will enhance it. After taking the third eye-opening tincture, sit quietly for an hour. The effects of this tincture are permanent.

# Moon Signs,
# Phases, and
# Tables

# The Quarters and Signs of the Moon

Everyone has seen the moon wax and wane through a period of approximately twenty-nine-and-a-half days. This circuit from new moon to full moon and back again is called the lunation cycle. The cycle is divided into parts called quarters or phases. There are several methods by which this can be done, and the system used in the *Herbal Almanac* may not correspond to those used in other almanacs.

## The Quarters
### First Quarter

The first quarter begins at the new moon, when the sun and moon are in the same place, or conjunct. (This means that the sun and moon are in the same degree of the same sign.) The moon is not visible at first, since it rises at the same time as the sun. The new moon is the time of new beginnings, beginnings of projects that favor growth, externalization of activities, and the growth of ideas. The first quarter is the time of germination, emergence, beginnings, and outwardly directed activity.

### Second Quarter

The second quarter begins halfway between the new moon and the full moon, when the sun and moon are at right angles, or a ninety-degree square, to each other. This half moon rises around noon and sets around midnight, so it can be seen in the western sky during the first half of the night. The second quarter is the time of growth and articulation of things that already exist.

### Third Quarter

The third quarter begins at the full moon, when the sun and moon are opposite one another and the full light of the sun can shine on the full sphere of the moon. The round moon can be seen rising in the east at sunset, and then rising a little later each evening. The full moon stands for illumination, fulfillment, culmination, completion, drawing inward, unrest, emotional expressions, and hasty actions leading to failure. The third quarter is a time of maturity, fruition, and the assumption of the full form of expression.

### Fourth Quarter

The fourth quarter begins about halfway between the full moon and new moon, when the sun and moon are again at ninety degrees, or square. This decreasing moon rises at midnight and can be seen in the east during the last half of the night, reaching the overhead position just about as the sun rises. The fourth quarter is a time of disintegration and drawing back for reorganization and reflection.

# The Signs
### Moon in Aries

Moon in Aries is good for starting things, but lacking in staying power. Things occur rapidly, but also quickly pass.

### Moon in Taurus

With moon in Taurus, things begun during this sign last the longest and tend to increase in value. Things begun now become habitual and hard to alter.

### Moon in Gemini

Moon in Gemini is an inconsistent position for the moon, characterized by a lot of talk. Things begun now are easily changed by outside influences.

### Moon in Cancer

Moon in Cancer stimulates emotional rapport between people. It pinpoints need and supports growth and nurturance.

### Moon in Leo

Moon in Leo accents showmanship, being seen, drama, recreation, and happy pursuits. It may be concerned with praise and subject to flattery.

### Moon in Virgo

Moon in Virgo favors accomplishment of details and commands from higher up, while discouraging independent thinking.

### Moon in Libra

Moon in Libra increases self-awareness. This moon favors self-examination and interaction with others, but discourages spontaneous initiative.

### Moon in Scorpio

Moon in Scorpio increases awareness of psychic power. It precipitates psychic crises and ends connections thoroughly.

### Moon in Sagittarius

Moon in Sagittarius encourages expansionary flights of imagination and confidence in the flow of life.

### Moon in Capricorn

Moon in Capricorn increases awareness of the need for structure, discipline, and organization. Institutional activities are favored.

### Moon in Aquarius

Moon in Aquarius favors activities that are unique and individualistic, concern for humanitarian needs and society as a whole, and improvements that can be made.

### Moon in Pisces

During moon in Pisces, energy withdraws from the surface of life and hibernates within, secretly reorganizing and realigning.

# January Moon Table

| Date | Sign | Element | Nature | Phase |
|------|------|---------|--------|-------|
| 1 Fri 9:41 pm | Leo | Fire | Barren | 3rd |
| 2 Sat | Leo | Fire | Barren | 3rd |
| 3 Sun 9:52 pm | Virgo | Earth | Barren | 3rd |
| 4 Mon | Virgo | Earth | Barren | 3rd |
| 5 Tue 11:58 pm | Libra | Air | Semi-fruitful | 3rd |
| 6 Wed | Libra | Air | Semi-fruitful | 3rd |
| 7 Thu | Libra | Air | Semi-fruitful | 4th 5:40 am |
| 8 Fri 5:00 am | Scorpio | Water | Fruitful | 4th |
| 9 Sat | Scorpio | Water | Fruitful | 4th |
| 10 Sun 1:10 pm | Sagittarius | Fire | Barren | 4th |
| 11 Mon | Sagittarius | Fire | Barren | 4th |
| 12 Tue 11:54 pm | Capricorn | Earth | Semi-fruitful | 4th |
| 13 Wed | Capricorn | Earth | Semi-fruitful | 4th |
| 14 Thu | Capricorn | Earth | Semi-fruitful | 4th |
| 15 Fri 12:17 pm | Aquarius | Air | Barren | New 2:11 am |
| 16 Sat | Aquarius | Air | Barren | 1st |
| 17 Sun | Aquarius | Air | Barren | 1st |
| 18 Mon 1:17 am | Pisces | Water | Fruitful | 1st |
| 19 Tue | Pisces | Water | Fruitful | 1st |
| 20 Wed 1:36 pm | Aries | Fire | Barren | 1st |
| 21 Thu | Aries | Fire | Barren | 1st |
| 22 Fri 11:39 pm | Taurus | Earth | Semi-fruitful | 1st |
| 23 Sat | Taurus | Earth | Semi-fruitful | 2nd 5:53 am |
| 24 Sun | Taurus | Earth | Semi-fruitful | 2nd |
| 25 Mon 6:11 am | Gemini | Air | Barren | 2nd |
| 26 Tue | Gemini | Air | Barren | 2nd |
| 27 Wed 9:01 am | Cancer | Water | Fruitful | 2nd |
| 28 Thu | Cancer | Water | Fruitful | 2nd |
| 29 Fri 9:10 am | Leo | Fire | Barren | 2nd |
| 30 Sat | Leo | Fire | Barren | Full 1:18 am |
| 31 Sun 8:23 am | Virgo | Earth | Barren | 3rd |

## February Moon Table

| Date | Sign | Element | Nature | Phase |
|------|------|---------|--------|-------|
| 1 Mon | Virgo | Earth | Barren | 3rd |
| 2 Tue 8:42 am | Libra | Air | Semi-fruitful | 3rd |
| 3 Wed | Libra | Air | Semi-fruitful | 3rd |
| 4 Thu 11:56 am | Scorpio | Water | Fruitful | 3rd |
| 5 Fri | Scorpio | Water | Fruitful | 4th 6:48 pm |
| 6 Sat 7:04 pm | Sagittarius | Fire | Barren | 4th |
| 7 Sun | Sagittarius | Fire | Barren | 4th |
| 8 Mon | Sagittarius | Fire | Barren | 4th |
| 9 Tue 5:43 am | Capricorn | Earth | Semi-fruitful | 4th |
| 10 Wed | Capricorn | Earth | Semi-fruitful | 4th |
| 11 Thu 6:24 pm | Aquarius | Air | Barren | 4th |
| 12 Fri | Aquarius | Air | Barren | 4th |
| 13 Sat | Aquarius | Air | Barren | New 9:51 pm |
| 14 Sun 7:23 am | Pisces | Water | Fruitful | 1st |
| 15 Mon | Pisces | Water | Fruitful | 1st |
| 16 Tue 7:30 pm | Aries | Fire | Barren | 1st |
| 17 Wed | Aries | Fire | Barren | 1st |
| 18 Thu | Aries | Fire | Barren | 1st |
| 19 Fri 5:55 am | Taurus | Earth | Semi-fruitful | 1st |
| 20 Sat | Taurus | Earth | Semi-fruitful | 1st |
| 21 Sun 1:47 pm | Gemini | Air | Barren | 2nd 7:42 pm |
| 22 Mon | Gemini | Air | Barren | 2nd |
| 23 Tue 6:29 pm | Cancer | Water | Fruitful | 2nd |
| 24 Wed | Cancer | Water | Fruitful | 2nd |
| 25 Thu 8:08 pm | Leo | Fire | Barren | 2nd |
| 26 Fri | Leo | Fire | Barren | 2nd |
| 27 Sat 7:52 pm | Virgo | Earth | Barren | 2nd |
| 28 Sun | Virgo | Earth | Barren | Full 11:38 am |

## March Moon Table

| Date | Sign | Element | Nature | Phase |
|------|------|---------|--------|-------|
| 1 Mon 7:31 pm | Libra | Air | Semi-fruitful | 3rd |
| 2 Tue | Libra | Air | Semi-fruitful | 3rd |
| 3 Wed 9:11 pm | Scorpio | Water | Fruitful | 3rd |
| 4 Thu | Scorpio | Water | Fruitful | 3rd |
| 5 Fri | Scorpio | Water | Fruitful | 3rd |
| 6 Sat 2:36 am | Sagittarius | Fire | Barren | 3rd |
| 7 Sun | Sagittarius | Fire | Barren | 4th 10:42 am |
| 8 Mon 12:13 pm | Capricorn | Earth | Semi-fruitful | 4th |
| 9 Tue | Capricorn | Earth | Semi-fruitful | 4th |
| 10 Wed | Capricorn | Earth | Semi-fruitful | 4th |
| 11 Thu 12:42 am | Aquarius | Air | Barren | 4th |
| 12 Fri | Aquarius | Air | Barren | 4th |
| 13 Sat 1:44 pm | Pisces | Water | Fruitful | 4th |
| 14 Sun | Pisces | Water | Fruitful | 4th |
| 15 Mon | Pisces | Water | Fruitful | New 5:01 pm |
| 16 Tue 2:32 am | Aries | Fire | Barren | 1st |
| 17 Wed | Aries | Fire | Barren | 1st |
| 18 Thu 12:29 pm | Taurus | Earth | Semi-fruitful | 1st |
| 19 Fri | Taurus | Earth | Semi-fruitful | 1st |
| 20 Sat 8:28 pm | Gemini | Air | Barren | 1st |
| 21 Sun | Gemini | Air | Barren | 1st |
| 22 Mon | Gemini | Air | Barren | 1st |
| 23 Tue 2:16 am | Cancer | Water | Fruitful | 2nd 7:00 am |
| 24 Wed | Cancer | Water | Fruitful | 2nd |
| 25 Thu 5:39 am | Leo | Fire | Barren | 2nd |
| 26 Fri | Leo | Fire | Barren | 2nd |
| 27 Sat 6:57 am | Virgo | Earth | Barren | 2nd |
| 28 Sun | Virgo | Earth | Barren | 2nd |
| 29 Mon 7:21 am | Libra | Air | Semi-fruitful | Full 10:25 pm |
| 30 Tue | Libra | Air | Semi-fruitful | 3rd |
| 31 Wed 8:41 am | Scorpio | Water | Fruitful | 3rd |

# April Moon Table

| Date | Sign | Element | Nature | Phase |
|------|------|---------|--------|-------|
| 1 Thu | Scorpio | Water | Fruitful | 3rd |
| 2 Fri 12:53 pm | Sagittarius | Fire | Barren | 3rd |
| 3 Sat | Sagittarius | Fire | Barren | 3rd |
| 4 Sun 9:07 pm | Capricorn | Earth | Semi-fruitful | 3rd |
| 5 Mon | Capricorn | Earth | Semi-fruitful | 3rd |
| 6 Tue | Capricorn | Earth | Semi-fruitful | 4th 5:37 am |
| 7 Wed 8:51 am | Aquarius | Air | Barren | 4th |
| 8 Thu | Aquarius | Air | Barren | 4th |
| 9 Fri 9:48 pm | Pisces | Water | Fruitful | 4th |
| 10 Sat | Pisces | Water | Fruitful | 4th |
| 11 Sun | Pisces | Water | Fruitful | 4th |
| 12 Mon 9:31 am | Aries | Fire | Barren | 4th |
| 13 Tue | Aries | Fire | Barren | 4th |
| 14 Wed 6:55 pm | Taurus | Earth | Semi-fruitful | New 8:29 am |
| 15 Thu | Taurus | Earth | Semi-fruitful | 1st |
| 16 Fri | Taurus | Earth | Semi-fruitful | 1st |
| 17 Sat 2:08 am | Gemini | Air | Barren | 1st |
| 18 Sun | Gemini | Air | Barren | 1st |
| 19 Mon 7:39 am | Cancer | Water | Fruitful | 1st |
| 20 Tue | Cancer | Water | Fruitful | 1st |
| 21 Wed 11:42 am | Leo | Fire | Barren | 2nd 2:20 pm |
| 22 Thu | Leo | Fire | Barren | 2nd |
| 23 Fri 2:24 pm | Virgo | Earth | Barren | 2nd |
| 24 Sat | Virgo | Earth | Barren | 2nd |
| 25 Sun 4:16 pm | Libra | Air | Semi-fruitful | 2nd |
| 26 Mon | Libra | Air | Semi-fruitful | 2nd |
| 27 Tue 6:28 pm | Scorpio | Water | Fruitful | 2nd |
| 28 Wed | Scorpio | Water | Fruitful | Full 8:19 am |
| 29 Thu 10:36 pm | Sagittarius | Fire | Barren | 3rd |
| 30 Fri | Sagittarius | Fire | Barren | 3rd |

## May Moon Table

| Date | Sign | Element | Nature | Phase |
|------|------|---------|--------|-------|
| 1 Sat | Sagittarius | Fire | Barren | 3rd |
| 2 Sun 6:00 am | Capricorn | Earth | Semi-fruitful | 3rd |
| 3 Mon | Capricorn | Earth | Semi-fruitful | 3rd |
| 4 Tue 4:52 pm | Aquarius | Air | Barren | 3rd |
| 5 Wed | Aquarius | Air | Barren | 3rd |
| 6 Thu | Aquarius | Air | Barren | 4th 12:15 am |
| 7 Fri 5:34 am | Pisces | Water | Fruitful | 4th |
| 8 Sat | Pisces | Water | Fruitful | 4th |
| 9 Sun 5:29 pm | Aries | Fire | Barren | 4th |
| 10 Mon | Aries | Fire | Barren | 4th |
| 11 Tue | Aries | Fire | Barren | 4th |
| 12 Wed 2:48 am | Taurus | Earth | Semi-fruitful | 4th |
| 13 Thu | Taurus | Earth | Semi-fruitful | New 9:04 pm |
| 14 Fri 9:18 am | Gemini | Air | Barren | 1st |
| 15 Sat | Gemini | Air | Barren | 1st |
| 16 Sun 1:46 pm | Cancer | Water | Fruitful | 1st |
| 17 Mon | Cancer | Water | Fruitful | 1st |
| 18 Tue 5:06 pm | Leo | Fire | Barren | 1st |
| 19 Wed | Leo | Fire | Barren | 1st |
| 20 Thu 7:58 pm | Virgo | Earth | Barren | 2nd 7:43 pm |
| 21 Fri | Virgo | Earth | Barren | 2nd |
| 22 Sat 10:50 pm | Libra | Air | Semi-fruitful | 2nd |
| 23 Sun | Libra | Air | Semi-fruitful | 2nd |
| 24 Mon | Libra | Air | Semi-fruitful | 2nd |
| 25 Tue 2:17 am | Scorpio | Water | Fruitful | 2nd |
| 26 Wed | Scorpio | Water | Fruitful | 2nd |
| 27 Thu 7:15 am | Sagittarius | Fire | Barren | Full 7:07 pm |
| 28 Fri | Sagittarius | Fire | Barren | 3rd |
| 29 Sat 2:44 pm | Capricorn | Earth | Semi-fruitful | 3rd |
| 30 Sun | Capricorn | Earth | Semi-fruitful | 3rd |
| 31 Mon | Capricorn | Earth | Semi-fruitful | 3rd |

# *June Moon Table*

| Date | Sign | Element | Nature | Phase |
|---|---|---|---|---|
| 1 Tue 1:08 am | Aquarius | Air | Barren | 3rd |
| 2 Wed | Aquarius | Air | Barren | 3rd |
| 3 Thu 1:34 pm | Pisces | Water | Fruitful | 3rd |
| 4 Fri | Pisces | Water | Fruitful | 4th 6:13 pm |
| 5 Sat | Pisces | Water | Fruitful | 4th |
| 6 Sun 1:50 am | Aries | Fire | Barren | 4th |
| 7 Mon | Aries | Fire | Barren | 4th |
| 8 Tue 11:41 am | Taurus | Earth | Semi-fruitful | 4th |
| 9 Wed | Taurus | Earth | Semi-fruitful | 4th |
| 10 Thu 6:11 pm | Gemini | Air | Barren | 4th |
| 11 Fri | Gemini | Air | Barren | 4th |
| 12 Sat 9:50 pm | Cancer | Water | Fruitful | New 7:15 am |
| 13 Sun | Cancer | Water | Fruitful | 1st |
| 14 Mon 11:54 pm | Leo | Fire | Barren | 1st |
| 15 Tue | Leo | Fire | Barren | 1st |
| 16 Wed | Leo | Fire | Barren | 1st |
| 17 Thu 1:41 am | Virgo | Earth | Barren | 1st |
| 18 Fri | Virgo | Earth | Barren | 1st |
| 19 Sat 4:13 am | Libra | Air | Semi-fruitful | 2nd 12:30 am |
| 20 Sun | Libra | Air | Semi-fruitful | 2nd |
| 21 Mon 8:14 am | Scorpio | Water | Fruitful | 2nd |
| 22 Tue | Scorpio | Water | Fruitful | 2nd |
| 23 Wed 2:10 pm | Sagittarius | Fire | Barren | 2nd |
| 24 Thu | Sagittarius | Fire | Barren | 2nd |
| 25 Fri 10:21 pm | Capricorn | Earth | Semi-fruitful | 2nd |
| 26 Sat | Capricorn | Earth | Semi-fruitful | Full 7:30 am |
| 27 Sun | Capricorn | Earth | Semi-fruitful | 3rd |
| 28 Mon 8:52 am | Aquarius | Air | Barren | 3rd |
| 29 Tue | Aquarius | Air | Barren | 3rd |
| 30 Wed 9:10 pm | Pisces | Water | Fruitful | 3rd |

## *July Moon Table*

| Date | Sign | Element | Nature | Phase |
|------|------|---------|--------|-------|
| 1 Thu | Pisces | Water | Fruitful | 3rd |
| 2 Fri | Pisces | Water | Fruitful | 3rd |
| 3 Sat 9:44 am | Aries | Fire | Barren | 3rd |
| 4 Sun | Aries | Fire | Barren | 4th 10:35 am |
| 5 Mon 8:29 pm | Taurus | Earth | Semi-fruitful | 4th |
| 6 Tue | Taurus | Earth | Semi-fruitful | 4th |
| 7 Wed | Taurus | Earth | Semi-fruitful | 4th |
| 8 Thu 3:51 am | Gemini | Air | Barren | 4th |
| 9 Fri | Gemini | Air | Barren | 4th |
| 10 Sat 7:38 am | Cancer | Water | Fruitful | 4th |
| 11 Sun | Cancer | Water | Fruitful | New 3:40 pm |
| 12 Mon 8:53 am | Leo | Fire | Barren | 1st |
| 13 Tue | Leo | Fire | Barren | 1st |
| 14 Wed 9:15 am | Virgo | Earth | Barren | 1st |
| 15 Thu | Virgo | Earth | Barren | 1st |
| 16 Fri 10:24 am | Libra | Air | Semi-fruitful | 1st |
| 17 Sat | Libra | Air | Semi-fruitful | 1st |
| 18 Sun 1:42 pm | Scorpio | Water | Fruitful | 2nd 6:11 am |
| 19 Mon | Scorpio | Water | Fruitful | 2nd |
| 20 Tue 7:48 pm | Sagittarius | Fire | Barren | 2nd |
| 21 Wed | Sagittarius | Fire | Barren | 2nd |
| 22 Thu | Sagittarius | Fire | Barren | 2nd |
| 23 Fri 4:39 am | Capricorn | Earth | Semi-fruitful | 2nd |
| 24 Sat | Capricorn | Earth | Semi-fruitful | 2nd |
| 25 Sun 3:38 pm | Aquarius | Air | Barren | Full 9:37 pm |
| 26 Mon | Aquarius | Air | Barren | 3rd |
| 27 Tue | Aquarius | Air | Barren | 3rd |
| 28 Wed 4:00 am | Pisces | Water | Fruitful | 3rd |
| 29 Thu | Pisces | Water | Fruitful | 3rd |
| 30 Fri 4:42 pm | Aries | Fire | Barren | 3rd |
| 31 Sat | Aries | Fire | Barren | 3rd |

# *August Moon Table*

| Date | Sign | Element | Nature | Phase |
|---|---|---|---|---|
| 1 Sun | Aries | Fire | Barren | 3rd |
| 2 Mon 4:13 am | Taurus | Earth | Semi-fruitful | 3rd |
| 3 Tue | Taurus | Earth | Semi-fruitful | 4th 12:59 am |
| 4 Wed 12:54 pm | Gemini | Air | Barren | 4th |
| 5 Thu | Gemini | Air | Barren | 4th |
| 6 Fri 5:50 pm | Cancer | Water | Fruitful | 4th |
| 7 Sat | Cancer | Water | Fruitful | 4th |
| 8 Sun 7:23 pm | Leo | Fire | Barren | 4th |
| 9 Mon | Leo | Fire | Barren | New 11:08 pm |
| 10 Tue 7:01 pm | Virgo | Earth | Barren | 1st |
| 11 Wed | Virgo | Earth | Barren | 1st |
| 12 Thu 6:43 pm | Libra | Air | Semi-fruitful | 1st |
| 13 Fri | Libra | Air | Semi-fruitful | 1st |
| 14 Sat 8:26 pm | Scorpio | Water | Fruitful | 1st |
| 15 Sun | Scorpio | Water | Fruitful | 1st |
| 16 Mon | Scorpio | Water | Fruitful | 2nd 2:14 pm |
| 17 Tue 1:34 am | Sagittarius | Fire | Barren | 2nd |
| 18 Wed | Sagittarius | Fire | Barren | 2nd |
| 19 Thu 10:17 am | Capricorn | Earth | Semi-fruitful | 2nd |
| 20 Fri | Capricorn | Earth | Semi-fruitful | 2nd |
| 21 Sat 9:37 pm | Aquarius | Air | Barren | 2nd |
| 22 Sun | Aquarius | Air | Barren | 2nd |
| 23 Mon | Aquarius | Air | Barren | 2nd |
| 24 Tue 10:11 am | Pisces | Water | Fruitful | Full 1:05 pm |
| 25 Wed | Pisces | Water | Fruitful | 3rd |
| 26 Thu 10:49 pm | Aries | Fire | Barren | 3rd |
| 27 Fri | Aries | Fire | Barren | 3rd |
| 28 Sat | Aries | Fire | Barren | 3rd |
| 29 Sun 10:35 am | Taurus | Earth | Semi-fruitful | 3rd |
| 30 Mon | Taurus | Earth | Semi-fruitful | 3rd |
| 31 Tue 8:19 pm | Gemini | Air | Barren | 3rd |

# September Moon Table

| Date | Sign | Element | Nature | Phase |
|------|------|---------|--------|-------|
| 1 Wed | Gemini | Air | Barren | 4th 1:22 pm |
| 2 Thu | Gemini | Air | Barren | 4th |
| 3 Fri 2:50 am | Cancer | Water | Fruitful | 4th |
| 4 Sat | Cancer | Water | Fruitful | 4th |
| 5 Sun 5:45 am | Leo | Fire | Barren | 4th |
| 6 Mon | Leo | Fire | Barren | 4th |
| 7 Tue 5:53 am | Virgo | Earth | Barren | 4th |
| 8 Wed | Virgo | Earth | Barren | New 6:30 am |
| 9 Thu 5:01 am | Libra | Air | Semi-fruitful | 1st |
| 10 Fri | Libra | Air | Semi-fruitful | 1st |
| 11 Sat 5:21 am | Scorpio | Water | Fruitful | 1st |
| 12 Sun | Scorpio | Water | Fruitful | 1st |
| 13 Mon 8:52 am | Sagittarius | Fire | Barren | 1st |
| 14 Tue | Sagittarius | Fire | Barren | 1st |
| 15 Wed 4:30 pm | Capricorn | Earth | Semi-fruitful | 2nd 1:50 am |
| 16 Thu | Capricorn | Earth | Semi-fruitful | 2nd |
| 17 Fri | Capricorn | Earth | Semi-fruitful | 2nd |
| 18 Sat 3:35 am | Aquarius | Air | Barren | 2nd |
| 19 Sun | Aquarius | Air | Barren | 2nd |
| 20 Mon 4:15 pm | Pisces | Water | Fruitful | 2nd |
| 21 Tue | Pisces | Water | Fruitful | 2nd |
| 22 Wed | Pisces | Water | Fruitful | 2nd |
| 23 Thu 4:47 am | Aries | Fire | Barren | Full 5:17 am |
| 24 Fri | Aries | Fire | Barren | 3rd |
| 25 Sat 4:17 pm | Taurus | Earth | Semi-fruitful | 3rd |
| 26 Sun | Taurus | Earth | Semi-fruitful | 3rd |
| 27 Mon | Taurus | Earth | Semi-fruitful | 3rd |
| 28 Tue 2:10 am | Gemini | Air | Barren | 3rd |
| 29 Wed | Gemini | Air | Barren | 3rd |
| 30 Thu 9:46 am | Cancer | Water | Fruitful | 4th 11:52 pm |

# October Moon Table

| Date | Sign | Element | Nature | Phase |
|------|------|---------|--------|-------|
| 1 Fri | Cancer | Water | Fruitful | 4th |
| 2 Sat 2:21 pm | Leo | Fire | Barren | 4th |
| 3 Sun | Leo | Fire | Barren | 4th |
| 4 Mon 4:00 pm | Virgo | Earth | Barren | 4th |
| 5 Tue | Virgo | Earth | Barren | 4th |
| 6 Wed 3:52 pm | Libra | Air | Semi-fruitful | 4th |
| 7 Thu | Libra | Air | Semi-fruitful | New 2:45 pm |
| 8 Fri 3:52 pm | Scorpio | Water | Fruitful | 1st |
| 9 Sat | Scorpio | Water | Fruitful | 1st |
| 10 Sun 6:09 pm | Sagittarius | Fire | Barren | 1st |
| 11 Mon | Sagittarius | Fire | Barren | 1st |
| 12 Tue | Sagittarius | Fire | Barren | 1st |
| 13 Wed 12:17 am | Capricorn | Earth | Semi-fruitful | 1st |
| 14 Thu | Capricorn | Earth | Semi-fruitful | 2nd 5:27 pm |
| 15 Fri 10:24 am | Aquarius | Air | Barren | 2nd |
| 16 Sat | Aquarius | Air | Barren | 2nd |
| 17 Sun 10:52 pm | Pisces | Water | Fruitful | 2nd |
| 18 Mon | Pisces | Water | Fruitful | 2nd |
| 19 Tue | Pisces | Water | Fruitful | 2nd |
| 20 Wed 11:23 am | Aries | Fire | Barren | 2nd |
| 21 Thu | Aries | Fire | Barren | 2nd |
| 22 Fri 10:30 pm | Taurus | Earth | Semi-fruitful | Full 9:37 pm |
| 23 Sat | Taurus | Earth | Semi-fruitful | 3rd |
| 24 Sun | Taurus | Earth | Semi-fruitful | 3rd |
| 25 Mon 7:47 am | Gemini | Air | Barren | 3rd |
| 26 Tue | Gemini | Air | Barren | 3rd |
| 27 Wed 3:14 pm | Cancer | Water | Fruitful | 3rd |
| 28 Thu | Cancer | Water | Fruitful | 3rd |
| 29 Fri 8:39 pm | Leo | Fire | Barren | 3rd |
| 30 Sat | Leo | Fire | Barren | 4th 8:46 am |
| 31 Sun 11:51 pm | Virgo | Earth | Barren | 4th |

# November Moon Table

| Date | Sign | Element | Nature | Phase |
|------|------|---------|--------|-------|
| 1 Mon | Virgo | Earth | Barren | 4th |
| 2 Tue | Virgo | Earth | Barren | 4th |
| 3 Wed 1:19 am | Libra | Air | Semi-fruitful | 4th |
| 4 Thu | Libra | Air | Semi-fruitful | 4th |
| 5 Fri 2:16 am | Scorpio | Water | Fruitful | 4th |
| 6 Sat | Scorpio | Water | Fruitful | New 12:52 am |
| 7 Sun 3:28 am | Sagittarius | Fire | Barren | 1st |
| 8 Mon | Sagittarius | Fire | Barren | 1st |
| 9 Tue 8:37 am | Capricorn | Earth | Semi-fruitful | 1st |
| 10 Wed | Capricorn | Earth | Semi-fruitful | 1st |
| 11 Thu 5:32 pm | Aquarius | Air | Barren | 1st |
| 12 Fri | Aquarius | Air | Barren | 1st |
| 13 Sat | Aquarius | Air | Barren | 2nd 11:39 am |
| 14 Sun 5:24 am | Pisces | Water | Fruitful | 2nd |
| 15 Mon | Pisces | Water | Fruitful | 2nd |
| 16 Tue 5:59 pm | Aries | Fire | Barren | 2nd |
| 17 Wed | Aries | Fire | Barren | 2nd |
| 18 Thu | Aries | Fire | Barren | 2nd |
| 19 Fri 5:04 am | Taurus | Earth | Semi-fruitful | 2nd |
| 20 Sat | Taurus | Earth | Semi-fruitful | 2nd |
| 21 Sun 1:46 pm | Gemini | Air | Barren | Full 12:27 pm |
| 22 Mon | Gemini | Air | Barren | 3rd |
| 23 Tue 8:14 pm | Cancer | Water | Fruitful | 3rd |
| 24 Wed | Cancer | Water | Fruitful | 3rd |
| 25 Thu | Cancer | Water | Fruitful | 3rd |
| 26 Fri 1:01 am | Leo | Fire | Barren | 3rd |
| 27 Sat | Leo | Fire | Barren | 3rd |
| 28 Sun 4:34 am | Virgo | Earth | Barren | 4th 3:36 pm |
| 29 Mon | Virgo | Earth | Barren | 4th |
| 30 Tue 7:15 am | Libra | Air | Semi-fruitful | 4th |

# *December Moon Table*

| Date | Sign | Element | Nature | Phase |
|------|------|---------|--------|-------|
| 1 Wed | Libra | Air | Semi-fruitful | 4th |
| 2 Thu 9:44 am | Scorpio | Water | Fruitful | 4th |
| 3 Fri | Scorpio | Water | Fruitful | 4th |
| 4 Sat 12:59 pm | Sagittarius | Fire | Barren | 4th |
| 5 Sun | Sagittarius | Fire | Barren | New 12:36 pm |
| 6 Mon 6:16 pm | Capricorn | Earth | Semi-fruitful | 1st |
| 7 Tue | Capricorn | Earth | Semi-fruitful | 1st |
| 8 Wed | Capricorn | Earth | Semi-fruitful | 1st |
| 9 Thu 2:30 am | Aquarius | Air | Barren | 1st |
| 10 Fri | Aquarius | Air | Barren | 1st |
| 11 Sat 1:41 pm | Pisces | Water | Fruitful | 1st |
| 12 Sun | Pisces | Water | Fruitful | 1st |
| 13 Mon | Pisces | Water | Fruitful | 2nd 8:59 am |
| 14 Tue 2:15 am | Aries | Fire | Barren | 2nd |
| 15 Wed | Aries | Fire | Barren | 2nd |
| 16 Thu 1:49 pm | Taurus | Earth | Semi-fruitful | 2nd |
| 17 Fri | Taurus | Earth | Semi-fruitful | 2nd |
| 18 Sat 10:37 pm | Gemini | Air | Barren | 2nd |
| 19 Sun | Gemini | Air | Barren | 2nd |
| 20 Mon | Gemini | Air | Barren | 2nd |
| 21 Tue 4:22 am | Cancer | Water | Fruitful | Full 3:13 am |
| 22 Wed | Cancer | Water | Fruitful | 3rd |
| 23 Thu 7:51 am | Leo | Fire | Barren | 3rd |
| 24 Fri | Leo | Fire | Barren | 3rd |
| 25 Sat 10:14 am | Virgo | Earth | Barren | 3rd |
| 26 Sun | Virgo | Earth | Barren | 3rd |
| 27 Mon 12:38 pm | Libra | Air | Semi-fruitful | 4th 11:18 pm |
| 28 Tue | Libra | Air | Semi-fruitful | 4th |
| 29 Wed 3:49 pm | Scorpio | Water | Fruitful | 4th |
| 30 Thu | Scorpio | Water | Fruitful | 4th |
| 31 Fri 8:21 pm | Sagittarius | Fire | Barren | 4th |

# About the Authors

**ELIZABETH BARRETTE** serves as the managing editor of *Pan-Gaia*. The central Illinois resident has been involved with the Pagan community for more than seventeen years. Her other writing fields include speculative fiction and gender studies. Visit her Web site at www.worthlink.net/~ysabet/sitemap.html

**CHANDRA MOIRA BEAL** is a freelance writer currently living in England. She has authored three books and published hundreds of articles, all inspired by her day-to-day life and adventures. She has been writing for Llewellyn since 1998. Chandra is also a massage therapist. To learn more, visit www.beal-net .com/laluna

**NANCY BENNETT** has been published in Llewellyn's annuals, *We'moon*, *Circle Network*, and many mainstream publications. Her pet projects include reading and writing about history and creating ethnic dinners to test on her family.

**CALANTIRNIEL** has worked with herbs and natural healing since the early 1990s and became a certified Master Herbalist in 2007. She lives in western Montana with her husband and daughter while her son is off to college. She also manages to have an organic garden and crochets professionally. Find out more at www.myspace.com/aartiana

**KAAREN CHRIST** is a consultant providing research and writing services to social service organizations. She also writes children's stories and crafts poetry. She lives in Prince Edward

County, Ontario, with two beautiful children (Indigo and Challian), a Super-Dog called Lukki, and a magical boy-rabbit.

**DALLAS JENNIFER COBB** lives in an enchanted waterfront village where she focuses on what she loves: family, gardens, fitness, and fabulous food. Her essays are in Llewellyn's almanacs and recent Seal Press anthologies *Three Ring Circus* and *Far From Home*. Her video documentary, *Disparate Places*, appeared on TV Ontario's *Planet Parent*. Contact her at Jennifer.Cobb@ Sympatico.ca

**SALLY CRAGIN** writes the astrological forecast, "Moon Signs," for the *Boston Phoenix*, which is syndicated throughout New England. She can also be heard on several radio stations as "Symboline Dai." A regular arts reviewer and feature writer for the *Boston Globe*, she also edits *Button, New England's Tiniest Magazine of Poetry, Fiction, and Gracious Living*. For more, including your personal forecast that clients have called "scary-accurate," see http://moonsigns.net

**ALICE DEVILLE** is an internationally known astrologer, writer, and metaphysical consultant. She has been both a reiki and seichim master since 1996. In her northern Virginia practice, Alice specializes in relationships, health, healing, real estate, government affairs, career and change management, and spiritual development. Contact Alice at DeVilleAA@aol.com

**ELLEN DUGAN** is an award-winning author and a psychic-clairvoyant. Her Llewellyn titles include: *Garden Witchery: Magick from the Ground Up* and *Herb Magic for Beginners: Down to Earth Enchantments*. Ellen likes to unwind by working in her perennial gardens with her husband. She wholeheartedly encourages people get their hands dirty and discover the wonder of the

natural world that surrounds them. Visit her Web site at www
.geocities.com/edugan_gardenwitch

**JAMES KAMBOS** has had a lifelong interest in folk magic. He
has written numerous articles concerning the folk magic traditions of Greece, the Near East, and the Appalachian region of
the United States. He writes and paints from his home in the
beautiful Appalachian hills of southern Ohio.

**MISTY KUCERIS** has worked as a plant specialist over the last
several years for various nurseries in the Greater DC metro-
politan area. As a plant consultant, she meets with homeown-
ers to assess their property and gardens. She also lectures at
garden clubs and senior citizen centers giving guidance and
advice on how to create healthy home gardens and lawns. At
the time of this printing, Misty's gardening Web site is under
construction. However, you can reach her at Misty@Enhan-
ceOneself.com with any questions.

**KRISTIN MADDEN** is a bestselling author of several books on
parenting, shamanism, and paganism, including the Llewellyn
books *The Book of Shamanic Healing* and *Dancing the Goddess
Incarnate*. A Druid and tutor in the Order of Bards, Ovates,
and Druids, she is also Dean of the Ardantane School of Shamanic Studies. Kristin's work has appeared in print, on radio,
and television in North America and Europe. She is also a
homeschooling mom, wildlife rehabilitator, and environmental educator.

**AMY MARTIN** is a journalist and writer of over twenty-five years
experience. Amy released *Hibachi Herbal Magic* on Moonlady
Media, and she's working on a book on poison ivy. A leader in
earth-centered spirituality in north Texas for over sixteen years,
Amy and her nonprofit group Earth Rhythms have presented

seasonal events that include the acclaimed Solsticelebrations She may be reached through http://www.moonlady.com/

**JIM MCDONALD** lives in Michigan, and offers a perspective of herbalism that blends folk and indigenous views of healing with the Vitalist traditions of nineteenth-century western herbalism. He hosts www.herbcraft.org and is currently writing a book about herbs in the Great Lakes area. Jim is a community herbalist, a manic wildcrafter, and a medicine maker. He has been an ardent student of the most learned teachers of herbcraft—the plants themselves.

**LISA MCSHERRY** is the author of *Magickal Connections: Creating a Healthy and Lasting Spiritual Group* (New Page, 2007) and *The Virtual Pagan: Exploring Wicca and Paganism Through the Internet* (Weiser, 2002). The senior editor and owner of Facing North: A Community Resource (www.facingnorth.net), she is also a frequent contributor to pagan publications. You can contact her at lisa@cybercoven.org

**SUE J. MORRIS**, founder and creator of Sue's Salves, combines her knowledge of organic gardening, natural healing, medical herbalism, nutrition, and astrology. Sue focuses on connecting the energies of the planets with the medicinal properties of plants. Sue also publishes the "Planting by the Moon" calendar, a day-to-day guide for all gardening activities based on the lunation cycle. She resides in central Pennsylvania, where she grows all of the plants for her line of products. Visit her Web site at www.suesalves.com

**SUSAN PESZNECKER** is a hearth pagan and a child of the natural world in all of its magickal guises. Areas of expertise include astronomy, herbology, healing, stonework, nature study, and folklore. As a fourth-generation Oregonian, Susan is an aficionado of the rock art of Northwest Coastal and Columbia Plateau First People. She loves to read, camp, and work in her organic garden. She makes her home in Milwaukie, Oregon.

**DANNY PHARR** is an author and instructor. He is also the founder of the Wings of Fire Seminars, which provides individuals with a safe environment to discover joy, encourage personal achievement and growth, and engage in life-changing experiences. His first book, *The Moon and Everyday Living*, was published in 2000.

**SUZANNE RESS** has been writing fiction and nonfiction for an eclectic array of publications for more than twenty-five years. She is an accomplished self-taught gardener and silversmith/mosiacist. She lives in the woods at the foot of the Alps in northern Italy with her husband, two teenage daughters, wolf dog, and two horses.

**LAUREL REUFNER** lives in gorgeous Athens County, Ohio, with her husband and two daughters. Attracted to topics of history and mythology, she is working on her first book. Keep up with her at her blog Tryl's Meanderings at trylsmeanderings.blogspot.com/

**JANICE SHARKEY** is an aromatherapist and astrological gardener. She loves scented plants and, most of all, herbs. When she's not gardening, she's making stained glass panels or writing. One of her ambitions is to get her children David and Rose and her husband William to spend more time in the garden.

**MICHELLE SKYE** is a founding member of the Sisterhood of the Crescent Moon, she is active in the southeastern Massachusetts pagan community, presenting various workshops, classes, and apprenticeship programs. An ordained minister in the Universal Life Church, she performs legal handfastings, weddings, and other spiritual rites of passage.

**ANNE SULA** grew up in the Connecticut River Valley of New Hampshire. Currently, she lives and works as a freelance journalist in Minnesota.

**SUSUN WEED** began studying herbal medicine in 1965. Today, her work appears in peer-reviewed journals and magazines like *Sagewoman*. Her first book, *Wise Woman Herbal for the Childbearing Years*, was published in 1985. Her worldwide teaching schedule includes herbal medicine, the psychology of healing, nutrition, and women's health. Learn more at www.susunweed.com/

# Essential Herbal Wisdom

Healing practitioner Nancy Arrowsmith will take you on a fascinating, in-depth exploration of herbs in *Essential Herbal Wisdom*. As entertaining as it is practical, this comprehensive illustrated guide covers everything from herb gathering prayers and charms to detailed herbal correspondences for fifty powerful herbs. Each herb is described in detail, with tips for growing, gathering, drying, and storing, as well as on the herb's culinary virtues, cosmetic properties, medicinal merits, veterinary values, and household applications.

ESSENTIAL HERBAL WISDOM
504 pp. • 7 x 10
978-0-7387-1488-2 • U.S. $29.95   Can $34.95
To order call 1-877-NEW-WRLD
www.llewellyn.com